TEACHERS AND SCHOLARS

TEACHERS AND SCHOLARS

A Memoir of Berkeley in Depression and War

Robert Nisbet

Transaction Publishers
New Brunswick (U.S.A.) and London (U.K.)

Library of Congress Catalog Number: 91-32636
ISBN: 1-56000-034-1 (cloth)
Printed in the United States of America

Library of Congress Cataloging-in-Publication Data

Nisbet, Robert A.
    Teachers and scholars: a memoir of Berkeley in depression and war / Robert Nisbet.
       p.   cm.
    ISBN 1-56000-034-1
    1. University of California, Berkeley — History. I. Title.
LD759.N57   1992
378.794'67 — dc20
                                       91-32636
                                         CIP

Contents

Preface

This is a memoir I have written, not a history and only incidentally an autobiography. My book is a memoir of the Berkeley I knew more than half a century ago; more particularly the Berkeley I entered as a freshmen in 1932 and departed from a decade later when as an assistant professor I went into the army and became part of World War II. Obviously the decade was an important one in my life, encompassing as it did my ascent from callow adolescent to the start of a life career as an academic.

The decade was also a vital one in the life of America. It began with the Great Depression that had been triggered by the Crash of '29 and didn't end until we were as a nation well into World War II. Berkeley made for a rich window through which to see a Western world in the throes of depression and war. There were ideologies galore: liberalism, capitalism, socialism, communism, fascism, and in America, Huey Long's Share the Wealth, Dr. Townsend's Thirty Dollars Every Thursday, and Upton Sinclair's End Poverty in California — EPIC.

The thirties was a critical decade in the life of the University too. It was the final decade of what, for want of a better term, I call the Old Berkeley. Berkeley in the thirties wasn't crucially different from the Berkeley of the 1890s. There were more students, more departments, more faculty and more buildings. But in conceived and accepted mission, the Berkeley of the 1930s wasn't significantly different from what Berkeley had been at the turn of the century. That mission was, in a word, teaching. All else in the Old

Berkeley was secondary, ancillary, to the teaching of undergraduates primarily. Research was expected of every faculty member; without it promotion was difficult and exceptional. But the chief importance of research was widely held to be its elevating effect on one's teaching—which didn't militate against the occasional appearance of a titan in research such as Andrew Lawson, Ernest Lawrence, and Herbert Evans.

Today Berkeley is, proudly, a research university, so declared by its faculty and administration, so appraised by other colleges and universities. It is not unfair to say that just as research was generally conceived in the Old Berkeley as ancillary to teaching, so in the New Berkeley is teaching regarded as ancillary to research—though that in no way precludes the existence of splendid teachers on occasion.

Berkeley is a much grander, richer, place today than it was in the 1930s. There are those who believe that in the process of becoming grander, Berkeley has perhaps lost something in consensus, community. Perhaps. Others, however, argue persuasively that Berkeley has only diversified and enriched itself. Perhaps that is true. Perhaps *both* are true.

It is not, however, the purpose of this memoir to argue the case for either Berkeley, the Old or the New. I have known both Berkeleys and found much in each to respect—and, for that matter, to criticize. My intent here is to limn as best as my abilities permit the Old Berkeley I knew intimately in the 1930s, as student and faculty member. It occurred to me a couple of years ago that I am bound by age to be one of a now fast-diminishing number who knew that Berkeley as not merely students but as fledgling members of the faculty. If I didn't tell about the Berkeley of five and six decades ago, who would or could?

Hence this memoir. I hope it has in it at least some of the interest for the reader that it has had for me as the writer. The writing has brought with it, the inevitable stretching of memory muscles and the reawakening of images now beginning to fade but still, I believe, alive. I loved the Old Berkeley. But that is no warrant for gilding the lily or exuding vapors of idle romanticization. There was the bad as well as the good in the Old Berkeley.

Prologue

Although this book is a memoir of the university at Berkeley, not an autobiography, I should say something about myself the memoirist. What I say will be brief, and confined to the essentials of my life before I entered Berkeley as a freshman in 1932.

I was born in Los Angeles, 30 September 1913. I never actually lived in the city; I was there solely for my birth, as I shall explain shortly. Nineteen-thirteen was, as I learned later, both a good year and a bad year for Los Angeles. It was the year that Owens River water from 250 miles north in the High Sierra, stolen fair and square, as patriotic Angelenos were wont to say, came cascading down into upper San Fernando Valley, then a parched desert, at the rate of 26,000,000 gallons a day, thus making possible the transition from an overgrown pueblo to an American city. It was the year too of the Great Freeze that nearly destroyed southern California agriculture and turned the attention of many thousands from rural to urban pursuits. Finally, 1913 was the year in which Willard Huntington Wright, who had grown up in the city's environs and gone east, wrote his famously devastating article in Mencken's *Smart Set* on Los Angeles, the city of frauds, faith healers, and furriers-become-movie moguls.

My mother had been born a few miles from Los Angeles and it was her cherished city throughout her life. The reason I was there briefly was that she and my father lived in Maricopa, a desolate little town on the west side of the San Joaquin Valley, the desert side

1

in those years. She was bound, and my loving father therefore was too, that she would not have her first born in such topographically and horticulturally squalid circumstances, that she would go the hundred miles or so required to reach Los Angeles and deliver her first amid civilized people and folkways. There was also the fact that she, though not my father, was a devout Christian Scientist and in Los Angeles her baby could be born in a Christian Science nursing home, without doctors and the threat of medicines. Then it was, for my father's job, back to Maricopa.

This town, forty miles west of Bakersfield, sat in a sea of sage-brush, as complete a desert town as one could have possibly found. There were no lawns, flower gardens, or trees apart from a couple of weather-beaten, but miraculously still alive, pepper trees in the town. Weather swung abruptly from a baking, almost mind-numbing, arid summer heat to winter, with its freezing winds from the north showering the place with tons of dust and debris. No spring or fall; only winter to summer and vice versa. Instead of groves of trees surrounding the desiccated marketplace that was the village there were hundreds of oil derricks, each with its sump of black gold that could glisten sufficiently to fool birds by the hundreds at times into thinking it water and drop on it for refreshment. Always there were the creaking and groaning sounds of walking beams that, rising and falling methodically, drew the oil up from hundreds of feet below. There were no gushers in my time in Maricopa, but there had been somewhat earlier — Lakeview One and Lakeview Two, as they were known. They must have been exciting: raw oil from the deep forced by tremendous pressures up through the pipes that when their caps blew off under the pressure became like weapons, discharging the oil hundreds of feet in the air where winds could blow it in every direction for dozens, sometimes hundreds, of square miles. The gushers' gift to Maricopa was en-crustations of oil that took the place of paving for streets and walk-ways, effective enough in the cold winter but turned into soft squishy, sticky pulp in the hot summer.

I shall come back to Maricopa presently. When I was five years old, something miraculous happened. My parents and two-year-old brother and I moved from the California desert to Macon, Georgia, then as charming a small city as one could possibly come on in the South. This was my father's birthplace and where his parents, my grandparents, lived and had lived for many years. My grandfather, as nearly as I can recall, filled the combined positions of registrar and assessor for little Bibb County, for which the city of Macon was responsible. He became instantly fascinating to me simply because he had fought in the Civil War, as a Confederate of course. It pleases me to say that he liked me. Otherwise he wouldn't have asked my mother to change my middle name to his, thus making two Robert Alexander Nisbets for a couple of years in Macon. So, happily, did my grandmother like me. She was the first grandmother I had ever known. She was my grandfather's second wife, the first having died in childbirth, leaving him with three small children. The young woman he married was named Cora Solomon; she had been born and reared a Jew, but prior to her marriage to my grandfather she converted to Presbyterianism, the Nisbet family religion, the cost of which to her was the rigorous, almost brutal, indoctrination that was then required for a Jew to become a Christian, or at least a Presbyterian.

Three children were born to them, my father being the last — and clearly most favored — of them. It was a big house they lived in, all of three stories, with bedrooms galore, a large sitting room or parlor — but, mirabile dictu, a *used* parlor, one in which large groups sat around even when it wasn't wedding or funeral time, or raining hard. In good weather, the large front porch, high up off the street, was, as was standard operating procedure in those years, the invariable haven of the family, along with relatives and friends when they called.

My mother had her third son while living in Macon, barely escaping with her life in the process. There were complications, twins, one of which died in birth, other problems, some no doubt stemming from her somewhat too old midwife. It was all done at home, of course; if Macon had a hospital — many towns and small cities didn't in those years — my mother wouldn't have gone to it. Her reason would have been her Christian Science, but whatever the reason, she was wise to stay out of any and all hospitals of that day. Antisepsis was only just becoming known in a great many places at that time, and there were surely more deaths than lives saved in the vast majority of hospitals in 1918. The lessons in medicine that came out of World War I would make for a substantial difference in the death rates of hospitals in the 1920s and after.

I began school in Macon. In the South typically there were seven rather than eight grades in grammar school. The result was that they managed to teach more, to "larn" us more in a single grade than was the case in California. All I know is that by virtue of the Macon first grade, I got off to a start that stood me in good stead for a long time after we went back to California.

By the time we went back, after a little more than two years in Macon, I was a Southerner. I couldn't help it. My grandfather's interest in me, his wonderful tales of his boyhood in Alabama, of his service as a very young infantryman in the Confederate army, his accounts of General Robert E. Lee, the beautiful portrait of Lee that hung in the living room and was lent to my school each year when Lee's birthday came around, with the whole school filing silently by the portrait in the school lobby, his gracious, almost courtly manner, his obvious devotion to my grandmother, all this took its toll on my just-begun Westernism. I should add that my grandmother helped considerably in the making of this Southerner. She, as a tiny girl, had known what it was to live in the very path of Sherman's march to the sea, the operation that broke the South's back in the war. She told of all the women and girls in her large extended family taking with them to bed nights the family silver and other valuables. It was widely believed that while Sherman's soldiers would pillage and burn as well as kill, they would not molest girls and women in their beds.

Once married, once separated for life from the people from whom she was descended, she became the instant matriarch of my grandfather's house. The love, the mutual courtesy, the trust and respect they had for each other, the respect and affection too for both of them in the community, in church, wherever, made an impression on my mother that was profound. Thereafter, whenever she spoke of Mother or Father, it was not her own parents— who had both died in her girlhood—she was thinking of but my grandfather and grandmother. The only time I ever saw my father cry was when in 1927 the word was telephoned from Macon that his mother had died.

But it was more than family that made me into a sworn Southerner. The tales told by my two grandparents were enough to make me a Confederate forever; the military strain is never very far from the Southern mind, or the mind of that age. I couldn't bear the thought that the North had won the war. Until I was at least seven years old I kept hoping to find the history book that would assure me that not the North but the South had really won the Civil War. I found family as it existed in the South — replete with many degrees of relationship, almost incessant visiting, gossiping, and locating obscure relatives in the past and present — fascinating. (I must add here that I got over that predilection for family within a very few years after returning to California.) The Negro in the South was of course a new and often baffling phenomenon to me. I had never seen a black person prior to going to Macon at age five. I was made to assimilate the fact that they were different and had to be treated differently, at once guarded against and protected. It was all right for white and black boys to play together, go swimming, fishing, etc. but only up to a certain age, about eleven; then absolutely no more. I humiliated myself one day when a lot of family were around the house by telling my grandmother in front of them all that a "lady" was at the back door. Looking mystified, my grandmother hastened to the back, to return a few minutes later with the word that it was "Old Hazel," to wit, a black woman calling for her food handout. I was saved from the derision of my aunts and cousins by my grandmother's presence. Later she explained, or tried to explain, the nature of my gaucherie, but I didn't have the impression that her heart was in it. Neither would have been my grandfather's. Both, as I realized many years later, were prime examples of what Myrdal called "an American dilemma," that is possessed of a deeply moral American philosophy of individualism and equality but possessed also of a time-honored impulse to observe the local mores of one's family, class, and people.

We lived in Georgia for only a little over two years, but for a child of six and seven, just starting school, two years can have a very considerable effect. It was a long time after we went back to California before I got over the feeling, the strong feeling, that I was a Southerner. In fact, I probably didn't get over it altogether. As I look back on grammar and high school years, I was forever reacting positively to what I understood states' rights to be, to charges that

Southern whites tyrannized and exploited blacks, and indeed to the whole Southern way of life, so often ridiculed in the rest of the country.

I was at Berkeley when the Southern Agrarians' *I'll Take my Stand* fell into my hands. The quickness with which I found myself agreeing with most of it was probably sufficient evidence that my road to political conservatism began with a considerable dosage of Southern Conservatism, the result of a couple of years in Macon. To the South I can no doubt blame or credit the fact that years later when I was a graduate student in search of a subject for the Ph.D. dissertation, I ended up with conservatism, albeit European, not of the American South.

After two years and my grandfather's death from the flu that was raging across American and indeed the world, we moved back to Maricopa. This time my father was manager and sole permanent employee of a retail lumberyard. Part of his income was use, rent free, of the house that sat squarely in the lumberyard. There were two bedrooms — reduced effectively to one by virtue of the other's being the office for the business — a living room and dining room, a kitchen and a small bathroom with tub and basin. There was for us, as for all other residents of Maricopa, a backyard privy about fifty yards from the back porch, no small distance, especially on the freezing, windy nights of winter.

Memory quails at the recollection of exactly how five of us slept in a small one-bedroom house. We were nevertheless a contented, reasonably happy, middle-class family. My mother had her church friends, my father his monthly poker gathering, which consisted of the little town's butcher, realtor, haberdasher, Piggly Wiggly manager, and pharmacist.

School was outstanding. All subjects were sturdy, time-tried disciplines or pursuits of the mind. The single goal of schools then was that of filling ignorant minds with the literacy that was a minimum essential of life. Just that. No overtures to humanitarianism, values, and life adjustments except insofar as some sense of these came from the strict standards that were imposed upon what one read and wrote in class. There was no nonsense about therapy. My knuckles still remember the feeling of the teacher's ruler — sharp edge if the offense had been marked — coming down hard on them.

Not only were schools excellent in the oil-producing Westside Desert, what with tax revenues and serious, conscientious elected county supervisors, but so were public libraries. Maricopa had a small but excellent library, a saloon (confined, of course, under Prohibition to near-beer and soft drinks) on one side of it and an open field of sagebrush on the other. I take nothing away from school when I say that the public library was where I really learned to read. How dull seemed all school readers when one could devour Zane Grey, Edgar Rice Burroughs, the Henty books, even Tom Swift and the Rover Boys, at the library — or at home, given the kind of highly supportive parents my two brothers and I were blessed with. My father had not finished high school; the wanderlust had gotten to him, much to the sadness of his doting parents who could easily have put him through college. He didn't seem like a person only partially schooled. Due undoubtedly to the civilized family life he knew, where conversation was almost incessant and language reflecting the best of English grammar and vocabulary was the rule, he had a sufficient start on life, at least for that day. He read little apart from a newspaper, but he honored reading almost to a fault. As a typically crafty child, I noticed that when I had a book in hand and open I was nearly exempt from household chores. All my father had to say was "Robert's reading" if there was a call from my less credulous mother to do this or that.

She did a great deal of reading, starting with the sacred works of Mary Baker Eddy. She didn't force her religion on her children, and apart from a year or two in Sunday School, my brothers and I were exempted — also from my father's lukewarm Presbyterianism. I have always thought, though, that something of Christian Science rubbed off on me. That religion, at least as found in the devout, breeds in its communicants a quiet and altogether certain self-confidence. The religion emphasizes a perpetual salvation for the devout. Christian Science endows the believer with not only immortality but with success in life. Second in importance, I think, was the relative absence in our bathroom cabinets of all the nostrums, salves, cough syrups, and similar dosages that tens of millions of Americans took from tens of thousands of miles of shelves in confident belief that each new potion, whatever aimed at, was bound to be miracle working. Americans, ever since the early nineteenth century, have been very possibly the most drugged people on earth. I have taken my share of medicines during my adult lifetime, but I am sure I would have thrust far more pills, tablets, powders, and draughts of foul-tasting potions down my throat had it not been for the stern attitude at home in my childhood regarding medicines.

My father was not a Christian Scientist; in fact he could wax critical about what he felt was that church's elevation of Mrs. Eddy to a position at least equal if not slightly higher than Jesus Christ. He was a backslid Presbyterian; I have no recollection of his ever going to any church save for the occasional required funeral or wedding. My mother and father made, from any pragmatic point of view, excellent parents so far as their children's health was concerned. There was an unwritten pact between them: As long as illnesses of the children were minor, my mother's Christian Science could take over, with or without auxiliary aid of a practitioner. But if illnesses threatened to be serious, my father's views would take effect and a doctor would be called for help. I remember in my own life the dreaded German measles that kept me out of school for six weeks; I remember mumps, chicken pox, frequent colds with heavy coughs, and two early illnesses that doubtless were the ones that left tuberculosis scars on my lungs. I remember untold headaches at one point in life. But, on the evidence, I was never "seriously" ill, meaning that I never had a doctor. My mother and presumably a practitioner now and then handled all. The first doctor I ever saw professionally was at Cowell Hospital at Berkeley. And the first aspirin tablet I ever took — and, I recall vividly, with almost instant relief from the headache (I've taken a thousand or more since) — was also at Berkeley my first year there.

On balance, I think the combination of views on medicines and doctors represented by my mother's and father's views was salubrious. The medical and apothecary professions when needed; but only then. I must not forget one more boon in my life from Christian Science: *The Christian Science Monitor,* which my mother subscribed to, along with the *National Geographic* magazine, throughout her life. The *Monitor* she read cover to cover, and she was easily the best-informed parent I knew during grammar and high school years. In poring over it, she was of course fulfilling that part of Mrs. Eddy's religious instructions to her followers that included the importance of a clean, honest, and objective newspaper, but she was also inevitably taking some pleasure in knowing more about national and international events than almost anyone around.

Education was supreme among the lares and penates of our hearth. My father and mother—the more so no doubt because of their own limited schooling—talked of little else, it often seemed, at meal table but how my brothers and I were doing in school; were we studying sufficiently; what courses did we like best, etc., etc. There was never the slightest doubt in my mind but that, no matter how low the family income might be, I was going to college. That was gospel at home, and I absorbed it. Berkeley came early into my life. I found myself naturally and spontaneously cheering for Cal over Stanford, USC, and the others. The words "Wonder Team" were often heard in our house. Archie Nisbet just *had* to be a second cousin at least. When I was about eight years old and the family was vacationing in the north, we visited Berkeley—Cal of course, to everyone in those years, from the Atlantic to the Pacific in this country—and a couple of enchanted hours walking over the ample greensward from one beautiful building to the next, taking in the Campanile including its elevator ride to the top, the magnificent Memorial Stadium, the Greek Theater, with student actors actually on the stage that day, the old halls like South and Bacon—I can't remember whether North Hall was still standing; I think it was—and the glades and trees with names I had never heard of, lots of good looking, friendly students to be seen—all this left on me a stamp that would never disappear. Henceforth it was Cal, Cal, Cal, and nothing else for me. It would be about ten years before I saw my first Cal football game, with the Cal Aggies and the Olympic Club in the early fall of 1932 when I was a freshman, but from the time I had my first visit to the campus, I spent a lot of time every autumn imagining what it was like to actually see a college game.

Another family move when I was in the middle of the sixth grade took us to Santa Cruz. It was and is a lovely city. The sudden change in topography and climate was almost traumatic. It was the great naturalist Helmholtz who once said that a sudden move from Siberia to the Senegal without stops would lead to loss of consciousness in any human. Something of that, in the benignest possible way, was involved in my family's move from Maricopa to Santa Cruz. The climate was matchless the year round. So was the scenery. On the west, coming right up to a lovely beach for swimming, was the Pacific Ocean; to the east were the densely wooded, green hills that ascended into the Santa Cruz Mountains and into which frequent hiking and camping trips were taken by Santa Cruzans. A more complete contrast to Maricopa it would be impossible to imagine. The schools were excellent and so were the libraries, beginning with the main library downtown and a branch near where we lived out Soquel Avenue. I reached twelve shortly after settling in Santa Cruz and promptly joined the Boy Scouts, the fulfillment of a dream that had begun with reading *Boy's Life* each month in Maricopa. There were occasional rides on Sundays up to San Francisco, with some of us in the family opting with my father for a baseball game — the minor league San Francisco Seals then the attraction — and the rest, Golden Gate Park with its thrilling De Young Museum and enchanting Japanese Tea Garden.

In the summer of 1926, just before the eighth grade for me, we moved again, this time to San Luis Obispo, situated halfway between San Francisco and Los Angeles and in its way quite as fetching a town as Santa Cruz; smaller (about 8,000 pop. then) and somewhat farther from the ocean and its beach but with some highly redeeming hills and mountains in every direction that formed the delightful valley in which the small town nestled. Apart from a Union Oil refinery and tank farm, there was no industry, farming, or retail business furnishing the entire economic structure of the town. I should add, though, that it was the main stop for the Southern Pacific trains that ran between San Francisco and Los Angeles. It was to San Luis Obispo that William Randolph Hearst brought his famous parties of movie actors by private railroad car, there to be transferred into a fleet of Packard taxis that Hearst maintained solely for the fifty-mile drive north to his castle in the Santa Lucia mountains overlooking the Pacific. Some of the town's recreation was afforded by the arrival, usually late at night, of one or another Hearst party — preceded by leak or rumor for the benefit of the locals. One never knew whether, by staying up past midnight, there would be rewards in the sight of Marion Davies to begin with but two or three dozen other stars as well.

I spent high school in San Luis. Its academic offerings were as fine as those of Maricopa and Santa Cruz. It's no wonder there were so few private schools in California then; public education was just too great a bargain no matter how well off a family might be; even so there were three girls I knew slightly and one boy who were sent off to private school; doubtless they loved their schools—Miss Head's in Berkeley, Thatcher in Ojai—but they always seemed lonely, somewhat stiff, and uncomfortable during the holidays and long summer when they were at home; hardly surprising; one lived with one's school pals in holiday and summer as well as during school sessions.

For the college bound there were four years of Latin—Caesar, Cicero, and Vergil after the first year. There had been two of Greek until a year or so before I entered high school in 1927, taught by the then superintendent of schools, Mr. Mayberry. There were four years of English Lit., math, science, history, beginning with a full year of ancient history, four years of Spanish and two of French. Physical education was required of girls and boys alike, the latter excused only if they were active in competitive sports. There were orchestra and band for those interested, the instruments and uniforms furnished by the school; there were clubs—restricted, however, to those built around a subject or theme such as Latin, science, literature, and the like. Purely social clubs were barred, most especially any that might aspire to becoming a high school Greek letter fraternity, then barred by law in the California schools.

High school was for me what it has been for millions of other Americans, a profound emotional experience as well as an intellectual regimen. I recall a book published in the 1970s with the beguiling title *Is There Life After High School?* I never chanced to see it, but from reviews and occasional radio talk-show commentary I gather it had a quite successful existence for a year or two. It deserved to, for the title alone captures a feeling vast numbers of American boys and girls have known at the mere thought of high school—setting of Freshman Reception, Junior Prom, Senior Ditch Day, and Class Night; nurturing ground of first true romances, a time when one could get over, at last, disdain-covering-fright in the presence of girls and come to be almost monomaniacal about a given female. I have known people in their seventies who still held on tightly to their high school annuals, going through them nostalgically at least once a year. The American comprehensive, coeducational high school is unique on this earth.

If one never was able to go beyond the public high school — and I estimate that not more than 5 to 10 percent of high school students in the twenties did — you still had been exposed to a good deal of what is important in the world, society, and the individual by the time you finished high school. The howlers in civics, history, and literature we are forever reading about today in one national study or another simply didn't exist for the most part sixty years ago. Curricula were too tight, too compulsory. If they erred it was on the side of strictness of curriculum and of examinations.

There was another cultural influence afloat in the twenties and then on through the next two or three decades, an influence that necessarily raised the level of the public's awareness of Western civilization and its roots and development over the centuries. I am referring to — of all things — Hollywood! If you were, as tens of millions of Americans were, an avid moviegoer in the twenties and thirties, you did indeed have your share of slapstick, Western cowboys, ridiculous melodramas, and shallow romances; but you also had a rather remarkable procession of historical films, films that highlighted romance, sex, violence, and derring-do, to be sure, but that also featured (because the producers couldn't escape from it) the historical setting, the time, the epoch, in a word — history.

Without leaving my chair I can summon up vivid recollections of *Babylon and Tyre, The Ten Commandments, Intolerance* (D. W. Griffith's masterpiece of comparative history), *Ben Hur, The Decline and Fall of the Roman Empire, When Knighthood was in Flower, Ivanhoe, Henry VIII, Elizabeth and Essex, Disraeli, Clive of India,* and many others; all motivated by marketing and crowd-pleasing forces, without doubt, but episodes nevertheless in the Western epic. And if we laugh disdainfully today at recollections of some of the scenes in Hollywood's historical films such as Mae Murray saying "What big muscles you have, Sampson" as he stood fatefully before the temple, or a self-important military captain addressing his medieval troops, "Men of the Middle Ages: You are about to begin the Hundred Years War," or whatever, we were at least picking up the crumbs of historical information that, on the evidence of frequent national tests, are so lacking today from the general intellectual fund of the American people.

I can say truthfully that before I entered high school I knew something, however small, about the Fall of the Roman Empire, Feudalism, the Magna Carta, Agincourt, the War of Roses, the Tennis Court Oath, the Terror, and sundry other episodes in Western history. And what I knew came as often from the movies, the historical movies Americans then so delighted in, as from the reading I did from well-stocked public libraries. The twenties and thirties remain Hollywood's golden age. Of course there was dross. There must have been dross even in ancient Athens' golden Age of Pericles. But overall there were (the exceedingly popular) movies about the historical past and about other continents and peoples of the world.

No one realized it at the time, but the twenties was a bona fide cultural renaissance, a very feast. We all know about the Roaring Twenties, the Boom Era, the Jazz Age, and the like. We all know that it was a short-lived period of economic prosperity with predictions rife throughout that such prosperity would be endless. What we are less likely to remember or realize about the twenties is that it was an authentic cultural flowering, one whose intellectual fertility would extend through the Depression decade of the thirties. The twenties was a renaissance in several areas, all fundamental in American life: literature including the novel, poem, and critical essay, with names like Hemingway, Dreiser, and Lewis; Frost, Robinson, and Jeffers; Mencken, Brooks, and Huneker to draw from regularly; in music, meaning chiefly jazz, blues, and swing with Ellington, Cole Porter, Gershwin, Berlin, Louis Armstrong, Bix Beiderbecke, and Jack Teagarden to hear on the radio if one couldn't reach or afford their usual night club haunts; in the art of the film, in a word the movies, which like jazz was exported to the entire world in the twenties and included such names as D. W. Griffith, Vidor, and von Stroheim, Chaplin, Keaton, Pickford, Fairbanks, the Gishes, and Garbo; and finally the twenties renaissance included, for most Americans, the world of sports, college, and professional; no other decade before or since has come even close to matching the number of heroes—still heroes, be it noted, to this day—of the luster of Jack Dempsey, Red Grange, Babe Ruth, Knute Rockne, Bill Tilden, Helen Wills, and Bobby Jones.

The talent of the Twenties didn't have to go unsung. Publishers like Knopf, Harcourt Brace, Random House, Scribner, and others rose to the literary occasion and published widely and supportively. The public libraries (including the small but excellent one in San Luis Obispo) also rose to the renaissance and regularly stocked the major works of the day. As if by divine act, a new, national medium came into existence, radio, for the works of musical composers and instrumentalists and singers of the Jazz Age; also for the works of dramatists, and above all those of comedic genius.

Thanks to the public library and to the habit of reading now thoroughly ingrained in me, I read the novels and stories of Hemingway, Dos Passos, Fitzgerald, Willa Cather, Ellen Glasgow, Louis Bromfield, and a good many others almost as quickly as they came off the presses. Will Durant's *Story of Philosophy* stirred me deeply. The Philo Vance murder mysteries began appearing (*The Green Murder Case* was, I believe the first) and made a lifelong devotee of the genre of me.) I won't pretend that James Branch Cabell's *Jurgen* was on the library shelves, or David Graham Phillips' *Susan Lenox,* but our librarian was quite willing to order them on loan for me despite the notoriety in which each was held, the first for its extravagant sexual symbolism, the second for its harsh, uncompromising picture of prostitution-in-poverty in Chicago. Mrs. Ames had her limits, though, as I discovered when, with a straight face, I asked her to order *The Memoirs of Fanny Hill,* having read a tantalizing reference to it in *The American Mercury* which our library subscribed to. But Mrs. Ames' chilly (and obviously informed) response brooked no further plea from me. I had to wait for Berkeley and the University Library where it was kept in a special section known as Case O and not available to ordinary borrowers, before I at last got to the ineffable Fanny. The only reason I got to it was that by my sophomore year I was a student assistant in the library—of which more below.

To return to my reading during the Twenties Renaissance, there were also the magazines the library subscribed to. I've mentioned Mencken's notable production; we had additionally *Vanity Fair,* then at its peak, *Harper's, Scribner's, Atlantic, The Nation, Time* and *The New Republic,* among others. Mencken enjoyed, at least among those of us who aspired to be known as intellectuals, highest repute, and apposite quoting from Mencken (also of course from Dorothy Parker) was requisite of San Luis cosmopolitanism. Even if Mencken — or Nathan or Dorothy Parker or Ogden Nash — hadn't in fact said it, you could enhance nevertheless the appreciation of what it was you were about to say or pretend to quote by attributing the gem in advance to one or other of America's reigning wits and critics. Yes, even in little San Luis Obispo, we the aspiring cosmopolites and sophisticates knew about the Algonquin Hotel in New York and its Round Table of endless wit, and we knew too of Broadway; drama reviews and notices in New York-based magazines insured that, leaving us attentive to the time when a Broadway hit would become a Hollywood movie and thus fare for us.

The Crash of '29 had little meaning and no particular impact upon my parents and their three sons. They owned no stocks or bonds. The Booming Twenties had passed them by; my father's salary as retail lumberyard foreman never went above 170 dollars a month. From the time I was a freshman in high school I worked summers, weed hoeing and ditch digging for the Union Oil Company, piling sacks of grain at the Southern Pacific Milling Company, and so on. There was good money to be made for about ten days at Christmastime by delivering packages from the post office. When the Depression hit, my father's salary dropped to 135 dollars a month; but under FDR's NRA it went back up to 150, as I recall. In any event, the now fabled stock market stories of the end of the twenties had not an iota's relevance to my family. We were quite possibly the only middle-class family in San Luis that was barren, during my high school years, of automobile, electric refrigerator, washing machine, and radio, one and all. My father's fortunes picked up considerably in the late 1930s, mirabile dictu, but he and we went through the whole of the legendary Booming Twenties living very modestly indeed.

Which didn't diminish our middle-class character in the slightest. I mean in the respects crucial to the middle class: a cohesive, affectionate family; a strong inclination for educational and other

kinds of success for the children; a considerable degree of permis-
siveness, especially in religious matters—but not moral, not in
respect to the values of honesty and overall decency. Jobs kept me
in enough money to dress more or less like other high school students and to date, attend dances, and in general have a damned
good as well as tutelary time in high school. And it was high school
without drugs, handguns, gangs, and teenage pregnancies. Truly a
golden age, a renaissance of all kinds.

1

Berkeley, 1932

I went up to Berkeley in the fall of 1932. For the vast majority of us then, admission was simplicity itself. All that was necessary was a diploma from an accredited high school with at least a B average in a prescribed list of strictly academic courses: history, English, foreign language, chemistry, physics, and then, upon formal application, you were suddenly in the clan of the Golden Bear. There were a few who became freshmen by qualifying on a standardized test or by special permission of the president, but their number in any freshman class was insignificant. Admissions at Berkeley was governed by the faculty, by a special committee of the Academic Senate. We didn't have to worry about such unimaginable things as ethnic quotas and the like.

Berkeley had the best academic calendar in the country in those years; it was made possible by the salubrious San Francisco Bay climate. While the rest of the country lay baking in the heat of August, the precious cooling breezes wafted through the Golden Gate (without bridge then) and made the campus seem like a mountain or sea resort. The fall semester began in early August, which meant that it ended just before Christmas, with all finals taken. Spring semester opened in early January and ended in May.

The academic air at Berkeley struck me as being quite as invigorating as the air we breathed. Gone forever now the straitjackets of grammar and high school curricula. I don't fault those. They are admirable at the proper phases of any individual's educational development. I wish they were wider spread in today's schools. But they don't have a proper place, it has always seemed to me, in college. I had been somewhat repelled when in my senior year of high school I visited a couple of the several well-known liberal arts colleges in southern California. There was too much of the air of in loco parentis, too many professors and deans trying to be big brothers or chums. There was none of that at Berkeley, and I thanked my stars then as I continue to today.

Not that there were no helping hands at Berkeley. Every student had a faculty adviser who was just that, an adviser not a surrogate Mom or Dad. You took any academic problems to him. If you didn't feel well, there was the first-rate Cowell Memorial Hospital, if you were hungry and needed part-time work, there was the Bureau of Student Occupations which took good care of the considerable number of us who needed additional income to stay in college.

Tuition was virtually nonexistent at Berkeley in the thirties. There was a mandatory twenty-five dollar registration fee each semester, perhaps a few small laboratory fees for those in the sciences, an optional ten dollar Associated Students membership card that took you gratis to all athletic, campus theater, musical, and other events during the whole academic year. But that was it. And if you didn't have the twenty-five dollars for registration, there were loan funds—though never as large as the Depression called for—to tide you over. Basically you were on your own, ready for adult responsibilities and thereby adult freedoms.

What most contributed to the invigorating academic air at Berkeley was the elective system. That system, founded at Harvard under President Eliot in the late nineteenth century and still regarded warily by many administrators and faculty members in America in the 1930s, was the very essence of academic Berkeley. What the great President Eliot had done was effectively declare all rigorous four-year programs, whether in the classics or the sciences, suspect. Such programs, Eliot thought, robbed the student of one of the most important of all freedoms: freedom of choice, freedom to choose from the rich assortment of courses in the Harvard firmament. Eliot's revolution gave the student himself the responsibility for programming of courses. As might be expected, there were many for whom this exercise in intellectual freedom bespoke sheer raw anarchy.

Happily, I thought and still think, Berkeley was one of the universities early on to follow Harvard in the elective pattern. When you arrived at Berkeley as a freshman you went right off to the college of your choice — the majority of us to Letters and Science, others to Engineering, Architecture, Chemistry, Agriculture, and so on. In L and S there were distribution requirements. But these weren't onerous and they guaranteed that anyone graduating from the college, properly had some exposure to literature, history, philosophy, and the sciences, biological and/or physical. These distribution requirements were formed of regular courses in the departments, taught by those of professorial status; not graduate students in roles of Assistants or Associates. Introductory courses in all fields were, in the thirties, commonly taught by the light and leading among Berkeley's professors.

Mercifully and wisely there were very few requirements of an all-University character. Subject A English was one, fulfillable by examination, of course; American History and Institutions, a relic of World War I, also fulfillable by exam; two years of ROTC for men students, and two years of Physical Education for both male and female students. Most of us were strongly opposed to all these except Subject A English. All others have long since been discarded, I believe (and hope).

But these University-wide requirements were relatively few and inoffensive by the standards of that day. One chose one's college, one's major within the college (to insure some degree of specialization) and the rest was free choice of courses under the elective system. How free one was may be illustrated by my clear memory of one semester when I chose courses in Greek Lit. (in translation), industrial organization, Shakespeare, Art Appreciation, and American political theory. I had no indigestion whatever as a consequence. The great Joel Hildebrand used to liken a good and free university to a buffet table or cafeteria. Make certain, said Joel, that all dishes (courses) are nutritious and then leave the actual selection and the pattern of selection to the diner (student). In more than a half a century of association with universities, from one coast to the other, I have never seen any reason for departing from Joel Hildebrand's advice.

There were more than a few, though, around the country who were or would have been horrified at the Hildebrand prescription. What, they would say in high indignation, entrust *any* selection of courses to the *student*??? What kind of anarchy, of intellectual chaos, must this not bring? For such enemies of the elective system there were two shining prophets in the thirties. The first was Robert Hutchins, Boy Wonder of Chicago, who became at age twenty-nine president of the University of Chicago. His almost instantaneous purpose became that of "saving" the undergraduate students from the "anarchy" of the elective system and the "professionalism" of courses taught by economists, literary scholars, biologists, physicists, and the like. He organized a new undergraduate college that was, by design, as separated in spirit and substance from the rest of the university as would have been a Trappist monastery. For their first three years no choice whatever was allowed students in their courses. Even in the fourth and final year not more than two elective courses were permitted. At the heart of their education in the Hutchins dispensation was the reading, or alleged reading of Great Books. In point of fact what the students read for the most part were excerpts specially printed from Great Books: hence the amused reference by many to Hutchins' Great Snippets. No matter what a majority of faculty at Chicago may have thought of the college, it was widely taken up as an ideal for undergraduates by outsiders in the U.S., by those who in a nutshell loathed the elective system and cherished a mandatory utopia.

Among these was Alexander Meiklejohn, the second prophet of the 1930s and equally a sworn enemy of the elective system. He set up an "experimental" college at the University of Wisconsin, one in which there would be none, or the barest minimum, of electives for the undergraduates. He chose to go a few steps beyond Hutchins. The first two years would be composed of "great books" but those of a special kind, illustrative or descriptive of ancient Athens. The second two years of the college would be similarly restricted, similarly mandated in the reading done and courses taken, but would deal with contemporary America. Suffice it to say that Meiklejohn's college failed, broke up, before Hutchins's did, but in each case a considerable mess was left behind that took years to clean up.

There were a few faculty members at Berkeley in the thirties who were impressed by one or the other or both Hutchins and Meiklejohn, but they had little if any influence on their colleagues. The very idea of an undergraduate, or even a lower division, college formed in which students would be barred from elective freedom, obliged to take an unvarying program of mandated courses, would have horrified most of the Berkeley faculty. I, even as an undergraduate, heard more than a few sharp criticisms of the two prophets, Hutchins and Meiklejohn.

There were other fads and fancies in academe in the thirties, one and all antagonistic to the spirit of the elective system and to courses as "specialized" and "narrow" as those in, say economics, political science, English, French, chemistry, or physics. What was wanted, it was said—though rarely if ever at Berkeley in the thirties—was "integrated" courses in which "artificial" boundaries within the social sciences or humanities were razed. The result, alas, where these allegedly integrated courses flourished was not any appreciable integration but simply stale, flat, and sprawling survey courses in which an economist would lecture for two or three weeks, to be followed by a political scientist, then a geographer, or whoever, for equal amounts of time, the result being like a plate of badly scrambled eggs. No such courses existed at Berkeley in the thirties.

Nor was there a sacred canon drawn from the literary classics of the Western world, one consisting of, say, the Ten Great Books, the reading of which was made a requisite for graduation no matter what field of knowledge one was by disposition committed to. I believe I am an authentic humanist—evidenced by books and articles I have written—but I have never been able to read a Great Book in cold blood. I was introduced to, and profoundly edified by scores of genuinely great books, from past and present, but always in warming intellectual contexts, meaning chiefly courses taught by learned faculty.

Berkeley in the thirties operated, as did such other, cognate universities as Harvard, Princeton, Michigan, and Stanford, on the historic assumption that the purpose of a university, as contrasted with a sect, a political party, or other instrument of purported redemptive truth, was that of laying before students the best that had been done and said by scholars and scientists dedicated to an understanding of the world and the individual. In this, Berkeley and other fine American universities were, in their varied ways, continuing the tradition begun in the High Middle Ages by such entities as Oxford, Cambridge, Paris, Salamanca, Padua, and Cracow among others. The Absolute, the eternally True and the Good could be left to the church. What the university sought was *knowledge:* knowledge in all its inevitably changing, developing way of cosmos, society, and man.

Berkeley was emphatically not the place—nor was any other genuine university in the Western world—for those who were seeking their personal identities, the meaning of life, a platform for large-scale social and moral revolution or unchanging, eternal truth. If, however, one was simply in quest of knowledge as this was to found in the humanities and sciences of the twentieth century, then Berkeley was an admirable place in which to reach adulthood.

One of Berkeley's curricular virtues was the fluidity and continuity of its three divisions of courses: lower, upper, and graduate. They were not, as they were in many universities of the time, sealed off from one another. There was in truth a kind of telescoping of the three divisions. Thus graduate students working toward the M.A. or Ph.D. could, indeed were expected and even urged to present some of their academic units of credit from undergraduate, upper division, areas. As an undergraduate and then in time a graduate student I found it stimulating to rub shoulders in a class open to both undergraduates and graduate students.

Upper division students could, when disposed and reasonably well prepared, obtain permission to enter a graduate course on occasion, even a graduate seminar. The permission of the faculty member concerned was, of course, vital, and I do not suggest that it happened very often. Nor was it considered eccentric or bizarre for an upper division student to wander into the introductory course of a field other than his own. This practice was encouraged. When I came to teach the introductory course in sociology, it was not at all uncommon to have seniors in the physical sciences enrolled. By the time they felt they had mastered the world of their own specialty, they were emboldened to tread in new and very different fields.

This, it occurs to me today, was integration with a difference. It was also, more importantly, intellectual freedom!

Heightening the newfound, zestful sense of individual freedom at Berkeley in the thirties was the very strong, if not entirely conscious, awareness of the University's *collective* freedom, its legal autonomy, in the state. The very appearance of the Berkeley campus suggested this autonomy, this "privateness" within the commonweal that the politicos of Sacramento managed. In this Berkeley was unique among public universities.

The style of Berkeley — building, landscaping, as well as intellectual-social style — was anything but what one characteristically found in state-created and state-governed collegiate institutions. Stanford, designed originally by the most expensive architects, had nothing in beauty over Berkeley by the 1930s. Structures of the elegance of the Greek Theater, the Campanile, Sather Gate, the Hearst Mining Building, the Hearst Gymnasium for Women, the Doe Library and within it the breathtakingly beautiful Morrison Library attested to a state university strikingly different from all that is usually connoted by that label. There were few if any signs of heavy-footed bureaucrats in Sacramento having had controlling influence. So did the wealth of greensward, glades, gardens, and groves of trees such as the eucalypti at West Gate tell one immediately that Berkeley was a public campus with a difference, a stunning reflection of private taste and design.

The university at Berkeley was the reflection of something else too, something constitutional-legal in structure, something rugged and durable. I refer to the unique position the University of California had among all state universities in the U.S. This was a position originally, in 1868 when the University was founded, granted by what was for many decades fondly, gratefully called the Organic Act. Under this act, the substance of which would be later incorporated in the State Constitution, the new university was almost totally freed from the governing powers of the State Legislature and Executive Office. The Organic Act and later the Constitution specified that the government of the University would be vested solely in a new Board of Regents composed in small part of State officers such as the governor, lieutenant governor and speaker of the assembly, but largely, overridingly by private citizens. Moreover all would serve long terms thus freeing them from some of the short term political pressures and crises. And, mirabile dictu, the Legislature would fund it all!

This was, especially in the America at the time of regnant populism, a stunning achievement. It was as if the authors of the Organic Act were significantly aware of the fact that in the history of freedom, corporate, collective freedom from state bureaucracy is as important as individual. The Regents had a great deal of the kind of freedom to govern that inhered in the boards of trustees of private universities. The Board of Regents was, and still is constitutionally at least, if less and less in practice, a virtually sovereign body over the University of California without obligation to seek ratification of its actions by legislature or executive. When, early on, the Regents decided to restrict enrollment to the top 12½ percent of California's high school graduates — a decidedly risky venture for a state university in an age when such action was instantly vulnerable to charges of elitism — their action stood. It was legal and constitutional, given the Organic Act that generated the University by California's government. Throughout the Midwest and elsewhere in the country, state universities were prevented from any such restriction of enrollment. They were and still are obliged to admit all students with high school diplomas, no matter in what fields of studies they had worked and with what grade average. The results were from the beginning foreseeable: large numbers of unprepared college freshmen flunked out unceremoniously and humiliatingly.

Berkeley's constitutional, quasi-public, quasi-private character, its autonomy from the state government, helped encourage donations to the Berkeley campus. Without knowing, or being particularly interested in, the unique constitutional status of the University — down through the thirties it was often referred to as the fourth branch of California government, so magisterial did it seem — alumni who became wealthy found it easy, as easy as if it were a Harvard or Yale, to identify with Berkeley and its chaste grandeur. Almost from the beginning Berkeley had an alumni association that was equalled only by the associations of the old, famous, private universities. Berkeley to this moment, is the most heavily endowed — by private money — of any of the state universities in America. And that fact derives almost entirely from the quasi-private nature of the university. What possible chance would Berkeley have had in winning from alumni such structures as the Campanile, Sather Gate, the Morrison Library, and Sather, Mills, and Flood endowed professorships if it had not the character and the sheer memorability of the historic private universities? Alumni donors would have been frightened away immediately if their proposed gifts had had to go through layer after layer of state bureaucracy.

Not all donors were by any means alumni. I think of Phoebe Apperson Hearst and also of her son William R. who gave in memory of his mother, the Greek Theater. When I first saw it, there was actually a Greek play, in the ancient Greek language being done. The players were lost on the massive stage and there weren't more than a dozen or so sitting in the audience. But Hearst's and the University's intent from the beginning was less a vehicle for plays in the Greek language than it was an elegant outdoor amphitheatre for a variety of functions ranging from Charter Day exercises to the old Bonfire Rally just prior to Big Games.

In addition to the buildings and monuments, wonderful open spaces between buildings, spaces made up of glades, groves of trees and shrubs, bridges crossing creeks, gardens and greensward all gave testimony to a richly endowed private university rather than a public one. The main glade, stretching from west to east, from Oxford Street and the magnificent eucalyptus grove all the way up to Memorial Stadium and the arboretum and source of Strawberry Creek had a specimen of virtually every kind of tree, shrub, bush, grass known in the world's temperate belt.

This is of course the glade that at the very end of the thirties when the University was desperate for classroom and office space, was brutalized by "temporary buildings" still there, I believe, looking like nothing so much as housing for an alien, invading army. But at the time there was no alternative. Another glade, perhaps the single most photographed part of the campus and the setting of Max Reinhardt's exciting, 1930s production of *Midsummer Night's Dream* starring Mickey Rooney as Puck, was Faculty Glade sited between Stephens Union and the Men's Faculty Club. In the thirties this glade had not yet lost by disease the handsome, superbly pruned and shaped trees that added measurably to the beauty of the glade.

Strawberry Creek, in several branches ran through the campus from east to west. There were eye-catching bridges, two of particular beauty, one by the south end of the Education Building, another approaching the Men's Faculty Club. At the southwestern corner of the campus stood the mighty eucalyptus grove that had been thickly planted early in the University's history. I pray that it survived the terrible blight of some years back that destroyed tens of thousands of eucalypti in the Bay Area. And I must not omit the Memorial Stadium, remarkably graceful for something that seated seventy thousand people, and popular with everyone except those whose houses had had to be razed and those whose houses had survived but whose punishment was the football masses making their way to the Stadium so many Saturday afternoons in the fall.

In the Thirties it was common to hear that Berkeley was one of the three most beautiful campuses in America, the other two being Princeton and Cornell, the first with its Lake Carnegie and buildings dating back to George Washington's time; the second with its spacious but still intimate liberal arts campus looking down on the magnificent Lake Cayuga. Berkeley was indeed in good company. But only a prejudiced mind could then rule Berkeley out in the beauty contest. Berkeley may not have had a lake, but from its superb site in the gently rising hills there was an incomparable view of the Pacific Ocean through the Golden Gate.

The Founding Fathers of the University of California had chosen well for the infant university's permanent site, the Berkeley hills, then empty save for an occasional farm house; this beginning in 1868, with North and South Halls soon to denote the new Athens of the West. One of Mrs. Hearst's gifts, well meant, was an international competition, with large a monetary prize, among architects for the best master plan of development for the tiny campus. Happily the resulting plan, elegant though it was, never had a chance to constrict growth, as well-meant master plans so often do if utilized.

In another, and important, respect the Berkeley campus exuded an air of the private—and also the urban. I refer to the dozens of shops, restaurants, coffee counters, clothing, and book stores that, especially on the south and north sides, hugged the campus. I remember William Wurster saying years later that every university, no matter how public its sponsorship, should have "fingers of private enterprise" threading it or else intimately clustered on its borders. Wurster was a Berkeley graduate in architecture, famous in time for his creations, and in his final years dean of architecture and the environmental sciences. He was also a world traveller and sharp observer. He had such places as the Sorbonne, Oxford, Cambridge, and Padua in mind when he referred to the importance of blending the private and public, the academic and the mercantile. I thought of Wurster's words when I spent a year teaching in 1956 at the University of Bologna in Italy; there classroom and other university buildings are interspersed among hotels, restaurants, book stores and the like, all privately owned.

In our own country, in addition to Berkeley, there are splendid examples of this intimacy of the public and private: Harvard Square immediately off the Yard, Princeton with the village immediately across the street, Yale and New Haven, etc. Pity the students at universities which, using everything short of a Great Wall of China, seek architecturally to prohibit any blending of the public and the private. One feels imprisoned.

The University and the town of Berkeley literally grew up together, closely together as Telegraph Avenue on the south side and Euclid on the north, with their shops, stores, and restaurants hugging the campus, made vivid to generation after generation of students. Telegraph in the thirties extended a block farther than it does today. Where today's Sproul Hall and Plaza sit on one side and the immense Student Union on the other, then sat a couple of dozen shops and restaurants on Telegraph's final block to the north. Narrow Alston Way to the left as one reached Sather Gate was the escape from what would otherwise have been a dead end at Sather Gate and the route to the downtown area.

Almost as famous in Cal student memories as Wheeler Hall and the Doe Library were some of the stores that lined the two sides of the final block of Telegraph. There was the Sather Gate Book Store on the left side almost immediately after one exited through Sather Gate. It was then, along with Campbell's in Los Angeles, one of the two finest book stores in California, notable for the European as well as American titles on its shelves. In between the Gate and the book store was Vaughan At Sather Gate, probably the best known of men's clothing stores in Berkeley. It strove successfully to be at fashion's edge and at the same time with generally affordable prices.

George Good was then located in that same block, on the right side as you walked from Sather Gate to Bancroft Way. His store was the class of Berkeley, worthy of comparison with Bullock and Jones in San Francisco and Brooks Brothers in New York. His prices, though, left the great majority of us in the ranks of window-gazers. It was hardly believeable to most of us in the Depression that suits could cost a hundred dollars and above, sport jackets at fifty dollars minimum, with few at that price, shirts ten dollars, neck ties three to five dollars. Needless to say, everything was most fetching to look at.

On down the block just beyond George Good, at the intersection of Telegraph and Bancroft was the Varsity. It was a combination restaurant, soda fountain, bakery, and confectionery. It was easily the most favored of hangouts for students during the thirties as indeed it had been for some years before. The chocolate cake was, it seems to me in long retrospect, at least as good as many years later I discovered Sacher's to be in Vienna. With fifteen cents you could nurse along a generous slice of Varsity cake and a small Coke for hours.

As notable as any place on that now-long gone block was the Black Sheep restaurant, on the east side of the street, with a winding stone staircase that took you up to the multi-roomed but still intimate restaurant where Fritzie, middle aged, of Eastern European descent (no one could be more exact than that) always greeted you. The place was famous for its European food flavors and aromas; not least among these were the special sweet rolls that were served in place of bread. It wasn't cheap: lunches ranging between forty-five and seventy cents, dinners a little higher. For the ordinary student such as myself it was a place for splurging: like Spenger's wonderfully noisy and happy seafood restaurant at the foot of University Avenue, right on the Bay. About two doors from The

Black Sheep was the newly opened Jules where milk shakes were a dime in the fall of 1932 and was accordingly well attended.

Other well-known places on or just off Telegraph in its final block or two were Dan Whelan's tobacco shop on the corner of Telegraph and Bancroft; the Campus Theatre, on Bancroft immediately off Telegraph, then showing mostly foreign films. The Berkeley Music House was across Telegraph from Dan Whelan's. It was very popular and for the best of reasons. It must be one of the most generous music havens in all history, certainly in Berkeley's. The owner's patience was endless. It never seemed to matter whether you actually bought a record or not. You asked for and got a certain record, took it into one of the several small soundproof cubicles, played it to heart's content, and then returned it as you walked out of the store to the owner who simply said thank you.

The north side of the campus also had its fingers of private enterprise, though nothing as impressive as the southside beginning with Sather Gate. When you walked through North Gate by the handsome old redwood shingle architecture building, you had a full block, no more, of Euclid shops and eateries ahead. Most interesting was the now long since razed Northgate Hotel, more nearly a shabby rooming house by the 1930s than a true hotel. There was at the corner of Euclid and Hearst the Euclid Apartments that I believe still exist. Except for the two studio apartments at street level, all apartments in the three-story building were uniform: a living room, dining room, each with folding double wall bed, a small kitchen and smaller bathroom. There was Jack's up at the corner of Euclid and Ridge Road, a favored hangout for northside students and a first rate drugstore with soda fountain on Euclid at Hearst. Nothing else was of much interest. Still the block of "fingers of private enterprise" did exist, and I'm sure we were grateful.

How fortunate Berkeley was in this respect, and continues to be, is best appreciated by contrasting a few other campus experiences within the University of California. UCLA agonized for many years, still agonizes, I assume, over the total lack of anything around the Westwood campus besides exceedingly expensive houses with protective zoning ordinances that forbid anything of

commercial character, anything that might have become a Berkeley Telegraph Avenue community or a Harvard Square. The
campus was miles from Westwood Village and even when you got
there, you were more nearly in the presence of what we think of
today as South Rodeo Drive off Wiltshire than a place of immediately adjacent shops, restaurants, coffee houses, and the like, all
oriented toward students.

The Riverside campus's experience has been little different except that no girdle of million-dollar houses encircles it. During the
twenty years I was there on the faculty, hapless students had a small
shopping center a mile away; then it was another mile or two to
reach the town. I believe Santa Cruz and Irvine are in much the
same positions. This is unfortunate. Nearly all of the great universities of the world, from Paris and Bologna in the Middle Ages to
Harvard and Berkeley have had, and have relished, the "private
fingers."

There is finally Stanford—as a positive force, I mean, in the
development of Berkeley. If Senator and Mrs. Leland Stanford
hadn't decided upon a university as the proper memorial to their
beloved, deceased son, Leland Jr., it would have been necessary,
one can't help think, for the gods of the new state university to
intervene and create a university like Stanford simply for the invaluable, almost indispensable competition between the two.
Competition among universities has been a constant in their thou-
sand-year history in the West: between Oxford and Cambridge,
Harvard and Yale, and so on. The founding of Stanford in 1891
gave Berkeley an uplifting rivalry almost from the very beginning
that was salutary to each.

Universities love competition, and not simply in sports. The real
heart of the competition lies in academic things—libraries, laboratories, impressive buildings, distinction of faculty. The act of the
Stanfords in creating, out of their great wealth, a new university
only a few miles to the south of Berkeley inevitably put the idea of
gifts and endowments in the minds of Berkeley alumni and well-
wishers. If Berkeley had Joseph LeConte and Bernard Moses, Stanford wanted and got David Starr Jordan and Thorstein Veblen. I
remember a Big Game not long after the war, Stanford was beating
Cal decisively at Berkeley and the Cardinal rooting section was

pouring it on. A man just behind me got up and shook his fist at the Stanford section, shouting "We got the Mark Twain Papers," an event that had happened only a week before.

The founding of Stanford, which opened in 1891, was a much publicized national event. When the Leland Stanfords got the idea of a university as a memorial to their young son, they both went to Harvard to consult President Eliot about the feasibility of such a memorial. Eliot graciously showed them about the Harvard campus, answering all their questions. Finally, Mrs. Stanford asked, with bated breath, how much would it cost, all this assembled academic glory, to duplicate? President Eliot thought and thought and finally said "about thirteen million dollars," at which Mrs. Stanford, almost beside herself with joy, said "We can do it, Leland, we can do it." Do it they did, in lovely Spanish architecture and very nearly a model opening faculty.

Competition between Berkeley and Stanford was immediate. No less than Berkeley, Stanford was committed by charter to the education of the poor. Stanford's first president was the distinguished scientist, David Starr Jordan. Although Cal was twenty-two years old when Stanford opened its doors, she had to wait a near decade for a president to match Jordan's stature. That was Benjamin Ide Wheeler, still greatest of all U.C. presidents. His decision to leave Cornell and a chair in Classics was no doubt fortified by knowledge in 1900 that only a few miles from the Berkeley hills was an already nationally famous private university called Stanford.

Without a Stanford University close by, Berkeley would have had no near rival, and rivalry is vital in the growth of universities and colleges. There was San Jose College, founded eleven years before Berkeley's inception, in 1857, but it was then nothing but a normal school, as it was called, that is, confined to teacher training. It was in no sense a burgeoning university. What Stanford and Berkeley both needed, as did and had Harvard and Yale, was friendly but stiff competition, in courses and curricula primarily but not insignificantly in sports. The first Big Game was played on a bleacherless vacant field in San Francisco in 1900. Almost from the start it was legendary.

Stanford was private, based solely upon private wealth and Berkeley, at least legally was public, The State University. But as I have said, Berkeley was a different kind of public university, given its constitutional autonomy and its many private gifts, and there thus wasn't all that much difference between private Stanford and public Berkeley. Both drew heavily from the Bay Area middle class. Both universities were based solidly on the liberal arts and sciences, with professional schools regarded as important but auxiliary to the central core of arts and sciences. Both from the beginning put high value on research; teaching was of course the primary function but it was made plain by Jordan at Stanford, as it had been by the earlier Joseph Le Conte at Berkeley that teaching was expected to be anchored in continuing research. Both universities were enthusiastic about intercollegiate athletics. Finally, Stanford was and remained for many years, as tuitionless as Berkeley. Part time jobs were regarded with as much respect by Stanford as Berkeley. Herbert Hoover and my own mentor at Berkeley, Teggart, were among Stanford's very first class in 1891 and both required jobs in order to stay in college. Hoover worked in the school laundry, Teggart as student assistant in the Library.

Rivalry, in contrast to war, is always laced with at least a few premises of cooperation, in society as well as nature. This was true of the two Bay Area universities. For many years there was a "gentlemen's agreement" not to raid each other for faculty. It was enough for the welfare of both and indeed of all California that either should manage to bring a renowned scholar-teacher from the ivied East out to the remote reaches of the West. Rail travel from Boston or New York to San Francisco took five days, and with only the telegraph, it is no wonder that California was thought of as a kind of insular possession of the United States. Given those difficulties underlying recruitment of Eastern academic stars, it would have been cruel and stupid for either Berkeley or Stanford to steal from one another through carefully calculated offers.

Another of the once-cherished patterns of collegiality between the two young universities was the annual dinner, always in San Francisco, of Berkeley and Stanford professors of the same academic field. That handsome custom was, I believe, another of the Depression's casualties.

But all such courtesies and civilities recognized, it was, by the end of the first decade of this century, the Big Game that most completely and satisfyingly embodied the Stanford-Berkeley mystique. Football rivalry carried with it the related rivalries of yell leaders and their yells such as Give 'em the Axe, Oski Wow Wow, and the exhilarating songs like Hail To California and Come Join the Band.

2

Bohemian Berkeley

Two striking aspects of the Berkeley of half a century ago — and indeed of the present time — are incomprehensible apart from the city across the bay, San Francisco. I am referring first to bohemianism and second to the spirit or culture of revolution, each deeply etched into Berkeley's being. But first I want to say something about San Francisco and its longtime, providential role as the Magna Mater, so to speak, of Berkeley's destiny.

In the thirties we revered the city by the bay just as had our predecessors, going back to the very beginning of Berkeley. It was The City. When you said you were going to The City there wasn't the slightest doubt where you were going: certainly not to Oakland but neither to Los Angeles or Fresno. (An older generation on the campus in the thirties often spoke of San Francisco as "town." One "went over to town" for theater, museum, or whatever).

We revered The City because of its exciting and wonderfully creative past, its roll of writers and artists, its Barbary Coast, theaters and restaurants, its air of cosmopolitanism, then so appallingly lacking Los Angeles, its historic revolutions in politics and culture, and, far from least, its bohemianism.

San Francisco was already a booming, buzzing metropolis when Berkeley was founded in 1868. Its wharves by the 1860s were crowded with ships rich in cargoes brought from all over the world to exchange for the gold and silver mined not far from San Francisco. As Mark Twain, Bret Harte, George Sterling, Jack London, and scores of other writers have told us in books and letters, San Francisco was a thrilling, ever-buoyant Mecca to the many thousands who had come or were coming from the east to the west.

San Francisco was born a city. It never had to go through the stages of crossroads, hamlet, village, small town, and so on in order to become a city. San Francisco was the quintessence of urbanism from the start, unlike pathetic Los Angeles, which was just beginning when the University was founded to emerge from pueblo status. It had no real harbor, no industry or commerce, was already becoming desperate for water, and was surrounded by nothing but family farms and retired folk from Iowa and other Midwestern states. Lazy, sleepy, dominated well into the nineteenth century by a hacienda mentality, Los Angeles was the very opposite of San Francisco.

Thousands fled San Francisco in 1849 when gold was discovered in places like Sonora, Calaveras, and Columbia. But they came back in record time to the City, having learned that there was potentially more gold in San Francisco, to be had from shipping, manufacture, stores, hotels, and restaurants than in the Mother Lode country. It was the popular writer, O. Henry who eventually put the seal of greatness on San Francisco. America, he said, had only three great and genuine cities: New York, New Orleans, and San Francisco. If there was a Barbary Coast in the City by the Bay, so were there impressive libraries, museums, book stores, opera houses, theaters, and elegant mansions to be awed by. There were writers galore: Mark Twain, Bret Harte, Jack London, Frank Norris. No wonder the infant university saw San Francisco from early on as Mecca.

In a way, it's unfair that San Francisco should have been from the start of the new university its Magna Mater, its Athens. For it was Oakland that housed the University for its first four years, from 1868 until 1872 when the move was made to the campus in the hills and to the first two buildings, South Hall and North Hall. More than that, however, was the priceless gift of little College of California, situated in Oakland, about ten years old, and dedicated to the liberal arts, to the University as it first campus, its first school or college of instruction. The University of California was a Land Grant University, which meant that, in return for free land owned or bought by the Federal government, a university would in effect consecrate itself to the practical arts and the applied sciences. If there is a single reason for the University of California's having forged so quickly ahead of other Land Grant, other state universities indeed, it lies in the fact that Oakland made it possible for the University to begin not in the agricultural and other applied arts, but the liberal arts and sciences.

But life is unfair. And fairness or no, the reality was from the beginning the close economic, social, and psychological liaison from 1872 on between San Francisco and the new, small university nestled in the beautiful, then otherwise virtually empty hills rising from the water front to Grizzly Peak. The sad but blunt and irremediable truth was then and has been ever since that, as Gertrude Stein—who lived on both sides of the Bay for some years—famously summed up the matter of Oakland, "there's no there there." In the thirties there were only two purposes in making the short streetcar trip on Telegraph Avenue to Oakland: The Fox Oakland theater, which had first-run movies and occasional vaudeville, and visits to the waterside bar—where the glitzy Jack London Square sits today—where Jack London a few decades earlier had done his celebrated drinking. Drinks were cheap and the grizzled bartender convinced us by the number of his stories that he had indeed served Jack and a few other writers and alcoholics as well.

But so much said, Oakland scarcely existed for Berkeley students. The tie between the City and campus had been tightened in 1906 when thousands of Berkeley students and faculty came to the help of San Francisco in the throes of the earthquake and fire. Mostly, though, it was the other way: gifts, donations, subventions from the City by the Bay to the proud and eager young campus to which middle class San Franciscans could now send their children by street cars and ferry boats and not have to pay a cent.

San Francisco's greatest gifts to the Berkeley campus were simply its libraries, museums, art galleries, theaters, opera and concert halls, and its abundant symbols of wealth and culture. It is a great thing for a university to grow up in or very close to a great city— think only of the majority of Europe's greatest universities and the cities of St. Petersburg, Cracow, Granada, Paris, Oxford—itself a thriving, bustling city in the Middle Ages and only a short distance from London — Harvard, Columbia, Chicago, and Berkeley among many others. Cities in the Middle Ages were the first havens of freedom — "The City makes Free" was proverbial in the medieval era and it is no accident that the Sorbonnes, Oxfords, Paduas, and like institutions grew up in the cities, not in the feudally dominated countryside.

San Francisco also had writers and artists in substantial numbers from earliest times. They came and went, as did Mark Twain for one, but they were deeply attached to the City. High among the signs of writers' and artists' attachments was the bohemia that grew up from earliest days in the new and endlessly fascinating city. It was doubtless inevitable that so much of cultural essence, of flavor and tempo from the early days of San Francisco would have the flavor of bohemia, for the new city welcomed a great variety of social and intellectual types, none of whom had much difficulty in accustoming themselves to the place. Early on they tended to cluster on Russian and Telegraph Hills and also in enclaves of North Beach. With the influx of the intellectually unorthodox, the downright rebels against conventionality of thought and behavior, another bohemia was added to the world's number of bohemias that included the Left Bank in Paris, Soho in London, the Trastevere in Rome, the French Quarter in New Orleans, and Greenwich Village in New York. It is entirely in keeping with San Francisco that when its political and business titans decided to form a club, they named it The Bohemian Club and to show their sincerity had special memberships at substantially lower initiation fees and dues for artists and writers; also for ten each from the faculties of Berkeley and Stanford. So characteristic was it that to the Bohemian Club in downtown San Francisco was added the famous Bohemian Grove, consisting of hundreds of secluded acres in the Russian River area where a considerable degree of bohemian behavior was virtually a condition of attendance at the annual summer encampment.

It is very sad today to see in parts of San Francisco once lush with small cottages, studio apartments, and rooming houses that formed the background of the often colorful lives of the intellectuals, painters, writers, actors, and other denizens of a true bohemia, nothing but exceedingly costly high-rise apartment buildings populated by bankers, merchants, brokers, and lawyers, and no more a genuine community than Market Street. Not much of San Francisco's once famed bohemia on Telegraph and Russian Hills, and out in North Beach, survived the First World War. That war symbolized the beginning of the drying up of native talent in the City. No longer were the likes of Jack London, Frank Norris, Ambrose Bierce to be seen and read. By the Second World War the old bohemianism, the writers and artists colonies, were in full retreat, headed for extinction.

It was Berkeley that came to the rescue, that provided habitat and also inspiration to bohemians old and new. There are two highly distinctive legacies received by Berkeley from her great patron, San Francisco. One is a revolutionary tradition or culture. I shall come to it in the next chapter. The other legacy, that of bohemianism, became one the City's numerous cultural-intellectual exports to Berkeley, from the beginning an enthusiastic importer. By the thirties bohemianism was a signal feature of the campus and also of its surrounding blocks. Styles of dress, vocations and avocations, living arrangements, dedication to art as God, compulsion to *épater le bourgeois,* loathing of the purely conventional, desire to be and look different, above all, a cultivation of the free spirit marked distinctly the secure place of bohemianism at Berkeley.

There are two, related reasons for the ease with which bohemia was assimilated by the campus across the bay from San Francisco; one is negative, the other positive, both ecological, as it were. The first, negative reason is the almost total lack of University housing during Berkeley's formative years. Beyond International House and Bowles Hall, each recent and specially constituted, there were no residence halls whatsoever on the Berkeley campus in the thirties. This absence of dormitories and with them regulated student life was often accounted a social and moral vacuum, one that disturbed parents. But for the bohemian spirit such absence was benign.

The second, and positive reason for the fact that San Francisco's storied bohemia could successfully diffuse through Berkeley, was the ring of cheap housing around the campus. There were rooming houses galore, the average monthly cost of a room eight to ten dollars, studio apartments, usually rehabilitations of otherwise empty basements of houses in the hills, and what were called garden cottages, small houses built in the back yards of larger houses which fronted on scores of streets. (Eventually fire ordinances prevented the building of these, but such ordinances didn't affect the hundreds already built in the city.)

It was this amplitude of cheap, private housing only minutes from Wheeler Hall and the library that made possible in an ecological way the reception from San Francisco and other cities in the country the bohemian communities. As fast as the city across the bay dried up in bohemian hospitality, Berkeley absorbed them. Thus the University at Berkeley was put in the company of cities in the world that included great universities like Paris, London, and Rome, cities with a Left Bank, a Trastavere, a Bloomsbury or Soho, and a Greenwich Village in New York, also on the perimeter of a campus, that of New York University. Berkeley like the others was a magnet for the nonconformist, *épater-le-bourgeois* types, whether students or nonstudents.

The bulk of Berkeley bohemia lived, thrived, and agonized in the rooming houses found on all four sides of the campus but chiefly on the south side, on Bancroft, Durant, Channing, and Haste. The saga of Berkeley owes much to these rooming houses, for it was their relative abundance and cheap rent that enabled Berkeley to rise out of the dreadful state of commuter campus and become a stable, resident student population. Nearly all of these houses were three-story, built as family homes early in the century but gradually becoming rooming and boarding houses as original families died out and a reasonably good living could be seen by owners of the old houses. I spent the first few months of my freshman year in a house on Channing, about a block west of Telegraph. It was ten dollars a month for a room, an additional twenty for board if you could afford it which I couldn't.

Besides the hundreds of rooms of this sort, and, I stress, within five or ten minutes walk to the campus, there were for the fortunate, studio apartments in substantial number. These rarely cost more than fifteen or twenty dollars a month, and they offered, of course, a small kitchen where you could eat at low cost by doing your own cooking, and a private bath. Finally, there were the garden cottages, small houses, usually one bedroom, living room, bath, and kitchen. These could be had in the Depression thirties at anywhere from twenty to thirty dollars a month, and without much looking.

Thus the so frequently overlooked (by historians and memoirists) base or infrastructure of Bohemia, whether on the Left Bank, Greenwich Village, or Berkeley. Without an amplitude of cheap housing, ranging from waterless walkups to fetching little garden cottages and studio apartments with all the necessities there can be no bohemia no matter how fiercely the desire may rage to excoriate convention and become known as a genius. Berkeley had this amplitude, this ring of potentially bohemian dwelling places, and, given the inspiration provided by San Francisco's Russian and Telegraph Hills, a true bohemia in the Berkeley hills was almost inevitable. It is doubtful that anything resembling the bohemia of yore in San Francisco is to be found today. Artists and intellectuals have largely vanished from the City, and where low-cost cottages and studios used to sit in North Beach and environs, there sit today extremely expensive co-ops and condominiums.

One of the charms of the faculty at Berkeley was the number of those known or strongly reputed to be lovers of the bohemian life. Of the best known or suspected, the names of J. Robert Oppenheimer in Physics, Haakon Chevalier in French, Alexander Kaun in Russian and, not least, Benjamin Lehman in English come to mind. Lehman enjoyed, if that is the right word, particular luminosity as a bohemian by virtue of his earlier marriage for a rather short time to the great actress, Judith Anderson. Although this had been lore among students for some time, it was only the shattering of Berkeley tranquility one Sunday morning by the San Francisco Examiner and its full story of the spoiled Lehman-Anderson marriage-romance that confirmed what had only been titillatingly suspected. In his early years Lehman had preferred actors to scholars.

One characteristic of the bohemian faculty at Berkeley that set it off from the rest was the faculty bohemians' zest for company among the nonacademic bohemians, artists and writers, mostly, in both San Francisco and the immediate environs of the campus. Faculty as a rule lived within itself. Town and gown relations had once flourished but not in the thirties, save for the bohemians.

They looked the part: Chevalier like a Left Bank professor at the Sorbonne, Kaun like a member of the Arts faculty at, say, the University of St. Petersburg, Oppenheimer like a young professor, or even student, at Heidelberg, Lehman like one or other of the painters and scribblers of Greenwich Village. Silently we cheered them. They were colorful and invariably rumored to nurse the souls of geniuses, just like those who figured in the novels of Floyd Dell, Romain Rolland, and Compton Mackenzie.

Students, or a minority of them, delighted in aping their bohemian faculty, as best as limited finances made possible. Student bohemians lived anywhere and everywhere they could conceivably afford. There was an old, abandoned, water tower at the top of Hearst Avenue, a block up from the intersection of Euclid and Hearst that with its room around seventy-five steps up to the top housed a succession of mostly bohemian types. I knew one of them; Tony or Anton his name, a change from the Albert he had been born to in the Midwest. He had graduated years before, in music, from the University but stayed on and on, composing to the best of his ability. His room was made comfortable with the usual accessories of the bohemians in the way of rugs, wall hangings, pictures, and so on. He had an electric, fireless cooker on which there was perpetually a meat-and-vegetable stew. Tony never washed the stew vessel; just kept adding new meat and vegetable when required. He joined the National Guard just for the money each month, but became enamored of it, went zealously to training camps, and when the war broke out began as a major.

One charming couple, Ajax and Gordena, made expensive peasant clothing for the stores in San Francisco, and also wore it themselves, to the esthetic improvement of Berkeley sidewalks. There was the whole Dyer-Bennett family in a large house in the hills just above the campus. The mother was, I believe, a follower of Isadora Duncan — so it was said, I can't really vouch for it — and a son, Richard, known as Dickie, played the lute professionally. And in a strikingly beautiful, castle-like house in the hills lived Sam Hume, Bohemian, an early graduate of Berkeley, Class of 1907, I believe, whose considerably younger wife, Portia Bell, was the daughter of the Pacific Gas and Electric president and business power in San Francisco. Portia was an impressive amateur painter and it was in the interests of improving her portrait work that she signed up for Medicine in Berkeley simply in order to study human anatomy minutely. She became in short order more interested in medicine than in art, and finally wound up in medical psychiatry with a strong penchant for Freud and psychoanalysis. She worked from her castle home in Berkeley. By fortunate accident I came to know her; she was beautiful and charming. I'm sure I'm not the only male to have fallen at least a little bit in love with her. She and I and a fascinating young architect did a series of radio talk shows over the Pacifica radio channel. This after the war.

Student bohemians mingled freely with student revolutionaries on the campus, with Eshleman Hall, the student publications building, the commonest center of both groups. Naturally there were bohemian revolutionaries, or revolutionary bohemians, but the distinction between the two I found to be essential at Berkeley. I don't mean that I ever encountered a bohemian who wore a Hoover or Landon button, but for more than a few who wrote for the Daily Cal, the Pelican, or spasmodic tracts, or who participated actively in the campus theater, the full flavor of revolutionary impulse was used up in the unorthodox life-style, the ostentatious live-in relationships between the sexes with their nose-thumbings at the institution of marriage, the exotic foods and drinks, the manner of dress, the kind of reading done, the writing—or painting, composing, or sculpting—making unnecessary further ego-trips to cell meetings of the Communists and the like.

Considering the complex of forces involved in Berkeley's campus bohemianism, it is as though Hegel's "cunning of reason" in history was operative. Consider the vital elements: first, what Herb Caen calls Baghdad by the Bay; second, the absence of University dormitories; third, the presence of the old houses on all sides of the campus, the studio apartments, the garden cottages; and fourth, the "fingers of private enterprise" that included first-rate book stores, record shops, painters' supplies, and so on. Between San Francisco and Berkeley there was a strong filial relationship, one that both partners took pleasure in.

No such relationship existed between Stanford and the City. The distance between the two wasn't significantly greater than between Berkeley and San Francisco. But the ecology was profoundly different. Stanford was conceived and planted within a thousand or more acres of open land deeded by Mr. and Mrs. Stanford to the university for capital. There was no place for a circle of cheap housing to develop. Moreover Stanford was by design well equipped with dormitories, for men and for women. Nothing comparable to Berkeley's Telegraph Avenue retail culture ever existed at Stanford. I doubt that it does today.

Much the same is true of UCLA. It is without any discernible bohemianism in its campus and off-campus culture, and it is without the necessary circle of housing that bohemianism requires. Where such housing might sit there is instead street after street, block after block, of the very poshest and expensive of sub-mansions. As at Berkeley in the beginning, no dormitories, and the depressing gift of being encircled by nothing but very high priced houses. There wasn't a cheap rooming house, a garden cottage, or studio apartment within miles. Few of the faculty could afford the houses that concentrically ringed the campus; none of the students could. For many years UCLA was a commuter campus, with students and faculty driving or bus riding many miles between university and their homes. At night the campus was like a graveyard. However, like Stanford and USC, UCLA has improved substantially in these respects since the Second World War. I congratulate them.

I hope the foregoing will not be understood as the writer's belief that only with a true bohemia can a college or university become great. This would be absurd. I have just mentioned Stanford; from the beginning a university destined to greatness. There are many others.

But I will not conceal my conviction that while bohemianism is not a requisite, it is for the most part a charming and valuable fillip — there is no other word — for any estimable university, consecrated as it must be to curricula and deep research. "It is so pleasant to receive a fillip of excitement when suffering from dull routine," wrote Trollope. And the nineteenth-century poet, John Boyle O'Reilly, almost forgotten today, wrote in his *In Bohemia:*

The organized charity, scrimped and iced
In the name of a cautious statistic Christ,
Oh, I long for the glow of a kindly heart and the
Grasp of a kindly hand;
And I'd rather live in Bohemia than any other land.

To return to San Francisco, once deservedly known as the Athens of the West, fountain of intellectual and cultural blessings for the new university at Berkeley, beacon to the eccentric and creative alike, it must be recorded that in one of history's strange reversals of fate, the city has been eclipsed in recent decades by the campus — the Berkeley campus. The city has lost none of its physical beauty; from every direction the skyline remains thrilling, the architecture in places breathtaking. But that is all there is today. The city's once vibrant cultural and mental life has withered sadly. Gone are the times when writers, musicians, and artists flocked to the city. Gone too, it would seem, is the spirit that produced the Mid-Winter Festival of 1893 and the magnificent Exposition of 1915 to which millions came from all over the world. By comparison the World's Fair of 1939 on artificial Treasure Island was a bust. Where are the writers and artists, along with other movers and shakers once so prominent in San Francisco's life? They are largely gone, as are the once-prosperous and nourishing manufacturing industries that vied with waterfront wharves as generating forces in the economy underlying the cultural ambience.

Los Angeles, for so long derided by San Franciscans as an overblown pueblo, without culture in any recognizable form, has manifestly overcome the fabled city by the bay. The day is long past when Herb Caen could regularly warn all San Franciscans flying down to Los Angeles for the day to take with them a bag lunch, there being little, Caen said beyond hotel restaurants and Boos Bros. cafeterias. Los Angeles at the present time leads its northern competitor almost embarrassingly in high cuisine. And also in distinguished museums, in art galleries and in the volume of art sold, in bookstores, musical offerings in every context from opera to chamber music, in distinguished universities and colleges, and just about all the other spheres of culture in which San Francisco once had unchallenged leadership in the West. How humiliating to

San Franciscans that starting in the 1930s and extending to the present, it was Los Angeles to which Europe's light and leading, the Manns, Huxleys, Stravinskys et al., took themselves after escaping their homelands.

It would be grossly negligent to omit mention, however, of the single exception to San Francisco's intellectual drought of the last three decades: Eric Hoffer. Longshoreman for many years, one of Harry Bridges' principal adversaries in the longshoremen's union, Hoffer became famous throughout the world of letters in the 1950s for his classic *The True Believer,* to be followed by *The Ordeal of Change* and other books extending into the 1970s. He stood virtually alone in San Francisco, but it is nice to relate that he stood far from unnoticed by his fellow San Franciscans—and Berkeleyans too with whom he spent occasional times as campus resident.

Berkeley has become, in a manner of speaking, San Francisco's redeemer. What the City by the Bay did for the fledgling Berkeley campus in the late nineteenth century is being returned with considerable interest at the present time. By the sixties both the radicalism and bohemianism San Francisco was once famous for had made Berkeley their habitat. For the intellectual excitement, the brilliant play of ideas once synonomous with the great city, we have to turn to Berkeley, and in lesser degree Stanford. The children have redeemed their mother.

3

Revolutionary Berkeley

San Francisco's second considerable gift to Berkeley was the spirit of revolution. I ran smack into it on the first day of classes in August 1932. Walking, along with hundreds of other students in the early morning, through Sather Gate, we were greeted by a group that identified itself as The Social Problems Club. Perhaps three dozen students formed a moving circle; each had a Free Mooney arm band; all were chanting more or less rhythmically "Down with the ASUC," a reference of course to the Associated Students of the University of California, in a word, the student government. It wasn't immediately clear to me what the bill of indictment of the ASUC consisted of, but it required little watching and listening to realize that this was a social problems "club" with a difference. I found it thrilling.

I would have been more thrilled had I known, could have known, that this infant revolution in 1932 was the second in a series of Berkeley revolutions that began in 1920 and is still going on in the nineties. No other university in America comes even close to Berkeley's revolutionary proneness. All in all there have been from 1920 to the present six notable revolutions.

The first was the Faculty Revolt of 1920, organized against an administration that combined flabbiness with periodic authoritarianism. Suffice it for the moment to say that the faculty revolt was remarkably successful; out of it came the Academic Senate that persists to this day and is still uniquely powerful among faculties of

47

American universities, powerful in a multiplicity of vital academic respects.

The second revolution in order of time is that of the 1930s, which I have just identified and to which I will return momentarily.

The third Berkeley revolution was faculty again. This broke out in the fall of 1949 and lasted for close to three years. It was a revolt by the faculty against a loyalty oath that the Regents had decided to impose upon each faculty member, thus, as the Regents hoped at any rate, turning off the occasional red-baiting attacks on the University from the outside. Good intention notwithstanding, the faculty fought the oath and won.

Fourth in the procession of Berkeley revolutions was the most famous, and most durable, of them all: the Student Revolution of the 1960s; the revolution that began at Sather Gate in early December 1964 and, before it had run its course, spread throughout the Western world. This revolution has long since entered into Berkeley lore.

Berkeley's fifth revolution had a fiscal core. It took place in the early 1980s and was sparked by hatred of South African apartheid. It took the organized form of a demand that University investments in not only South African corporations but American corporations doing business with any elements in South Africa be terminated forthwith. The result was a surrender by the Regents and a quick turn to the massive disinvestment required by revolutionary demand.

Revolution number six is ongoing. It is perhaps best identified as the revolt of the ethnics, primarily with respect to the admissions system of the University. Thus far, with the help of a strong minority of faculty members, the ethnics revolution has managed to alter drastically the student admissions system, imposing percentages if not actually quotas of the several ethnic minorities—African-Americans, Asians, Latinos, American Indians—that form parts of the California population. The revolution has also brought about the creation of new courses in ethnic culture and history made mandatory for graduation. Beyond these achievements, serious thought is being given to the establishment of mandatory percentages or quotas of ethnic graduation—as well as admission—from Berkeley.

Revolution, thy name is Berkeley. I repeat: no other university in the United States comes even close to Berkeley in the number and also significance of the revolutions during this century. To this day each of the revolutions has its continuing cohort of those who were there at the time, who rejoiced in it, and can wax nostalgic at the drop of a syllable. Some of the most politically and academically conservative faculty I knew in the forties and after, individuals by then in advanced years, were nevertheless proud and generally very voluble about the great Faculty Revolt of 1920 when the Regents were forced into major structural changes. Joel Hildebrand, for one, could become almost lyrical on that revolt.

The sheer number of revolutions at Berkeley suggests the existence of some kind of revolutionary yeast ever ready to rise, no matter what a given cause may be. If there is such a yeast, it has to be another bequest of San Francisco to Berkeley, one side by side with the bequest of bohemianism. It is hard to think of any city, even New York and Chicago and Denver, with the record of political tumult and agitation over issues and candidates that San Francisco had during its first seventy-five years. In the great influx of Europeans in the nineteenth century, there was a good sprinkling of *revolutionistes,* from Fourierists to Marxists. There were native voices: Lincoln Steffens, Fremont Older, Ambrose Bierce. Jack London, who spent one year at the university in Berkeley, turned Marxian socialist in 1894 after a short imprisonment for vagrancy. His was militant socialism from the outset; he somehow combined the principles he gleaned from Marx and Engels with convictions too of the ascendancy of sheer power, personal strength, and the superiority of the white race. His skill as a writer was fitful, but there was never any flagging, even after he had become relatively well off, of the revolutionary impulse.

There were others of radical thrust in the City's history: Tom Mooney, anarcho-syndicalist, advocate of direct, lethal action. He with Warren Billings were found guilty of a bombing of the 1916 Preparedness Day Parade. Both were sentenced to hang. Woodrow Wilson, however, in the face of powerful radical protest in the country, commuted the sentence to life in prison. Billings, by recanting and expressed willingness to accept a commutation, was released by the time I reached Berkeley. But not Mooney; he insisted upon a full pardon, which he eventually got in 1939 from Governor Olson but only after he had become successor to Sacco and Vanzetti in Boston as the major symbol of revolutionary protest, and of repression in the Western world.

Almost as famous as Tom Mooney in the history of San Francisco radicalism was Anita Whitney. The daughter of conservative, well-off, middle-class parents, she early became a convert to the syndicalist movement, carrying her message to the very citadels of the capitalist class. After falling afoul of the comprehensive anti-syndicalist law, she was arrested shortly after World War I ended, and given a long prison sentence after a brief trial. She had access, however, to enough money to appeal the verdict. Her lawyer was John Francis Neylan, then a highly successful Progressive lawyer, later, in 1950, to become the leading Regent in the battle with the Berkeley faculty over the loyalty oath. The Whitney case was a cause célèbre without question, and it became historic when Anita Whitney, with Neylan as her lawyer, carried the case all the way up to the Supreme Court which found her not guilty.

Neylan—"Black Jack" as he was widely referred to out of his presence—must have had mixed feelings about his spectacular success with the syndicalist Whitney. He was chief lawyer for the entire William Randolph Hearst publications network, deeply opposed, as nearly all the early California Progressives had become to all forms of the radical left, syndicalist, communist, whatever, but willing nevertheless in 1920 to take the Whitney case.

By the early thirties San Francisco had become second only to New York City in the influence of Marxism on intellectuals and labor unionists. Harry Bridges was easily the foremost figure in labor. A native of Australia, long identified with radical unions in shipping areas, deeply radical by temperament irrespective of whether he was actually a member of the Communist party, he was without question one of the two or three most charismatic labor leaders in the U.S. Sam Darcy, editor of the *Western Worker,* a spinoff of the orthodoxly communist *Daily Worker* in New York, was Bridges' close companion in matters of Marxian theology—the dialectic, class struggle, proletarian democracy, and so on—but Bridges accepted absolutely no advice from others when it came to leading a large and powerful union, the International Longshoremen's Union.

There were those — Eric Hoffer, fellow-longshoreman of Bridges for years but a strong dissident, was one of them — who said Bridges would have benefited had he been found guilty of passport violations and been put in prison a few years. There, wrote Hoffer, he would have learned something about real-life Americans instead of the cardboard proletarians Bridges was limited to seeing within his chamber of Marxism. No doubt true; but irrelevant given the adulation he got from tens of thousands of Bay Area workers.

Two signal events took place in 1934, both external to the Berkeley campus but highly catalytic all the same to campus politics and ideologies. The first was the historic General Strike in the summer, one of the few such strikes ever mounted in U.S. labor history. The second event was the campaign for governor, on the Democratic ticket, of Upton Sinclair, notable American socialist and a widely read author on both sides of the Atlantic. His platform was End Poverty in California (EPIC).

The strike was the more gripping of the two events. By virtue of a job, I was spending that summer at Berkeley and thus felt as though I had a first-row seat to the unfolding revolutionary drama of the general strike. Harry Bridges was the electric figure behind the strike, which was a widening of the conflict between the longshoremen's union and the Waterfron Association of employers that had been going on for a considerable length of time. There were those, communists included, who disapproved of a general strike on the ground that willy nilly such a strike would become a revolution but one without competent leadership and resources. But Bridges prevailed, and the general strike was ordered in July.

It was general indeed, involving factories, stores, transportation, and so on. Everything was closed down. This included all the streetcars, and in Berkeley an eerie silence descended upon usually noisy intersections like Bancroft and Telegraph on the southside and Euclid and Hearst on the northside, where streetcars were almost constant and extremely noisy when they made their sharp turns as at the corner of Euclid and Hearst where I was then renting a room. I can't remember with certainty whether deliveries of food and other necessities were made to hospitals and cognate institutions; I believe not; for it was that lack of humanity on the part of the labor councils that so quickly brought the citizenry to the peak of concerted opposition that theorists of the general strike have always feared. The police and firemen also went out on strike, though I don't recall how long.

It was exciting beyond belief, living in Berkeley and the whole San Francisco area that summer. Before the streetcars and ferry boats ceased operating, I made my way to the waterfront, or as near to it as a student-outsider was likely to get. To my somewhat fevered mind, it all suggested Paris in 1789 and St. Petersburg in 1917. The strike presented no problem to me. I stored up a week's supply of bread, cookies, canned vegetables and fruits, coffee, cigarettes, and the like, and, by then a student employee at the library, made my way regularly on foot the short distance from my room to the library. There we talked of little else while paging and charging out books but the strike.

Giving the workers and their unions, and the whole left wing in the Bay Area for that matter, added momentum was the WPA Writers Project in the East Bay. One of its principals was Joan London, duly sprung in all significant, including ideological, respects from the loins of her famous father, Jack. She was by the mid-thirties one of the most publicized members of the Communist Party. She also effected a special library permit for several dozen of her "fledglings," as she called the rank and file, as well as herself. They were given stack privileges for a short time; a time just long enough to outrage the faculty who used the stacks for their serious research. I was by then working at the loan desk occasionally, not entirely used up by paging of books, and there were frequent opportunities to talk to Ms. London. My mind was largely on her father, but hers wasn't; it was on the present, actual, vivid struggle for power between the workers and the reactionary capitalists.

The second event of enormous ideological significance in the thirties was, also in 1934, Upton Sinclair's socialist bid for the governorship of California. By early fall he was deemed to be a serious threat. There were no polls in those days, and this judgment was, as it turned out, based largely on sheer fright of conservatives in the state. Certainly the then heavily Republican and conservative moguls of Hollywood took fright and under their leadership a massive campaign against Sinclair was mounted, with numerous popular film stars put into roles of propagandists.

Sinclair lost the election, but his impact on radical circles was striking. Despite the assumption by most people that all radicals, including the communists, would give him, a lifelong socialist, help, the reverse turned out to be true. I remember being thunderstruck when I learned from my communist student acquaintances in the fall of 1934 that the Party had taken an utterly negative position on Sinclair. In fact the Communist party was working as positively for his defeat by the Republican Merriam as possible. The reason—and Marxists always had reasons; for them there were never accidents or inscrutable events—was that capitalism by 1934 was so torn and destabilized by its own contradictions that there was nothing left to fear from the bloated capitalists. Their day was over and they could be safely left alone to rot. The real danger, according to campus communists was no longer the capitalist class but rather the aggregate of liberals, social democrats, and socialists who were, at least in the eyes of the hard core, deeply orthodox communists of the day, the greater menace to progress—meaning of course communist progress. Just as the worst furies of Lenin and the Bolsheviks in 1917 in Russia turned, not upon the Czarists but rather the liberal and anti-Czarist Kerensky government and then the socialists and Mensheviks, so in the early 1930s, the communists everywhere expended their largest energies upon the defeat and destruction of liberal and socialist groups, not the owners and managers of capitalism.

The Berkeley campus communists followed to the last inch the Comintern's line of strategy. They assailed the Socialist Club on the campus; liberal groups, even those which made a strong point of their own support of communist rights; and faculty members known or thought to be strong liberals or socialists. They took particular delight, it seemed, in attacking from every point of view Professor Carl Landauer in Economics. He was a European refugee from Hitler, a charming and gentle human being—and a profoundly committed democratic socialist. All of which made him in communist fancy a Social Fascist, running dog of Hitler and Mussolini.

I learned about Social Fascism at communist cells. I went to a couple, courtesy of a good-looking girl on the campus whom I had come to like, one Hazel M. She lived with Edith A. in a basement studio apartment I had occupied for the better part of a semester, then gave up for a much cheaper room in order to try to straighten out my finances. Hazel and Edith succeeded me in the studio. They talked, it seemed, of nothing but Marxism and communism and their apartment was dense with books, journals, propaganda sheets, and the like, all clearly profound parts of their lives.

My interest in Hazel was as much personal as ideological. She was very pretty. Her interest in me, I soon discovered, was anything but personal. She was interested solely in making a convert to her religion, Marxism. To that end she and Edith invited me to go with them to the monthly cell meeting, held two or three blocks from the campus in a meeting room of a liberal and indulgent church, Episcopal, I seem to remember. The meeting was at night; there were perhaps twenty-five in attendance, a few faculty and the rest students, chiefly graduate. Presiding was a communist member of, as I recall, the milk drivers union, with headquarters in Oakland. He was probably a better driver than spokesman for the Communist Party, although he had assuredly learned his lines. No matter what subject was brought up from the floor, our presiding officer's answer was the same, beginning with "The Comintern has studied that carefully, and its position is . . ." Over and over he explained and reexplained the doctrine of Social Fascism, which I have already described briefly. Liberals and socialists were worse enemies now, he intoned, than the capitalist class, for it is in process of self-destruction and unless the socialists and their allies are destroyed, there will never be the dictatorship of the proletariat that Marx posits as the necessary step to the redemptive classless society.

About two of such cell meetings and, Hazel notwithstanding, I bolted from role of tyro in the communist movement at Berkeley. A more stupefying amalgam of blind orthodoxy and banality I had never encountered. I could imagine meetings of Deep South fundamentalists, the swamp fever types, in precisely the kind of discussions that went on at communist cell meetings, in Berkeley at least.

As I have noted, the principal trouble with Berkeley radicalism in the Thirties was its unitary mould. It was all Stalinism. There were no refreshing heretical types around, Trotskyists, Lovestonites, Schactmanites, and the other defecting but still radical groups so well known in New York and its environs. Berkeley communists, as I was amused to discover in later years, were regarded by their Eastern brethren as lacking in "dialectical insight" and also a sense of humor. "More Communist than Stalin" was in the East a common reference to Berkeley and Hollywood communists. Within in the limits of the Marxist Church, there were a few excellent articles from time to time in *Science and Society, The Communist, Partisan Review,* and other heavily Marxist journals. But none I ever saw that was written by a California communist. *The Pacific Spectator,* founded in Carmel by communist Ella Winter and her fellow-traveling husband Lincoln Steffens was pathetic and short-lived.

Berkeley student communists were sublimely compliant with all zigs and zags of the official Communist Party Line. There wasn't a zig or zag that they found impossible to taste, swallow, and gulpingly pronounce delicious to the campus — through the Daily Cal, Pelican, or hand bill. The zig of official Social Fascism was acceptable; so was the zag in the mid-thirties of the Popular Front. When a zig of monstrous proportions took shape in August 1939 with Hitler and Stalin become allies, communists, including Berkeley's, were unruffled. Precisely the same was true when in June 1941, following the German invasion of Russia, Stalin went back to being an adversary of Hitler and Nazism, the Berkeley communists had no difficulty in taking this zag in stride and pronouncing it ever so tasty. They were fervent isolationists, pronouncing the European war a mere corrupt adventure in imperialism, from August 1939 until June 1941, and definitely something for America to stay out of. But when the Comintern spoke, following Hitler's invasion of Russia, the Berkeley communists, like those everywhere, were ready to obey, and overnight posters appeared with "Second Front Now" mandated and the war itself one of Soviet-led democratic freedom. An imperialist war became in a day one to make the world safe for democracy.

However fatuous Berkeley communists seemed in matters of international war and politics, they were not fatuous in their forays and strategies of campus politics. Their prime objective, as I have already stressed, was to capture as much as possible of the ASUC. They had a considerable success in capturing, through ballot box and other means, an impressive number of important posts: the ASUC presidency, the editorship of the Daily Cal, and sundry other positions of campus importance in the late 1930s.

There were frequent verbal assaults—nothing more—upon President Sproul and the regents, all of them labeled of course as fascists, a word thrown around in the thirties with as much aban-don as "racist" is today. The student revolutionaries demanded abolition of the twenty-five dollar a semester registration fee, of the ten dollar charge for an ASUC card, and greater freedom, in fact, limitless freedom in bringing on to the campus for lectures mem-bers of the Communist Party. They gave support to the creation of cooperatives for student housing, making use of a few ancient but large houses in campus environs, which was a good cause but marred by the communist students' insistence that they control the cooperatives. As I recall, they also participated in the Fair Bear crusade, the not unworthy effort by the ASUC to bring wages students earned in their various jobs up to a higher level.

There was a "guide to courses" printed by the communists, a rather ramshackle affair done in red letters and warning students against the "reactionary" courses and their instructors, such as introductory political science under the "militarist" Professor Barrows, the introductory course in economics taught by the "cap-italist-imperialist" Ira B. Cross, and "Social Fascists" such as Carl Landauer.

There were abundant rallies outside Sather Gate. I can't recall Earl Browder or William Z. Foster, the two ranking hierarchs of the American Communist Party speaking anywhere near the campus in the thirties; Oakland, yes, and San Francisco, but not in the town of Berkeley. The University did offer one program on the Hoover-Roosevelt campaign for the presidency in the fall of 1932. It was held in the old Harmon Gym, which was packed. Chester Rowell, editor of the *San Francisco Chronicle* and at the time a Regent, Maurice Harrison, leading Democratic conservative, formerly a Regent, spoke for their respective candidates, as did a charming, eloquent young woman whose name slips my mind speak for Norman Thomas, Socialist. She got the largest applause from the students, but not, as I said above, in the ASUC straw ballot in late October, which Hoover won.

Not, I believe, on the faculty. I have no idea how things were on the faculties of engineering, agriculture, and other professional schools and colleges, but in the College of Letters and Science, liberals and social democrats predominated, and they went strongly for Thomas and FDR.

There were avowed, publicized Marxists on the Berkeley faculty, Oppenheimer in physics being one of them. It is a matter of doubt whether he, like his brother Frank, became a member of the Communist Party. But he was a declared Marxist. There was Haakon Chevalier in French and his wife, already mentioned, both admitted communists.

It would have been astounding if Marxism hadn't reached many, though never a majority of American intellectuals including university students and faculty members. For the country, the entire Western world, was awash in strikes, lockouts, episodes of naked repression and brute violence, and withal a widespread feeling, induced by Depression, fascism, and Soviet communism, that the end of one world had come and there was nothing to do but await the arrival of the next. And for such a state of mind, Marxism was redemptive; it had exactly the same function possessed by such world religions as Christianity and Islam. It offered explanation of how the breakdown had come about, a cast of saints and villains, and, above all, Marxism offered hope for the future: hope of a united world proletariat ushering in a classless, thus truly free, society. And on this earth, not in a next world.

I repeat, the Marxists and communists never reached in number more than a small minority. There were indeed conservatives and ordinary, nonactivist liberals to make up the majority at Berkeley even during the Depression thirties. But the significance of revolutions in history is never a function of mere numbers. It was a small minority that conducted the French Revolution of 1789 in Paris, the spasm of revolutions all through Europe in 1848, and, above all, the Bolsheviks under Lenin and Trotsky that overthrew the liberal Kerensky regime in late 1917 and so quickly instituted, from the top down, the Soviet Communist regime.

To return to Berkeley, the number of students who proclaimed themselves communists, who paraded under that banner, who sought positions of influence in the student government and virtually flaunted their proud association with the legacy of Marx and Lenin, was not large assessed in terms of head count. But in intellectual influence, in ability to mobilize crusades recurrently for an abundance of social and educational objectives, the communists — and I mean here as elsewhere, proclaimed, self-advertised communists, not liberals and populists who might have occasionally offended the American Legion or Daughters of the American Revolution — could on certain occasions be a decidedly significant intellectual force. This was especially true from 1936 up to about Pearl Harbor when the campus was transformed by the impact of the draft on male students.

Marxism stood at a higher level of prestige, as philosophy of history and mode of economic analysis in the 1930s than at any time, I would guess, in its history. This was true in Europe and Asia as well as in North and South America. In the thirties it was the so called "scientific" Marxism that predominated, that of the *Manifesto,* the *Gotha Program, Capital,* and kindred Marxian texts. This was the "masculine" Marxism of the impending Armageddon between Capital and the Proletariat, of workers on the barricades, and the forthcoming dictatorship of the working class led by the Communist Party. Over and over in the thirties we were treated to references, in handbills and letters to the Daily Cal, to "historical necessity," "historical materialism," "dialectical synthesis," not to forget Lenin's "democratic centralism."

It was, obviously, a somewhat different Marxism from the kind that is fashionable today — in America and Western Europe if not exactly in Russia and the Eastern European states. Today's Marxism has had the softening benefits of Lukacs and Gramsci, and is borne by English professors, not professors of political science and economics, in the name of "literary theory" and "deconstruction," concepts the Marxists of the thirties would have disdained had they known of them.

By the time I began teaching classes, first as a teaching assistant in 1936, responsible for sections of Teggart's Progress and Civilization course and then, after finishing graduate work, as an instructor, with my own courses, all personal interest in Marxism and communism had disappeared entirely. But these didn't by any means disappear from the classes and courses I taught. It was inevitable that almost any class in the social sciences would have a fertile sprinkling at least of students committed to and zealous about Marxism and to the noble path taken by Stalin, his purges, Five Year Plans, and other strategies assertedly given birth by the scientific principles of Marxism. They weren't dumb, these Berkeley student Marxist-communists, no matter how heavily Marxist dogmas rested on their minds. Trapping their professors into class arguments (beginning as innocent questions and ordinary discussion) was a favorite pursuit, and I lost my share of them simply by being out-debated. Still it was zestful, challenging, and, I assume, not without a certain interest to the other students in the class. By the mid-thirties there had developed a significant number of ex-Marxists and ex-communists such as James Burnham and Sidney Hook, and the editors of the rejuvenated *Partisan Review,* and even at Berkeley there were occasional signs of the effects of these brilliant and thoroughly informed heretics on the thinking of all but the most fundamentalist and dogmatic of the Berkeley communist minds.

Taking all of the six Berkeley revolutions I identified at the beginning of this chapter into comparative consideration, I have to say that the weakest and the least effective of them all was the revolution of the thirties. The heavy weight of communist dogma on the minds of the student radicals of the thirties prevented their achieving anything remotely like the New Left in the 1960s.

4

Color, Creed, and Gender

Any student on today's Berkeley campus who might make his way, via Wellsian time machine, back to the Berkeley campus of the 1930s would surely be first struck by the monochromatic hue of the thousands of faces on the campus. That hue was of course white; or 99.99 percent white. For those accustomed today to the mosaic of colors at Berkeley—black, brown, tan, gold, as well as white—the Berkeley of half a century ago would seem pallid, to say the least.

When you did encounter a student of dark color, the chances were great that he would be, not American born, but a visiting student from an African, Asian, Middle Eastern, or Latin American country, his way paid either by well-off parents or, as was more common, by his own government, in return for demonstrated scholarly aptitude and for his promise to return to his country after he had completed his degree work at Berkeley, usually in the agricultural, engineering, and scientific departments.

I didn't know or know of a single American-born black student at Berkeley in the thirties. I knew there had been a few over the years: the illustrious Walt Gordon and Ida Jackson for two. But they were before my time. And I knew there were middle-class black communities in the country as well as color-blind admissions offices. To no avail; Segregation was still a powerful force, psychological and social, in that day. Powerful in the black and white mind alike.

It wasn't very different with other ethnic groups. There were

61

many thousands of Filipinos in the state; I had known two at least in high school in central California. But throughout the thirties at Berkeley I saw, and came to know, only one. He had the fetching name of Aloysius Ignacio Macadangdang. He frequently studied in the Reserve Book Room, large and cavernous and with echoes when one of the student assistants would call out a name to indicate that the student's requested book had come in and was available. The assistants would virtually fight over who got to call out, sonorously, slowly, every syllable emphasized, Macadangdang's name. Sometimes a third "dang" would be added to heighten the effect. There would usually be a slight titter, though friendly titter, I thought, when Mr. Macadangdang would walk up to the loan desk. He was small, handsome, and immaculately dressed. He always smiled as though he enjoyed the impact of his name as much as anyone else present. I came to know him slightly, have coffee at the Co-Op once in a while with him. I was not surprised when I learned that he was from Manila and on a government scholarship.

I knew one Mexican student; he too fit the type of well-off foreign visitor, upper class, well educated. His name was Raul Magaña. He was well known for both his acute intelligence and his beautiful sister, Isabella, who came up from Mexico City two or three times a year to visit her brother and to shop at some of San Francisco's fine stores. Raul spoke excellent, almost accentless English. I heard from those qualified to judge that his native Spanish was pure enough to warrant Library of Congress recording. He was also a very good mimic. His imitation of Professor Alexander "Captain" Kidd of the Law School, which Raul was enrolled in when I knew him, was especially famous. I shall say more about Kidd later; here it suffices to say that in his explorations before class of the virtues and iniquities of American criminal law, Kidd's voice could reach virtual high tenor and in the following split second plummet to deep bass. Raul could imitate it almost perfectly. After he got his law degree he moved to Los Angeles where I learned in later years he became both a major legal presence and a very shrewd political operator. This was a change of the plans which had originally brought him to Berkeley. At that time he had fully intended to practice law in his native Mexico. He is, I believe, still thriving.

I saw one and one only American Japanese on the campus during the Thirties. I knew him, Tamatsu Shibutani, as an A student in one of my classes in 1941–42. He came, I believe, from a farming family located near Stockton and inevitably had known the caste-like segregation of the races and the social and economic discrimination that was at that time routine for the Japanese in California and the other Western states as well. He was remarkably free of any bitterness over what had been his childhood in the public schools. The fact that he was America-born, a citizen and an outstanding student at Berkeley didn't save him from the fate in early 1942 of all the rest of the Japanese population. Tamatsu had one piece of good fortune. After being sent with his family to a relocation center, as the internment camps were officially called, he managed to obtain permission to enroll at the University of Chicago, thus to complete, during the war, his undergraduate degree. Following that he began graduate-sociology work in Chicago's notable department and received his Ph.D. not long after the war. In 1950 he received an offer as assistant professor in sociology at Berkeley, to become within a very few years a highly respected teacher and student of race and ethnic relations.

It will be understood clearly, I trust, no exclusionary limiting policies or practices existed at Berkeley respecting blacks, Hispanics, Asians, American Indians, or others during those years in Berkeley. The University's admissions policy was color-blind. The policy knew only those who had and those who hadn't either a minimal B average in strictly academic high school subjects or else a qualifying score on the SAT or whatever standardized test was then used. There was always the route of applying to the President of the University for special admission. Although admissions and admissions policy were totally in the hands of a faculty board of admissions, the board customarily allowed the President a tiny number of student admissions to administer as he saw fit for the welfare of the University; for example admission of a much desired athlete who didn't quite have the recommending grades or score or the son or daughter of a loyal alumnus. But the President was obliged to account each year to the faculty board of admissions and he was bound to be quite circumspect in his use of special privileges. What was done was done in every college or university I have ever heard of.

I am bound to say that if in the 1930s any admissions system had been proposed along the lines of what has now become admissions policy at Berkeley — one based upon percentages of ethnic admissions matching the percentages formed by a given minority in the California population — it would have been rejected at just about every hand, student and faculty irrespective of political or social ideology, or anything else. The rise of minorities in college admissions and other areas of education, not to forget employment, has been the major story of social reform since the early 1960s. There was almost no such minorities-based struggle for rights and for serious social and legal reform of minorities' status in America until well after World War II.

There were certainly a few, tiny few, journalists, social workers, and writers aware of the depths of poverty and racial-ethnic discrimination in the thirties and even earlier. But the great white middle class — out of which most reform movements in American history have emerged — had its own problems in the Depression thirties: unemployment reaching twenty-five million, strikes, lockouts, sit-ins, the ever-present specter of homelessness and hunger, and, in many areas, a profound conviction of decline and fall. There wasn't room, presumably, in the national mind for the plight of the so-largely invisible blacks, Hispanics, and others; not on top of the agonizing problems of so many Americans.

There was also the strong tendency in the 1930s to see all social problems as simply emanations of what were at bottom strictly economic problems. When capitalism was overthrown, argued the Marxists, all other problems would take care of themselves. Conservatives said that when the business cycle turns, all will be once again right. There will an end of poverty; such problems will be automatically met once the economic problem is solved, solved by conference or by revolution. The hallmark of progressivist thought in the thirties was its almost total commitment to an economic determinism. The cry of all radicals and many liberals then was End Capitalism Now. In the early thirties I recall that the official position on blacks of the American Communist Party — following, naturally, the Soviet-dominated Comintern — was that a section of America, one comprising three or four states, be created after the

Revolution, as a nation within a nation, along the line of the Soviet Union's nationalities.

It was only in the 1960s that such mindsets began to change, at first slowly, then in revolutionary rush. That was when people began to recognize that even so general an economic prosperity as that which came over America after the Second World War still left many gaping sores seemingly untouched by either the ending of capitalism as in Russia or the heavy reform of capitalism as in this country. In the 1960s the Karl Marx of *Capital* was succeeded by the Marx of Alienation The Social Problem triumphed over the Economic. Why? Clio spoke, that's why.

Religion was a matter of little interest in the thirties to students, faculty, and administration alike. The University, in its deep desire to keep itself free of all ideological and sectarian currents of thought and prejudice, forbade bishops, preachers, and other proselytizers of religion from speaking on the campus just as it did political ideologues, that is, to proselytize. So long as religion was dealt with in scholarly and objective fashion, as in anthropology, history, and philosophy, it was as welcome as politics was in the Political Science Department. The Bible, the King James, of course, was the subject of a course in the English Department, usually taught by George Potter, an authority on the Age of the Stuarts, but it was taught precisely as any of the Restoration plays were: as a work of English literature; nothing more.

Students and faculty who wanted religion as a faith or creed didn't have far to go from the campus: a block's walk up from Northgate to Newman Hall if they were Catholic, a block or two beyond Sather Gate on the south to the Unitarian Church, one of the most beautiful pieces of architecture in University environs, another block to the three Protestant churches, Methodist, Presbyterian, and Congregational, and for one of Bernard Maybeck's masterpieces of architecture, another three blocks to upper Dwight Way to the Christian Science church, famous for its clerestory and the inside-outside feeling one had with respect to tall windows and the natural beauties of nature one felt almost a part of. And there was Hillel Hall on the north side of the campus for Jewish students.

But in the thirties there weren't many, it seemed to me, sufficiently interested in religion to walk any distance for whatever reason. Catholics at early morning mass at Newman Hall were probably the most observant of the students at Berkeley, though there weren't many of them, the majority of college-age Catholics preferring one or other of the Catholic universities in the Bay Area. The thirties was a religiously neutral age at best; skeptical is probably more accurate. Bull sessions of students didn't, in my experience, often include God and church. Politics, jobs, novels, and sex generally filled the sessions.

With a few exceptions, the Berkeley faculty was faith-deaf when it came to any organized religion. They were quite content to leave it a subject for ancient history, archaeology, and the study of primitive society. There would be a revival later on the Berkeley campus. It was all student. Requests in the 1950s began to be made by student groups for one or other of the religious notables of the day — Bishop Pike of San Francisco, Bishop Sheen of television fame, Paul Tillich, among others — to be invited by the University to speak on campus in their religious roles. For a long time, though, the wall of separation was as rigorously observed with respect to religious as political sectarianism. The revolution of the 1960s changed a good deal of that historic condition. Gradually the wall became more porous, religiously as well as politically.

A benign result of the extremely low intensity of religious consciousness at Berkeley in the thirties was the lowered tension between Catholic and Protestant and Gentile and Jew; tension all too evident in colleges and universities in the eastern part of the country. There, in those years, exclusionary quotas were common, affecting in many instances Catholic Irish as well as Jews. I am not suggesting that the Berkeley campus was altogether free of such tensions. The mainline fraternities and sororities specifically excluded Jews from membership. There were departments which didn't have Jews on their faculties, and never had had, as best as I could ascertain.

Down through the thirties, as I learned years later, departments of English in America were particularly loath to appoint Jews to their faculties. There was apparently a consensus that the "Jewish mind" — held to be by nature one of unalterable Near Eastern oriental cast — could not truly assimilate and reflect the esthetic values of English and American literature. In the 1930s the Columbia University Department of English appointed — chiefly at the urging of the University's president, Nicholas Murray Butler — its first Jew. His name was Lionel Trilling; he had been a brilliant student in English at Columbia and had written a detailed study of Matthew Arnold and his works that was almost instantly recognized in the reviews as classic. When he was notified of his appointment as instructor by the very liberal Mark Van Doren, he was warned not to see his good fortune as a springboard for bringing other Jews into the Department.

At the time of Trilling's appointment at Columbia, the first Jew in the department's history, there were two full professors in English of Jewish descent at Berkeley, Benjamin Kurz and Benjamin Lehman, both longtime members of the department, both honored and respected on the Berkeley campus. And four years later, in 1936, a third Jew was appointed as instructor, James Hart who would serve with distinction for more than fifty years at Berkeley as professor, scholar, and administrator.

There were other Jews at Berkeley in the thirties, most of whom had been there for many years: Jessica Peixotto in economics, emeritus by the thirties, as I recall but still very much a presence; William Popper in Near Eastern languages, Robert H. Lowie in anthropology, J. Robert Oppenheimer in physics (only recently appointed, already a celebrity); Max Radin and also Barbara Nachtrieb Armstrong, both professors of law in Boalt Hall. There were others; I have singled out simply the more notable and celebrated on the Berkeley campus.

Let me not forget to add instantly here the names of two other eminent Jews at Berkeley when I entered: Monroe E. Deutsch, provost and vice president, professor of Latin; and Charles Lipman, dean of the graduate division and professor of biology. Not often did one find in Midwestern and Eastern universities in America, those of comparable distinction to Berkeley, Jews in such high administrative posts — or, for that matter in such number on the faculty as at Berkeley, modest though that number must seem by today's standards.

I don't want to exaggerate. There were departments, many of them indeed, that were without Jews on their faculties and that had never apparently had them. Among such departments were philosophy, political science, history, geography, psychology, social institutions, French, German, Italian, and Spanish. Nor was Berkeley notably aberrant in the nonexistence of Jews in so many departments in the thirties and earlier. Anti-Semitism was about as strong in American academe down to the Second World War as it was in any other professional cohort in the country. This was particularly true of an academic field in which one might have thought the very contrary: sociology. Not until after the Second World War would the dikes against Jews in academic America start collapsing.

Berkeley's relatively good record prior to the war has to be seen as another consequence of the University's historically close relation with San Francisco. Except for Chinese and Japanese, San Francisco's treatment of races and ethnic minorities was generally excellent. Perhaps it was an offshoot of the city's notable bohemian cast. From the time of the Gold Rush, Jews formed an important colony in the city. From the start they were strong supporters of the new university across the Bay.

The plight of women, no matter how talented and well trained they may have been, was at least as difficult as was that of Jews in academic America in the thirties. The Second World War, which changed forever so many of the ancient habits and mores of the universities and colleges, had a discernible impact upon both anti-Semitism and anti-feminism. The thirties was the final decade of the largely unchallenged forces of both. I am not suggesting that either is completely expunged today on the American or any other national scene. But at least anti-anti-Semitism and anti-anti-feminism are thoroughly respectable; and no one can rationally deny that by almost any standard of measurement both Jews and women live and work in a far less trammeled atmosphere than existed fifty years ago.

I can recall exactly six women who, in a Berkeley faculty of several hundred, enjoyed membership in the professorial ranks at Berkeley in the 1930s. I am referring here to professorships in the main, the substantive, and solid academic disciplines—the humanities, social sciences, biological and physical sciences, and the major professional fields such as law, medicine, and agricultural science. There were lots of women working on the Berkeley campus, but they held secretarial positions, supervisorships in women's physical education, in the training of elementary school teachers, nursing, home economics, agricultural extension, and so on. Almost every foreign language department employed one or two women but they were in ranks of nonprofessorial assistant-ships, set to the teaching of the most elementary courses.

But throughout the thirties, in my clear recollection, there were no women holding professorial positions in such mainline liberal arts fields as philosophy, English, history, French, German, Italian, Russian, Latin, political science, physics, chemistry, mathematics, or music and art. Remarkable therefore is the existence during that decade of two women, both full professors in economics, one in law, one in social institutions, one in what was then called decora-tive arts, and one in home economics. I am referring respectively to Jessica Peixotto and Emily Huntington, Barbara Nachtrieb Arm-strong, Margaret Hodgen, Hope Gladding, and Agnes Fay Morgan. No one who ever took a course from any of these remarkable women will have altogether forgotten the experience. They were respectable scholars as well as top-level teachers. They made their own way to the top; there was of course no affirmative action in that day.

Undoubtedly the most brilliant of the six was Jessica Peixotto in economics. She was Jewish as well as female which doubled her achievement, it is only fair to say. Beyond that she was beautiful, especially so when she first came to the Berkeley campus in 1899 to teach, in her first year, courses in socialism, and sociology in her second year, a field then absent from the campus. Andrew Lawson —who had been ten years on the faculty in geology when Miss Peixotto arrived as a young woman—told me one day at lunch, almost pontifically, I thought: "The most beautiful woman to ever set foot on this campus." In that day, who can be sure, her beauty may well have been as big a barrier as her sex and Jewishness?

After her first two years she dropped both sociology and social-ism and commenced teaching and research in the field that would make her nationally famous: the quantitative study of the family, its budget—used as a measuring instrument—and the role of women in the American work force, and as an indicator of the relationship of the family to the economy and the political state.

Her work and her teaching attracted national attention; she played a key role in World War I when she was one of those appointed by President Wilson to important posts in the monitoring and supervising of women holding novel jobs in factories and offices. At Berkeley from the time she joined the faculty until her retirement in the early Thirties she had great influence in faculty affairs.

Three of the six women — Emily Huntington, economics; Margaret Hodgen, social institutions; and Barbara Nachtrieb Armstrong, law, were students of Professor Peixotto, three among the dozens of students she had turned out who were scattered in important jobs all over the country. That Margaret Hodgen — whom I studied under and became colleague to — should have wound up in the social institutions department, chaired by the formidable, irascible, and also, I am obliged to stress here, anti-feminist Frederick J. Teggart is not without humor. He appointed her for one semester back in the mid-twenties when his prized young colleague Nicholas Spykman, left at midyear for a tenured position at Yale. But principle vanished before pragmatic reality in Teggart's case. She was too good to let go after the stated one semester. She was a splendid teacher and scholar and became profoundly devoted to Teggart and his ideas. Many on the faculty thought she was a helpless pawn in Teggart's anti-feminist scheme of things. What nonsense. It is enough to refer to one matter alone in which she differed sharply with Teggart, and stood by her guns. He was a very conservative Republican in the thirties who hated FDR and all his works; Miss Hodgen was just as intensely an admirer of FDR and wholly in favor of the New Deal.

The two remaining women of the six I am referring to were Hope Gladding, full professor and chair of the decorative arts department, and Agnes Fay Morgan, full professor and chair of the home economics department. If Berkeley's home economics was starkly different from any other such department in the country, the reason lies solely with Professor Morgan. She was by professional training, not a home economist at all. She had her Ph.D. in chemistry, more particularly in organic chemistry; she had studied in Germany, had written first-rate papers in organic chemistry. But no chemistry department in the U.S., including Berkeley's, would accept her for professional appointment. For the reason we don't have far to search. She was, in a word, female.

Rather than cry in her tea, however, Miss Morgan took a professorship in the Home Economics department. With full cooperation of the administration and the chemistry department, she set about remaking her department. Conventional courses in homemaking, consumerdom, and the like were displaced by food chemistry, a venue from her point of view falling clearly within the organic chemistry she had taken her doctorate in. She was, in sum, as much a chemist at Berkeley as any of those inhabiting Gilman Hall — all male, of course. She became nationally known as a pioneer in food chemistry, and although home economics departments across the nation may have gnashed teeth at her heretical approach to their subject, Professor Morgan was a very influential member of the Berkeley faculty.

Looking back it is astounding to think of the number of departments at Berkeley in the thirties that didn't have and probably never had had a single woman on their faculties; after all, there *were* women philosophers, political scientists, students of comparative languages, of French, German, Italian, Spanish, historians, and even occasionally in the hard sciences. After the war — always a leveling force in human history — the number of women would begin to go up visibly. But not at Berkeley before the war. Nor anywhere else in the university world.

The truth is, from Berkeley and Stanford across the country to Harvard and Yale, the university in the thirties was overwhelmingly masculine, gentile, Protestant, and white. This was as routine in the makeups of faculties as of student bodies. Universities were at least as WASP in composition as were law offices, banks, and brokerage houses on Wall Street. It is only this national ambiance that makes Berkeley's record at the time seem noble.

But what about women students at Berkeley, of which there were many thousands? President Sproul called the University of California the greatest matrimonial institution in the state. Given the annual register of Cal women marrying Cal men, Sproul was very probably correct. In any event it is safe to say that the majority of women students at Berkeley while studying, learning, and taking pride in grade averages that *en bloc* outdid those of men students, saw deep down in their consciousness, the primary reason for their being at Berkeley as that of putting frosting on their natural nubility.

This to be sure could entail a sacrifice — of the native intelligence and usually superior maturity of the woman student to the preservation at all costs of her attractiveness to men students and her marriageability. Hence the not uncommon sight in the thirties at Berkeley (and many, many other institutions of higher learning) of the A average, obviously superior mind of the female playing the role of Dumb Dora in public. In this self-caricature, the brilliant female student was generally cheered on by her parents who may have been impressed by their daughter's accomplishments in her courses but nursed nevertheless the deep fear that such brain work would so desex her as to render her unfit for marriage.

Parenthetically I should point out that in the nineteenth century conventional opposition to college for women rested on two arguments. First, it was thought, college would tax the young woman's mind to the point of possible brain fever, even insanity. This absurdity didn't last long or convince very many. What did last and last, was the second reason for opposition to college for women: it would desex them, render them less attractive in the marriage stakes. Men, accustomed to masculine headship of families, sensitive to their own possible failings, would look with some dread on women who were or might be intellectually superior. College desexed women, rendering them less attractive as helpmeet in marriage. College, as must have been said occasionally by men, made women "uppity" and therefore impossible within the home.

Berkeley, I regret to say, hadn't progressed far, if at all, in the thirties with respect to masculine theories of female desexing. Women yielded as many "brains" among students in my experience as students and faculty members as did men. Not seldom the University Medalist at Commencement — meaning the student with the highest academic achievement in the class — was female. How, if she was marriage-minded, looking forward to home, husband, and children, such an Athene was able to cope, I can only surmise; to wit that she succeeded only by burying her past, that is, academic past.

My experience as a teacher, whether as T.A. or assistant professor, was utterly one-sided when it came to men and women who were members of fraternities and sororities. I had, not many but a clearly discernible few, sorority women who were straight-A students and who made it look easy. Not once, however, did I ever have a fraternity student in one of my classes who could rise to an A level instead of wallowing happily among those satisfied, proud indeed, to get a "gentleman's C." I have often wondered how, over the years, Fraternity John got along in wedlock with Sorority Jane.

Faculty members in my first-hand experience knew that their women students could be, often were, extremely bright and, even more important, highly promising as professional scholars, thoroughly qualified to work toward the Ph.D. in graduate school. But almost nothing came of such perceptions in the thirties. For women among graduate students—I discount here those women working for, say, a Master's in nursing or home economics—were exceedingly rare. In the three years when I was taking graduate seminars toward the Ph.D., I did not once encounter women in them.

I will end this brief section on a glorious exception to what I have just written. Her name was Josephine Miles. She was badly crippled from a childhood onset of polio, barely able to walk—more of a shuffle—from shelf to shelf in the library stacks. Above her twisted and shrunken body was a beautiful face, one that contained a splendid full-throated voice. She was working for her Ph.D. in English, a degree she got in at least customary time. Her brilliance, and also her poise in classroom, were notable. She became the first woman member in the history of the Berkeley English department. Her rise to the full professorship, it is worth adding, was swift, on the basis of teaching that had positive impact upon students of all levels—who adored her—and a natural bent toward scholarship, in her case the seventeenth century in England. Beyond those conventional virtues was that of being a first-rate, nationally recognized poet.

World War II had a considerable effect upon the faculty's acceptance of women as serious graduate students. By 1942 the campus was fast becoming a feminine institution, and the war was beginning to look nearly endless. The light and leading of male students were off to war, or war-related work, and from the faculty's point of view that left a major problem: who would take their graduate seminars; who would work toward advanced degrees; who would be their teaching and research assistants? Women, that's who! I don't want to exaggerate the salutary effect of war on the nurturing and encouragement of female professional status, but in one form or other this effect has long been noted by scholars. It will suffice here to say that after the war, beginning almost immediately indeed, even with the males returned, females occupied a much larger piece of graduate and M.A. and Ph.D. space at Berkeley.

More than any other modern events, the two world wars, especially the second one, broke down hallowed prohibitions that had for so long blocked the aspirations of minorities, including women. The Civil War had this effect in some degree; I mean with respect to the propriety of women holding jobs — teaching, nursing, work in the mills, and so on. The First World War had even greater impact in this direction; after all, four million young men overseas left a gaping hole in the conventional American work force. But it is World War II that has proved to have had the greatest effect, and nowhere has this been more vivid than in the graduate and professional schools of the country — starting, we are privileged to say, with Berkeley. What feelings must have crossed the minds of women professors such as the six I described briefly above, women who had somehow made it the hard way and lived to see the graduate halls becoming almost as female-populated as male.

5

Coping with the Depression

We could have done a lot worse during the Great Depression than live in California and attend the university at Berkeley. Hard times there were indeed for many. But the times were not as hard as they were in the upper midwest and northeast of the U.S., areas heavily industrialized and staggering under the burden of unprecedented unemployment; or in the Dustbowl of Oklahoma and Arkansas, or the cotton-poor South.

California was still largely unindustrialized in the thirties. The great majority of Californians lived as their forebears had, in small towns, even villages. There were only two cities of mark, Los Angeles and San Francisco, in both of which the severest ravages of economic depression in California were to be seen. Such places as San Jose, San Diego, and Fresno were small and self-contained, their borders sharply delimited and environs composed not of densely populated suburbs but farms, orchards, and fields. The balance between agriculture and commerce was not notably different in California in the thirties than it had been at the turn of the century. Freeways, smog, and long-distance auto commuting were still largely unknown.

The University fared decently, all things considered. True, classrooms and labs could be crowded; ugly, wooden "temporary" buildings were thrust into the magnificent glade that stretched from Westgate all the way through the campus to the Memorial Stadium; indeed beyond, to the superb botanical garden and the source of

Strawberry Creek that ran east to west through the campus all the way eventually to the Bay.

Faculty posts were too often left empty when their occupants retired or died. Or else they were filled by the University's own recent Ph.D.s, who could be appointed at instructor levels at low salaries. For the Ph.D.s such a fate was of course a joyous one, for it was a time when even Ph.D.s in physics, chemistry, mathematics, and the biological sciences were going jobless for indefinite periods.

Supporting funds for scholarships, never abundant at Berkeley, were at record lows during the period. The same was true of funds for books. President Sproul, not an academician, rose heroically to the occasion and personally earmarked significant sums in the budget to prevent the University Library from becoming weakened in its acquisitions, thus crippling the library for decades ahead. Sproul's many years as the University's representative in Sacramento helped considerably in financing Berkeley through the Depression.

Things were bad, but tall tales have come out of the Depression such as that from Pauline Kael, student during the thirties at Berkeley and who several decades later "recalled" students, homeless and hungry, obliged for want of University housing to "sleep under the bridge on the campus." Bridge? I knew the campus pretty well, including its two or three small bridges crossing Strawberry Creek, but for the life of me I can think of no bridge under which any species but fish could have slept. Or done much else.

Romanticized exaggerations aside, there were indeed hungry and otherwise underprivileged students at Berkeley. There was scarcely a week, it seemed to me, when at least one acquaintance didn't drop out, forced out by lack of income from home or job. I learned in later years that the wonderful Cowell Hospital on the campus — another noble gift by private citizens — did its bit. Most of the students who reported dizziness, faintness, exhaustion were found to be suffering from nothing more complicated than severe, raw hunger, near-starvation. Cowell customarily put such students up under its sick-roll listings, feeding them heroically until they were back on their feet and ready for a fresh start. Dr. William Donald was then head of Cowell and a splendid humanitarian as well as physician he was.

Institutionally, Stanford was harder hit than Berkeley during the Depression. This came chiefly from shrunken resources from its investments and land holdings, but also from deficient leadership. The president, Ray Lyman Wilbur chose to go on leave for four years to become Hoover's Secretary of the Interior. When he retired, he was replaced by a businessman, Donald Tressider who knew nothing of academe. The mistake was compounded when Tressider appointed as his vice president an educationist. The quality of faculty declined badly, buildings and grounds, once palatial, became decrepit, and curriculum suffered. Not many in the country knew how badly Stanford fell, and kept falling until its spectacular rejuvenation began in the 1950s.

By comparison, Berkeley prospered. The state of its buildings and grounds remained generally good, and, of far greater importance, its faculty actually improved. Frederick Paxson and James Westfall Thompson, notable historians, were brought in; so was Howard Ellis in Economics, J.S. P. Tatlock in English, and J. Robert Oppenheimer in physics, a field already brightened by the prior appointment of Ernest Lawrence.

If memory serves, there was but one salary cut of the faculty during the Thirties, a stiff one, to be sure, of ten percent. But given the vastly lowered costs of living in a major depression, the faculty salary scale in those years was very good. Full professors received between $5 and $6 thousand — unless they held an endowed chair such as the Sather and Ehrman in History, the Mills in Philosophy, or the Flood in Economics in which case salary would be an extra thousand or two, depending on the endowment's yield. It was rumored that the medievalist Thompson, brought from Chicago, first occupant of the handsome Ehrman chair, received $9 thousand a year. Sproul, the president, got only $11 thousand, it was brought out when he had an offer of $25 thousand to come as president of a San Francisco bank (he turned it down and doubtless got a well-deserved increase in salary at the University).

Such salaries — and they were on a par with most of the major universities in the country — seem lilliputian today when starting salaries at Berkeley are over $30 thousand and most full professors are in the $60 thousand range, with above-scale salaries to academic stars occasionally reaching $100 thousand and higher — all of these for the traditional nine-month academic year, leaving the individual professor free to earn as much more as he likes during the three months of vacation.

But salaries, taken without respect to context, are deceptive. Today's $70 thousand: a-year professor is obliged to pay hundreds of thousands for a house in the hills behind the University that went, when it occasionally changed ownership during the Depression, for anywhere from five to ten, at very most $15 thousand. Banks were only too eager to make mortgage loans to university-tenured faculty, even nontenured, as I recall very well.

In the thirties, with all the advantages of a deflationary economy to those on fixed or virtually fixed incomes, it was possible for a faculty member to live very well on salaries in the $4 thousand range for associate professors and $5 thousand for full professors. Such an individual could and usually did have a comfortable house in the Berkeley hills, off Euclid, Arlington and the like, a cottage, owned or rented summers in the High Sierra or at Carmel or other vacation setting, a car, sufficient income to make possible occasional visits to San Francisco for dinner, theater, or opera, and every seventh year, with support from a sabbatical, a few months in Europe.

Thinking of salaries paid at Berkeley and all major universities at this moment, it is almost beyond belief at first thought of scholars and scientists of the genius-level such as Gilbert Lewis, A. L. Kroeber, H. M. Evans, F. J. Teggart, getting under $10 thousand a year in the thirties. But income can't be divorced from outgo, and outgo was minimal in the thirties by comparison with our present age.

For a large number of students, part-time jobs were vital. Granted that costs of living were low: ten dollars a month for a room, sometimes shared with another student, and food, if you looked around and didn't gorge, perhaps twenty a month. But thirty dollars a month bulked large for more than a few of us. My parents somehow squeezed out twenty-five a month to send me; how they did it—there were four mouths to feed—out of my father's total income of $150 a month, I'll never know. But even in the Depression, twenty-five wouldn't quite stretch, no matter how spartan an existence you led.

Thus, along with many hundreds of other students I haunted the Bureau of Student Occupations in Stephens Union. My first job came just as classes began; a hashing job at the Acacia House. There was another hasher to work with, Roger S. For three meals a day— without cash supplement—we set the tables for twenty-five, served the food, cleared the tables, and washed and dried all dishes and pots and pans. This three times a day. By hurrying our own eating and cutting corners, Roger and I could still make nine o'clocks and two o'clocks in classes. It was desolating when in a month we lost our jobs at Acacia to two house members suddenly strapped for money. I hashed once more, in a sorority, which was much nicer work than in the fraternities, but it was only filling in for a week or two for another student, ill in Cowell. Then I had a piece of luck. Another student, a friend, and I went into a newly opened little cafe on Telegraph, between Vaughan's and the Sather Gate Book Store, for a hamburger and coffee (twenty cents), and a man named Slim who was owner, chef, waiter, dish washer, and sweeper of the place came over to us, moved the toothpick from one side to the other of his mouth and asked us if either could type. We could, and for about a month, until the hapless Slim went broke and left town without notice, my friend and I got two meals a day for typing menus.

Things improved the second semester at Berkeley. Four of us, all friends, rented one of the Euclid Apartments at Hearst and Euclid for forty dollars a month, ten dollars apiece, and did our own cooking. The apartment had a living room and dining room, each with a pull-down wall bed. Almost all studying was done of course at the library, three minutes away. Food was cheap at the small grocery up the street—bread eight cents a loaf, five cents when day old, carrots a penny a bunch, a lamb chop, when splurging, a dime, and so on. My principal memory is of a concoction we dignified by the name of Red Bread which we had almost every lunch. It consisted of a large can of tomatoes (twenty cents) and a finger-crumbled loaf of day-old bread (five cents), cooked until the contents simmered. To it was added a green salad, that is, one head of lettuce (three to five cents) and a shredded bunch of carrots (usually one cent). The happy result of this mode of living was a food bill for each of us that never reached ten dollars a month. As long as my parents could send the twenty-five dollars each month and I could get an occasional job for extra spendable money, I was well off by Depression-at-Berkeley standards.

At the very beginning of my second year at Berkeley I had one of the luckiest windfalls of my life: to wit, notice that I had a job as student assistant at the library loan desk. I had applied the year before; those jobs were among the most sought after at Berkeley. At a stroke it was possible to relieve my strapped parents of their twenty-five a month and, for the first time in my eighteen years of living, be self-supporting.

For the next three years, leading up to graduation, the Doe Library was the center of my life. There were three distinct boons that went with a job as student assistant at the loan desk. First, obviously, it was a secure source of income. Assuming good behavior, anyone holding the job had tenure, so to speak; tenure that would last not only to graduation but during any professional school enrollment that one might decide upon after getting the B.A. You could work as many hours a week as you wanted to, hours comfortably chosen with an eye on schedule of classes for that term, and, using weekends and late night hours, earn forty dollars a month; a bonanza, it seemed to me. Over perhaps a couple of dozen student employees, some of them veterans of more than a few years at the job, were three professional librarians, two of them women, wives getting their husbands along in law school, all three as engaging and nonbureaucratic as anyone could wish for in a boss.

The second boon of the job was for me the simple fact of having over a million volumes in the nine interior floors of what were universally known as The Stacks. I had loved libraries from childhood, libraries ranging from a few hundred volumes to a few thousand. Now, wonderful to behold, a great library that I was free to roam as well as work in and to charge out books galore. My education thenceforth came almost as much from the hours spent in the library as in the classroom.

There were frequent periods when traffic was low, the number of pages at work substantial, and I found no difficulty in combing through the nine floors of books, browsing in sections that interested me, reading snatches of books with beguiling titles, and carrying a small armload each night down to the checkout counter and then home. I would find out a few years later when I was doing graduate work for the Ph.D. that my years as book page and of devoted, happy browsing, greatly enhanced my career as first apprentice, then journeyman, and finally master scholar.

Third among pleasures and profits was the companionship with other pages among student assistants. Willy nilly, the workroom behind the loan desk became a kind of fraternity house and it was quite possible to think of those you worked with, chatted with, joked with, borrowed from, lent to, and so on as your brothers, without the burden of Greek Letter affiliation.

From then on, with the virtually tenured library job, I had the freest life I had ever known: free of economic worry, including food and housing, primarily, but free, with this anchoring security, of parental and other small town constraints, free now to take full advantage of the free air of Berkeley.

Life on the campus could be benign indeed in the thirties for those who could manage the twenty-five to forty dollars a month needed for minimal well-being. The university in America was a wonderful window through which to see the world breaking apart, as it could seem at times, from internal domestic strains and conflicts or else those generated by people abroad like Mussolini and Hitler. It was a jungle out there, we must have thought if not said. In the University, though, was relative peace, even tranquility. True, there were the struggles on the campus between the political Left and Right. But these were almost wholly student struggles, and no one was obliged to pay much attention to them.

As for life in general on the campus, behold: no drug problems; in all my years as student I never once saw so much as a marijuana joint smoked. There was boozing in some measure, chiefly in the fraternities, though not by any means exclusively. Before Repeal, bootleggers were frequent visitors, always well paid. But I heard of no cases of alcoholism. Struggles of gays and lesbians, to the extent that they existed at all, were invisible. There were of course no minorities in conflict with others or themselves; simply because there were no minorities to speak of.

As if to atone for Depression, there was a cultural renascence going on in America during the thirties, its seeds having been planted during the preceding decade. In literature there were the novels of Fitzgerald, Hemingway, Dos Passos, Dreiser, Lewis, and Thomas Wolfe; in poetry there were Eliot, Pound, Frost, Robinson, Moore, and Robinson Jeffers who lived in nearby Carmel where he built his wondrous tower; in criticism there were Edmund Wilson, Van Wyck Brooks, Joel Spingarn, Bernard De Voto, and Mencken (albeit in something of a slump in the thirties).

The popular arts were in full swing in the decade. Cole Porter, Irving Berlin, Duke Ellington among many popular composers were at the height of their powers. It was without parallel the decade of the great orchestras, those of Benny Goodman, Artie Shaw, the Dorseys, Whiteman et al. In the Bay Area, chiefly San Francisco, there were Phil Harris at the St. Francis, Anson Weeks at the Mark Hopkins, Tom Coakley first at the Claremont, then the Palace Hotel, and Tom Gerun at the Baltabarin. All of them came on each night for radio half-hour presentations. There were a lot of people, including Berkeley students, to dance to these orchestras on weekends. You hoped to double date with someone who had a car, but lacking that convenience, it was an easy and popular way just to go over to the City by ferry and streetcar. Cover charges and set-ups at the hotels were cheap in the Depression, and there was always a high spirit about hotel dancing by students — who included Stanford and Santa Clara students most weekends.

Movies were at the height of their appeal in the thirties. Unemployment, hunger, and straitened finances notwithstanding, Americans went by the tens of millions to movies. There were some splendid ones to see: *Wuthering Heights, Gone With the Wind, Stagecoach, It Happened One Night,* not to forget the Laurel and Hardys, the Marx Brothers, and all the screwball comedies so named. Prices were low: fifty cents for first-runs at the United Artists on Shattuck, thirty-five at the California, about the same at the U.C. and the Campus.

The thirties was a great decade for radio. Sets were cheap, especially second-hand ones of which there were many for some reason; you could rent a set for two or three dollars a month. Nobody, it seemed, was ever very far from a radio of some kind, for the programs were diverse and exceedingly well publicized: there were the comedies of Jack Benny and Fred Allen, the early newscasters — who can forget the Richfield Reporter at ten o'clock every night?

—the Saturday Metropolitan Opera, Toscanini and the NBC Symphony, the Chicago Round Table, among many others.

Intellectual life on the campus was quickened and catalyzed by a constant flow of outsiders coming to lecture, mostly evenings, sometimes late afternoons. Most of these were free to students and faculty. They included T. S. Eliot, Thomas Mann, Niels Bohr, Walter Lippmann, Edith and Sacheverell Sitwell—who took turns at the Wheeler Aud podium, Edith at one point while her brother was speaking munching a half-eaten cheese sandwich she pulled out of her purse—and many others from Europe and Asia as well as from the U.S.

Looking back a half century, I still think the two most brilliant, exciting lectures I heard during the Thirties were given by T. S. Eliot in the fall of 1933—it cost seventy-five cents but with my new job in the library I could afford it—and Harold Laski in the spring of 1939. Eliot lectured on poetry and recited from his own. I had never heard poetry spoken as Eliot did, dryly, in an almost incantatory monotone that at first irritated my ear, then pleasured it. Wheeler Aud, the admission charge notwithstanding, was packed. Eliot was on one of his periodic lecture tours that usually began with events such as the Lowell Lectures at Harvard and the Stafford Little Lectures at Virginia. He was handsome, charming, but above all impressive.

The Laski lecture three years later, also in Wheeler Aud and before the largest audience, I would guess in that auditorium's history—we stood densely at the back, sat in the aisles, and were so quiet during Laski's lecture that one could have heard the proverbial pin drop—was riveting in content and manner of delivery. He was, even by British standards, an arresting speaker. His subject was Europe and the possibilities of war. The time, as I recall, was April, 1939. Although he didn't actually the predict in so many words that the Second World War would break out in four or five months, when war did so break out, many of us thought back on Laski's lecture. A very small man, dressed in a funereal suit, all black, he became a commanding and memorable presence the moment he began speaking. In retrospect, I have to say the lecture was vastly better than any of the books he was writing in those late years of his career.

The genius behind Berkeley's first rate fare of lectures was William Popper, Professor of Near Eastern languages and chairman of the Committee on Arts and Lectures, a post he was willing to hold for many years. Every evening lecture I ever attended would find Professor Popper there almost as though a personal host.

Berkeley had a long tradition of first-class lecturers coming to the campus. It began with Benjamin Ide Wheeler in 1899 when he came as president of the University. An easterner himself, he recognized immediately the problem presented by Berkeley's distance from the east coast where the greater number of America's intellects and leaders lived. Having a regular stream of visitors from distant places, reflecting diverse backgrounds and orientations was, Wheeler knew, vital to any intellectual center.

Wheeler went to work on it, and within a very few years succeeded in getting endowment money from wealthy San Franciscans for the express purpose of paying high fees to distinguished scholars, statesmen, and other notables along with first class travel accommodations and Bay Area hotels to match. Woodrow Wilson was a regular and popular speaker at Berkeley from the time he was president of Princeton. There were others, many others, to match. Lecture series were begun, the most famous of which were the Sather and the Hitchcock.

The University Theater soared under Irving Pichel when I arrived at Berkeley. He was a lustrous figure on the campus, especially among left-wing intellectuals, whether student or faculty. His talents proved too great for Berkeley with its then-primitive theater facilities, and by the mid-Thirties he was directing and producing in Hollywood.* The meagerness of theater facilities at Berkeley deserves heavy emphasis. There weren't any, putting it bluntly. Most plays were given in Wheeler Aud, the stage being the slightly raised platform in the front of the auditorium, on which sat the rostrum for professorial use. Dressing rooms were the halls between the back entrance of Wheeler Aud and one, repeat one, of the offices in the basement near the entrance. What "stage" embellishments there were for a given play had to be taken down each night after the

---

* Pichel was succeeded by the talented Edwin Duerr around 1934.

performance in order to restore the auditorium to pristine classroom use the next morning. Despite the lack of a genuine theater and proper accoutrements, there were some excellent productions during the thirties. One that still stands out for sheer technical quality was Odets' *Waiting For Lefty.* It was riveting to the several hundred of us who formed the audience. There were some excellent student actors in the thirties one of whom was Gregory Peck. I have already mentioned film critic Pauline Kael who was an undergraduate during the late thirties; she was even then prominent in Berkeley literary circles, as I recall. Ralph Edwards of future radio and television fame was also a student at Berkeley in the thirties. The precedent that Jack London at the beginning of the century and Irving Stone in the twenties set, that is, to go from academe to fame and success as novelists was not often followed, and Berkeley was much slower than Stanford to go in for creative writing and a permanent literary circle. But even so there was George Stewart of the English department and considerable luster on the side as novelist; there was Julia Altrocchi, wife of the chairman of the Italian department, and a few others including the author, whose name slips my mind, of the wonderful crime thriller, *Murder in the Stacks.*

Music was something of a loss at Berkeley in the thirties. There was the Cal Band but the less said of it the better. It was fine on a football Saturday, at least by California standards, but the idea of a concert band was foreign to the place. The Music department was small and lean; devoting itself largely to theory and music history. It lived in a small redwood house on the campus about where the westside of Dwinelle is found today. For musical offerings there were the occasional appearances, at a fee, of a concert pianist or string ensemble. For those staying on summers as I did once I had the library job, there was the Coolidge Quartet, sponsored by the Library of Congress, to appear each summer for a couple of weeks.

What was true of music was true of art. The Department of Art specialized in the theoretical and historical; not the practical. There were a couple of faculty like Eugen Neuhaus and Jacques Schnier who were known for their paintings and sculptures respectively, but such works were regarded as strictly extracurricular, not something properly belonging to a university organized around teaching and scholarship.

There was, finally, as the universal magnet of Berkeley culture, the football team. The thirties was the last decade in which college football was the all in all. By the late forties pro-football would be developing rapidly and building up the kind of mesmerized audiences we are familiar with today.

Football at Berkeley had had a near-sacred place in college life since the Wonder Teams of the early 1920s, teams which put not just Berkeley but the Pacific Coast generally on the football map of America. As a child in the early twenties I could recite name for name the players on the Wonder Teams. Actually, *the* Wonder Team, so accepted by eastern as well as western sports writers, was the team of 1920. It boasted such names as Brick Muller, Pesky Sprott, Stanley Barnes, Dan McMillan, my namesake Archie Nisbet who could punt almost the length of the field (as Brick Muller could similarly pass a football). In the 1920 season Cal scored 510 points, surrendering but ten to the entire aggregate of opponents. This was the high point of three highly successful seasons. Berkeley never hesitated to run up the score, once beating St. Mary's College 124–0.

Behind it was the sainted Andy Smith, to this day The Coach in Berkeley's history. He had coached successfully at San Diego High School prior to beginning at Berkeley in 1919. When he went to Berkeley he took most of his championship high school team, including the whole of the backfield, with him, thus inaugurating Cal's greatest succession of football seasons. From his very first year Andy Smith had heroic and charismatic stature on the campus. Even a few faculty members, notably Gettell in Political Science, who had had distinguished college football careers, volunteered to help the great Andy. When he died prematurely in the twenties not only Berkeley but much of the whole Bay Area went into full mourning.

Cal's preeminence would change of course in the Twenties. Andy Smith was the first of the big time, well-salaried coaches to reach the Pacific Coast. So impressive were the results that Stanford soon followed with Pop Warner and USC with the "Head Man,"

Howard Jones, each as wrapped in tradition to this day in their respective institutions as Andy Smith with Berkeley. By the middle of the twenties, Berkeley was clearly brought down to size. The famous tie game with Stanford in 1924 signaled that. There was a brief flare-up of distinction in the late Twenties with Benny Lom and Lee Eisen performing valiantly. But Berkeley had no Ernie Nevers of Stanford or Morley Drury of USC to boast of.

Until 1938 when the Thunder Team of Vic Bottari, Johnny Meek, Sam Chapman, and Dave Anderson came into view and actually ranked number one in the country, football at Berkeley was uneventful, almost dull, despite the appearances of a few able individuals such as Hank Schaldach and Arleigh Williams. Rarely did a Berkeley offense break with its almost mind-numbing sequence of plays beginning with each first down: a buck over the center, an effort to break tackle by another buck, then either a pass or sweeping, invariably unsuccessful end run, concluded, of course, by a punt. Thus it went, possession after possession, for the entire game.

All the same, football was by far the favorite sport of students and faculty alike at Berkeley as at just about every other college in the country. In the thirties the Big Men on Campus were almost routinely football players. There was a certain unconscious wisdom in this. After all, it was football above any other force that had lifted certain universities into national prominence. Academic purists dislike being reminded of this, but it was not scholarly letters but sudden football prowess, replete with earnest proselytizing and alumni gifts to the favored, that lifted first Harvard, then a succession of other universities into national instead of traditional regional influence. What Harvard began before World War I in the way of becoming overnight a feared football scourge was followed in the twenties by Yale, Michigan, Berkeley, and a number of other institutions. Longtime regional status as academic institutions was succeeded by national status. Without question it was the Berkeley Wonder Teams that raised Berkeley to national attention. Teaching and scholarship followed.

Nowhere was the status of football more illustrious than at the University of Chicago under its genius-founder president William Harper. No university president has ever created a great faculty—

in every field — more expeditiously than Harper did at Chicago after he took over. Thanks to John D. Rockefeller money and resolve, he made a small Baptist College into a university that was, department for department, professor to professor, the greatest in America through the 1920s. But Harper was quite as assiduous and talented in building a football team that dominated for years the whole Midwest. He chose Amos Alonzo Stagg, the first household name among football coaches and, far from blanching at the thought of preferments going to players, he rented a private railroad car once a year during a vacation period to take the Chicago football team across the country, stopping frequently so the team could work out to the vast enjoyment of many thousands of spectators. As Harvard and Chicago went, so did Berkeley, Stanford, USC, and a host of other institutions in America go, to the immense delight of millions of students and alumni.

When Robert Hutchins became a successor to the great Harper as president, he put the same care into the destruction of football at Chicago as an intercollegiate sport that Harper had into its building. That proved to be quite as grievous a blow to a great university as almost anything else Boy Wonder Hutchins did. Happily, Berkeley had no academic Robespierres in power in the thirties, and we could conclude the Age of Depression with the cornucopia of delight yielded by the Thunder Team.

6

The Decline of Honor

I saw two very different kinds of "honor" erode during the thirties, both casualties in considerable measure of the Depression. The first was the honor system, as it was known at Berkeley and many other colleges and universities in the United States. Under this system each student pledged that he would neither cheat, aid others in cheating, or steal from fellow students. In return for this pledge administrations forebore proctoring of examinations and cloakrooms.

The second type of honor was attached to the Greek Letter houses, the fraternities and sororities on American campuses. In a country such as the U.S. where aristocracy in the European sense was nonexistent, Greek Letter societies in colleges and universities joined lodges and civic groups of various kinds in conferring "honor" upon those privileged to be elected or otherwise made members.

The honor system was a product for the most part of the late nineteenth century. It arose in American colleges, or many of them, as a liberal reaction to the often harsh system of discipline imposed upon students by college administrations. Under it a student pledged that he wouldn't cheat and declared that if he observed any student in the act of cheating, he would rise and publicly challenge the cheater or thief, as the case might be. Finally, the whole system was to be policed by the organized student body itself alone, with no intervention by the faculty or administration permitted. When the honor code was at its height, all that was necessary in the punishment of a cheater was for the honor or judicial committee, as it was variously known, to satisfy itself that the student was guilty as charged and then level the punishment, which ranged from simple censure to suspension for a limited period of time all the way to dismissal from the University. If either suspension or dismissal was involved in the retribution, the honor committee itself, not the administration, dispatched word of its finding to the registrar.

It is important to understand that from east coast to west coast the honor system in colleges and universities applied only to cheating in examinations and other forms of testing and to stealing, pilfering of books, coats, and other personal items in the coat rooms scattered about the campus. Specifically the honor system did not apply to such other infractions of morality or decency as brawling or what was called wenching. In this respect the American honor system was rooted in the historic code of the gentleman. A gentleman might attempt to seduce women, get drunk occasionally, even fight or duel with an enemy. He could do all of these and never risk being drummed out of the order of the gentleman. The very idea of a gentleman cheating or stealing was virtually oxymoronic. No true gentleman could cheat or steal; if he did, that was instant proof that he was not and never had been a true gentleman.

But the honor system was based also, and probably more widely (except in the American South where the mystique of aristocracy and thereby of the pure gentleman prevailed among upper-class families) on the middle class, Puritan-based, morality that featured honesty, rectitude, trustworthiness, and all around decency without any special reference to gentlemen and aristocrats.

At Berkeley the honor system was, if not actually instigated by President Wheeler early in his term, at least powerfully encouraged and reinforced. I believe it is fair to say that the honor system at Berkeley was in full swing from about 1900 to the beginning of the Depression. When I reached Berkeley in 1932 the system was not yet dead by any means but was, in the words of the dean of men in an interview in the Daily Cal, "gravely to be considered." The blunt fact was, more and more students were becoming unhappy about the vaunted honor system. It didn't seem to be working. Cheating in examinations and the stealing of books, sweaters, coats, and the like from the various coat rooms were escalating by the mid-thirties; or so it was believed by a widening number of students. Letters in the Daily Cal calling for an ending of the "bankrupt," "moribund," or "hypocritical" honor system became more numerous each year. What was wanted was a proctoring of exams by the faculty members actually giving the courses or by graduate students paid to wander up and down aisles to either deter cheating or else catch it when it occurred.

The result—a common one in history when moral values and conventions are involved—was a mixed bag by the beginning of the thirties. In my freshman year in 1932–33 I saw both systems, the honor system and the proctorial system, when exams, especially finals were given. In History 4A-B, taught by Palm, the proctorial system existed. In the same term, however, Anthropology 1A, taught by Olson, and containing about the same number of students—around three hundred—that the history course did, conducted its final exam strictly by the honor system. From the time the exams were passed out and the professor asked if there were any questions and then left immediately, we, the students were on our own. We were pledged by our own self-administered oath on the back of the blue book not to cheat and we were also pledged to warn or if necessary report any student guilty of cheating.

There lay the rub: the warning or reporting. Women students were more likely to call out than men students were when cheating was observed. But what became almost blindingly evident by the middle of the decade of the thirties was that no one relished personally applying this sanction. The Depression, with its daily toll of pathetic victims—unemployed driven to stealing to support their families, children of the Dust Bowl, and other heartbreaking occurrences—stimulated in the American people a new psychology of understanding, of sympathizing, of forgiving a great many of the malefactors of the time. This same attitude, of seeing victims, children of tragic necessity instead of dishonest, crooked, guilty individuals, passed into the universities; or at least among large numbers of students. The result was, as I have noted, students became more and more reluctant to enforce the honor code.

Cheating increased during the thirties, primarily a result of the new desperation induced by the Depression for good grades. The day of the gentleman's C was past. The ravages of the Depression gave a new respect for jobs and for all that was necessary to get jobs after one had received one's B.A. Students aiming at law school, medical or business school, or simply immediate jobs found that higher and higher grades were required. And to get higher recommending grades, students were willing when necessary to cheat in exams and other academic requirements.

The honor system was in crisis by the mid-thirties. One never knew when one signed up for a course whether the honor system would prevail in examinations or instead the proctor system. It is fair to say that by the end of the decade, rigor mortis was beginning to show. The overwhelming majority of students wanted no more of honor but rather an ample number of proctors. The Depression-generated passion for high grades had induced an almost open willingness to cheat to get them; and the Depression-induced compassion for victims had come close to destroying the all important willingness to bear the brunt of identification and policing of the system. The advent of World War II and, by 1942, the transformed character of the University, applied the coup de grâce. Finis.

A very different kind of "honor" was that underlying the popularity of fraternities and sororities in American higher education. But no matter how different from the kind I have just described, its fate was basically the same, that is, decline and fall, and so was the precipitating cause, that is, the Depression followed by World War.

I should make clear here that I was never a member of a social fraternity. I remember getting a telegram from someone I knew only slightly asking me to defer acceptance of any pledging until I had had an opportunity to talk to him and to see his fraternity at Berkeley, the name of which I don't remember. But that was a kind of grim joke. On twenty-five dollars a month and the need of hashing and other jobs, I was scarcely among the cohort from which rushees and then pledgees were chosen.

I will admit to a pang on reading the telegram. At the beginning of the thirties, following the Roaring Twenties, the average middle-class child in America was as sensitized to fraternities and sororities as to college itself. Through the twenties the fraternities were as close to an aristocracy as one could easily conceive. Such was the luster of Greek Letter societies, thanks in part to such popular writers as John Held, Jr., F. Scott Fitzgerald, and a dozen or so writers of lesser renown in all the most widely read magazines, that a considerable number of American youths, male and female, tended to see Greek Letter affiliation as the very capstone of a college education. Countless were the middle-class expectations, parental included, of making a "good" house without difficulty; and countless too were the heartaches, the chagrin, the sense of humiliation, when one didn't make one of the best of either fraternities or sororities, was instead relegated to one or other of only marginal respectability, or, worst of all, failed to pass the searching scrutiny of house members when being rushed.

Tirelessly the Greek houses, incessantly reminded by national offices of these organizations, strove to affirm and emphasize the high *honor* that immediately accrued to any young man or woman who had been pledged and would now for a whole semester, at least, combine with academic course work the protean energies required to be thought worthy by the end of the pledge-term and thus, oh, thank you, God, be privileged at last to enter the inner sanctum of the fraternity or sorority for good, forever, into eternity. It is hard to guess what the response would have been from any young Theta or Kappa or Deke or SAE, had they been told about the Englishman who having been elected or appointed to the Royal Society, said, "the best thing about it is there's no damn nonsense about honor." In America you simply *had* to be honored, to be changed from earthling to demigod, by the high and sacred mantle dropped upon your shoulders when investiture time finally came and you had been judged worthy by your henceforth peers. The fraternity or sorority house was at once chapel, guild, fief, and sacred community.

That is, more or less, over the years, until the Depression fell upon America and leveled so many ranks off and on campuses. Under the fierce ravages of unemployment, lowered wages, salaries, and profits combined with the new egalitarianism that became an inevitable ethic of FDR and the New Deal, social differentiation, if not actually social class and inequality, took something of a fall.

Fraternities, then in time sororities, had multiplied in the late nineteenth and early twentieth century. Greek motifs were popular in America — in architecture, statuary, and not least, in letters by which to denote the numerous and diverse economic, political, and cultural societies which were springing up like mushrooms when Tocqueville made his historic visit to America in the early 1830s. As we know, he thought these among the most distinctive, and also salutary, features of American democracy. In a country where dukes, earls and viscounts did not — could not under the Constitution — exist it is understandable that individuals will devise other ways of conferring honor upon themselves in order to stand out from the populace. Hence, in the U.S., the divers means by which Americans, once the new republic was securely anchored, founded groups in which membership was deemed an honor to individuals. Tocqueville, in one of his ironic observations writes of Americans he interviewed who stoutly insisted that in America all people were absolutely equal but who would then seek to make evident that *they* nevertheless stood out from the common multitude.

The rapid growth of Greek Letter houses in the colleges went along with the equally rapid growth in society of lodges, sodalities, and literary and other cultural societies, many of which used Greek letters for identification. The older colleges weren't always enthusiastic about the new fraternities. They already had their Porcellians, Skull and Bones, and the like.

It was very different, however, in the literally hundreds of colleges that rose and spread across the country in the nineteenth century, from Maryland and Delaware all the way to California. The hunger for status and honor found ready relief almost everywhere in the burgeoning fraternities and soon sororities. At first, no doubt, these bodies could be thought of simply as Christian-based mutual aid societies, but by the late nineteenth century during the Gilded Age and the enormous uprush of wealth that went with it along with the rise and spread, too, of High Fashion — best exemplified by the Four Hundred in New York City and by the inhabitants of Newport—the Greek Letter societies became more and more enveloped in the air and privileges of aristocracy.

During the twenties, as I have already suggested, the Greeks were at the height of their evolution to wealth and power. At Berkeley the social difference between a Greek and a Non-Org was wide and kept getting wider under the aegis of the booming twenties. Not only were fraternities objects of celebration, even awe, to readers of popular novels and magazines, Tin Pan Alley picked them up. "The Sweetheart of Sigma Chi" and the "Maine Stein Song" were broadcast by radio all across the land. American girls loved sorority songs especially when sung or crooned into their ears by American boys.

Then there was the differential power in government. Student government counted for a great deal at Berkeley; it had ever since it was created and then respected by President Wheeler during the first twenty years of the century. The fraternities (considerably more than the sororities in that day of supreme male chauvinism) virtually had a monopoly on student government by the 1920s. They were organized, prosperous, and convinced of an effortless superiority that made stewardship of the campus their natural right. There weren't many, if any, student body presidents, editors of the Daily Cal and the literary magazine, functionaries of any importance whatever who weren't members of the fraternity and sorority houses in the 1920s at Berkeley. Throughout the decade how the fraternities went politically was signal to how the campus went in any matter involving voting.

The fraternity-sorority system was the worst kind of aristocracy, the kind, in Tocqueville's words about the pre-Revolutionary French aristocracy, "that loves the trappings of power even more than power itself." Through unceasing propaganda out of the national offices of the campus societies, the members began to actually believe in the superior clay of which they were formed and in the right on the one hand to rule and on the other to live as voluptuously as they chose. Scholarship was all right up to a point, but one had to be careful not to be tagged a "greasy grind," one who gave more attention to his academic responsibilities than to those of the House. How one held one's liquor, knew one's house ritual, behaved at sorority or fraternity parties, collected female "scalps" at genteel date-rape occasions, dressed, and appreciated old-boy jokes about women and certain minorities, all these had come to be regarded as being just as important to the fraternity man, the whole man, as were the courses he took.

Getting into a "good" house could be the obsessing concern of parents for their college-bound offspring. It was said that fathers would steal or kill if necessary to make it possible for Junior to become a Deke; and that mothers would figuratively take to the streets if such were necessary to get a bona fide Theta or Kappa in the newspaper at home. I can attest that during my high school years in the late twenties, nurtured as I was on the abundant stories in the slick magazines about College & Greek House (they were never separated in *Vanity Fair, The Saturday Evening Post,* and *Colliers*), I could feel on occasion slightly sick at the thought of going off to college and not being able to get into a fraternity.

All that, or most of it was swept away by the broom of economic depression cum egalitarianism. The Depression undermined the economic foundation of the Greek houses, and as is so often the case when honor is under assault by wretched circumstances, tended to bring out the worst in those able to maintain themselves in their houses. Pride of membership too often metastasized into arrogance and snobbery. I was acquainted with several women students who had begun college at Berkeley as pledges and then members of sororities only to be forced by heavy financial adversity at home to withdraw from membership and take jobs of one kind or other as the sole means of completing work for the B.A. Such unfortunates learned searingly the meaning of snobbery and bogus aristocracy when they found themselves thereafter looked through by those who before the fall had been their "sisters." The ancient code of total separation of the lady from work of any kind reared its head to the last.

It is hard today to remember the power and the glory that once attended Greek Letter membership. I assume that sororities and fraternities still exist, at least as postal addresses, telephone numbers, and abodes of room and board. But the Depression made them essentially moribund and World War II—when the veterans returned afterward — applied the finishing blow to fraternities and their proffered "honor." Today, far from being cushions of romance and honor, we read about fraternities chiefly for barbarous hazing customs and squalor of living conditions that bring them to sanitary prosecutions. Sic transit . . . !

7

Sproul

Among the natural forces on the Berkeley campus in 1932 when I entered Berkeley was the robust, buoyant personality of Robert Gordon Sproul, president since 1930. Of Sproul it was said, in paraphrase of a famous compliment to a California orange, "Doubtless God could have created a better president of the University of California, but doubtless God never did."

Like a great many other students I saw him first when a University Meeting was called during the second week of classes. It was oriented toward new students, principally freshmen of course, and there was excitement in the air as we walked down to the gym listening to the brisk chimes of the Campanile.

Sproul looked like the president of a great university when he climbed the steps leading up to the platform and strode masterfully to the podium. There was no microphone; none was needed even for that immense hall given Sproul's voice, which would to the end of his life be called "booming." His talk, of about twenty minutes, was devoted to welcoming the new students with a few anecdotes about Berkeley and its history. I remember to this day the story with which he began his remarks. "Recently there was a want ad in a California newspaper for a Stanford B.A. or his equivalent. Mystified, some readers wrote in asking what was meant by equivalent. 'A USC Ph.D. or a Cal sophomore' was the reply." With that story and the roar of laughter and applause that greeted it, we were in Sproul's hands. To stay, I might add, for as long as we knew him. He was already famous up and down the state for his oratorical eloquence. I heard him on many occasions over his public career, and it seemed to me that he was never better than when he was addressing large student gatherings or, in decidedly different key, the Academic Senate. Sproul never confused his speaking missions. He could boom to large student rally assemblages and with equal facility he could modulate tone and temper to an audience of academics. His diction matched his voice.

He served as president of the University for twenty-eight years, an almost unbelievable length in current times when any president who survives ten years becomes a heroic figure. Even in those years the length of Sproul's presidential tenure was extraordinary. He was also, it should be stressed, the first nonacademic to become president of the University. All his predecessors, among them LeConte, Gilman, Wheeler, Barrows, and Campbell, had been scholars and scientists. He was also the first president who had done all of his collegiate work at Berkeley.

Born in San Francisco in 1891, one of two sons (the other, Allan, would become a banker, rising to the post of President of the Federal Reserve in New York), Robert Sproul commuted throughout his undergraduate years from San Francisco. His parents were thoroughly middle class but of the most moderate means. Sproul majored in engineering, and gave himself generously to campus activities. He was never a fraternity member, but waged successful campaigns for a number of elective offices in the ASUC. He was also an avid miler on the Berkeley track team. From the strain of trying to win every mile event in the track and field season, he acquired the corrugation of wrinkles on his forehead that stayed with him all his life.

He graduated in engineering with the B.S. in 1913. His first job was in the city engineer's office in Oakland. He didn't enjoy it, and when he learned that the post of assistant cashier was open back on the Berkeley campus, he applied for and got it without delay. He never left Berkeley again. During the twenty years following his beginning job he became cashier, comptroller, and than administrative vice president, the position he held when he was chosen by the Regents for the presidential chair in 1932.

He was an immediate hit with the alumni, students and the

majority of citizens in California, so many of whom had heard him speak in behalf of the University, and they included the members of the state government at Sacramento. As vice president he had also been effectively the University's lobbyist there, and had made many friendships that would prove to be sturdy ones during the depression years.

He was not, however, a popular choice with the majority of the older faculty. There was nothing personal that they held against the youthful Sproul; many knew him and liked him. But he was a nonacademic, one whose sole working experience with the university had been in business and financial offices. The University had never before had a nonacademic president. How could he possibly preside over a faculty meeting, attend academic professional meetings in the east, understand academic values? Were there not qualified members of the faculty—Joel Hildebrand, for one: distinguished chemist, dean, and already recipient of presidential offers from other universities? Even a few regents, I learned in later years, were not entirely happy with what they had done in choosing a nonacademic. Businessmen though they were, they were used to academic presidents. It has to be noted that Sproul, for all his successes in the office of president, was not merely the first but the last of nonacademic presidents at the University of California, thus far at least.

Sproul immediately strengthened himself in some measure with the faculty when he took office by appointing as provost of the Berkeley campus a classicist, a professor of Latin, Monroe E. Deutsch. Many years before, Deutsch had taught Latin in a San Francisco high school; among his pupils was the young Robert Sproul. Sproul never failed to mention, even to emphasize, this fact when he and Deutsch shared a speakers platform. Audiences clearly liked it.

Deutsch asked for and got the additional title of vice president of the statewide university after he had been in the provost's office a few years. Publicly the two men were never less than courteous and affable with one another. Privately, however, they were never close in their respective offices. Some said the two were simply temperamental non-alikes; others that Sproul had early on come to distrust Deutsch's judgment on important university matters, in one of which Deutsch had alienated permanently the notable Dean Gilbert Lewis, in Chemistry; others that a serious accident, a multiple fracture of Deutsch's hip shortly after he and Sproul took office, one requiring many weeks of hospitalization, had necessarily interrupted the all-important early period of adjusting to one another administratively, of laying out the respective spheres in which they would operate together in office. Whatever the reason, it did not escape notice among the more discerning faculty that there was a certain tension between the two men and a marked disinclination on Sproul's part to share his presidential powers with his provost. But none of this was public.

Deutsch, older than Sproul, reached retirement age shortly after the war was over, and it is perhaps indicative that although Sproul had more than a decade ahead as president, he never appointed a successor to Deutsch. Nevertheless, whatever the nature and origin of the estrangement — and whoever knows, it may have been little if anything more than the estrangement that is almost built into all relationships between presidents and vice presidents — the presence of Deutsch, a bona fide teacher and scholar, a Classicist in academic profession, had a great deal to do with reassurance of the faculty when the nonacademic Sproul took office in 1930.

Sproul's greatest stroke of fortune came, however, from the fact that at Berkeley ever since the Faculty Revolt of 1920, the great majority of purely academic affairs were, by Regents' authority, located squarely in the faculty's Academic Senate and not in the formal administration over which the President presided. I shall say more below about the 1920 revolution and the broad powers that a victorious faculty was accorded by the Regents. Here I want only to emphasize that in the 1930s, well after the establishment of the powerful Academic Senate, the academically inexperienced Sproul was greatly advantaged by a system in which most important, purely academic matters such as curriculum, admissions and degrees in course wouldn't fall within his presidential purview in any case. Effectively Sproul and all other presidents following the 1920 revolution and settlement were, by conventional standards in higher education in America, weak presidents simply by virtue of the powers transferred in 1920 to the faculty at the expense of the president's office. Both David Barrows and William Wallace

Campbell, Sproul's immediate predecessors as presidents served short terms and were clearly restive under the constraints of office which were the result of the 1920 revolution.

Yet Sproul always seemed a strong president, the result in part of some very important areas of responsibility—nonacademic areas such as student order, budget, finances, lobbying in Sacramento, buildings—that were his even after the 1920 Revolution and the personal manner of leadership he had been born with and that was heightened by his expansive voice. He could be stentorian with it. A favorite campus story concerned a time when he was still vice president, and in an office close to the president's in California Hall. One day when the crusty President Campbell heard Sproul's voice through a wall or two, he asked his secretary to find out who Sproul was talking to. When she came back, she said, Sacramento. Campbell barked, "Well, tell him for me to use a telephone."

Sproul took his public speaking seriously; and for good reason. Oratory was still a valued quality in any public figure then; it had not yet slipped down to its present status, which is essentially that of an antique survival. When he had an important speech to give, he always—having worked for days, even weeks on the content—rehearsed at home before a mirror; watching himself as he delivered the whole speech. He took pride in never having a manuscript or even notes in his hands, and in speaking solely from careful memorization.

In this he was playing with fire; nothing is less reliable in the long run than memory alone. Sproul's comeuppance came before a large association—I think the American Bankers Association—in San Francisco. At the midpoint of the address, memory failed Robert Gordon Sproul and for two or three minutes he was in very considerable embarrassment as he searched his brief case for the text he had just happened to have brought along. Never, thereafter, did he approach a major address without at very least detailed notes. But this said, he was still one of the two or three finest speakers I have ever heard anywhere.

He was impressive in his role of chairman of the Senate. Prior to Sproul, the chairmanship—that is, after the Faculty Revolt of 1920—had been elective, restricted to members of the Academic Senate, all of whom were and had to be, bona fide members of the faculty. Both Barrows and Campbell were members not from their presidencies but from the academic, professorial status they held. Sproul of course had no such status and would have been totally separated from the Senate—hardly a wise arrangement. Knowing this, Sproul requested, as a condition of his acceptance of the presidency, that he be made permanent, ex officio chairman. There were enough faculty who saw the wisdom of this—and with it the educative effect on Sproul of attendance at Senate meetings—to effect the change with a minimum of opposition.

He presided superbly. Before the Loyalty Oath controversy in the late 1940s and the huge attendances of Senate meetings that resulted, all Senate meetings were in 312 Wheeler, known as the Senate Room. It seated just under two hundred and was only rarely full at meetings. When it was learned that Sproul and not the elected vice chairman would be presiding, attendance noticeably improved. Sproul was handsome, poised, concerned only with facilitating actions by the Senate, and authoritative, if that word is understood as the very opposite of dominating.

Only once during his long presidency did Sproul stumble. That was with the Loyalty Oath in 1949, the severest crisis since that of 1920, and it differed markedly from the earlier revolt in that from the very beginning the Loyalty Oath battle was a matter of considerable public attention, not seldom becoming front page news in the San Francisco and Los Angeles newspapers. The Regents sought to buttress their longstanding policy of prohibition of employment of members of the Communist Party with an oath in which each faculty member would swear that he was not a member of any totalitarian party. It was one of the worst decisions ever made by the Board. By 1950 the ostensible struggle between the faculty and the Regents overlaid in fact civil war within the faculty and civil war within the Board of Regents. For there were diverse points of view in each camp. Sproul's position was equivocal at best, and he had foes on both sides, faculty and Regents. It was certainly the nearest Sproul ever came in his twenty-eight years as president to being unseated as president.

But to return now to the decade of the thirties, Sproul was close to the height of his popularity as that decade wound down. The alumni, students, legislature were still ardent in their affection for

Sproul and by 1940 he had almost completely removed doubts in the minds of faculty members; removed them by the impressive example he had set from the beginning of his term of office as the chief executive, the leader of a great university. Circumscribed though his presidential powers were by a uniquely powerful faculty, Sproul yet radiated the luster of personal leadership. He did this by a quick and adaptive intelligence to which was united a love of Berkeley that extended not only to the rest of the University of California but to the very idea of the university. He was no historian, but he had somehow acquired through habitual and wide reading a clear sense of just what a true university was and had been since the birth of universities in medieval Europe: a guild of teachers and students dedicated alike to the search for truth and acquisition of fresh knowledge in all the important areas of human life and belief. Like his great predecessor President Wheeler—who was in office all through Sproul's student days and the beginnings of his business-finance career in the University—Sproul saw the university as the proper abode of not only the liberal arts and sciences but also of professional schools and not least of organized student activities.

Sproul astutely and accurately saw presidential leadership as not a means of striking attention-getting postures in academic matters but rather as the giving of effect to policy views which reflected the consensus of faculty opinion. Leadership, as Winston Churchill's career in war made evident, need never be afraid, in its own interest, of reporting to, of deferring to parliamentary bodies. Throughout World War II Churchill reported regularly and faithfully to the War Cabinet and, when he felt it incumbent upon himself, to the House of Commons. At any given moment Churchill could have been wiped out as Prime Minister by a majority vote in the Commons. But these restraints and obligations notwithstanding, Churchill emerged from the war as incomparably its greatest leader.

Sproul, who had boundless admiration for Churchill, had much the same view of leadership in the university. He respected and never failed to observe the authority laid by the Regents in the corporate faculty, no matter how determinedly he may have held to a different position on an academic question. Even though the

English parliamentary system didn't exist at Berkeley, with a president constitutionally at the mercy of the Academic Senate, the moral weight of Senate confidence in a president was considerable, and so recognized by the Regents.

Just as Sproul was vigilant about possible incursions by the state legislature or other body into the constitutional autonomy of the University, that is, its power to govern itself, so was he attentive to the freedom of individual faculty members in their teaching and writing. In the thirties the principal antagonist of not only the Berkeley faculty but faculties over the entire country was the American Legion. It had become a significant influence in American politics after World War I, and with the onset of the Great Depression and the inevitable spread of radicalism in the country this influence cascaded into a very considerable power over public opinion. Local chapters of the Legion were urged by the national headquarters to investigate as best they could the patriotism of teachers in the schools and especially colleges. Berkeley had its share of that kind of attention, and Sproul was indomitable in his protection of the faculty's proper freedom even when the American Legion was at its most virulent. Politically, Sproul—who was proudly a Republican and a Presbyterian—held views almost identical with those of Earl Warren, one of the most popular governors in California history, and a contemporary of Sproul's at Berkeley.

Sproul was frequently compared invidiously with his contemporary, Robert Hutchins at Chicago. The two men had begun their presidencies within months of each other, Hutchins in 1929, Sproul in 1930. Hutchins served for twenty-two, Sproul for twenty eight years. Hutchins was somewhat closer to an academic background than Sproul, for after graduating from Yale he taught for several years at Lake Placid School and then served as secretary, then dean, of the Yale Law School. When, astonishingly, the trustees of the University of Chicago—then without question constituted by the finest all-round faculty of any university in America —offered Hutchins the presidency, he was not quite thirty years old when he accepted. Like Sproul Hutchins began with feelings by the faculty ranging from skepticism to distrust. Whereas Sproul in the course of a few years overcame faculty distrust and strengthened the University of California in manifest respects, Hutchins not only didn't overcome faculty skepticism but actually added to it, worsened it, losing in the process more than a few of the ablest members of the faculty and creating a unending climate of distrust and crippling hostility. The blunt truth is that Hutchins never really understood the nature of a university or, perhaps understanding it, disliked it. Sproul loved the university from the start and came to have an understanding of the institution that could, in performance, have scarcely been improved upon. When Sproul retired from office after his twenty eight years in the presidency he turned over to his successor, Clark Kerr, in 1958, a vibrant, strong, and ever-burgeoning university. The very opposite was, alas, the case with Hutchins and Chicago.

8

Lecturing as an Art Form

In the thirties when you heard a student extolling the merits of one of his teachers, the chances were a hundred to one that it was that teacher's lecturing virtues that were being hailed. Lecturing was held in high regard by both students and faculty at Berkeley then. I am aware that much the same value was put on the classroom lecture at Harvard, Yale, Michigan, Wisconsin, Cornell, and Stanford among other leading universities at that time. But nothing I have ever read or heard suggests that Berkeley had to take a back seat to any of them. The lecture was a veritable art form at Berkeley.

The time hadn't yet come at any major university in the country when teaching undergraduates, and especially freshmen, was held in disdain as an intrusion upon any true scholar's time. Nor had the time arrived when university administrations in their tireless search for research stars were willing to bargain away all teaching save perhaps a graduate seminar, this in the interest of sweetening offers in ways beyond the merely monetary. Everyone from the Sather Professor down to the lowly instructor taught at least two undergraduate courses a term. Introductory courses primarily for freshmen were very commonly taught by the most distinguished members of departments, who took manifest pleasure in the results.

Joel Hildebrand in chemistry and Raymond Birge in physics were both noted research scientists, both members of the elite National Academy of Sciences, recipients of honorary awards and medals galore. Both, however, taught for many years the introduc-

tory freshman course in their respective fields. Hildebrand told me
that for years the senior members of chemistry met once a week at
night to discuss and to plan and organize the best possible introductory course. To Hildebrand went the honor—and that is precisely how it was regarded, as an honor—of giving the lectures
before the entire class, usually numbering in the hundreds. Other
members of the faculty, senior members in many cases, presided
individually over laboratory sections.

By the 1920s the Berkeley chemistry department was ranked
among the top three departments in the country and unquestion-
ably the first in physical chemistry. Hildebrand's textbook in introductory chemistry was the most widely used for many years in both
the U.S. and abroad. There were some impressive research minds
in the department, starting with the longtime chairman, Gilbert N.
Lewis. By virtue of such minds the Berkeley department became a
famous center for graduate work. But such eminence never
dimmed the light of the freshman course.

So was it with others on the campus. For many years, Teggart
taught the beginning course in the social institutions department,
taught it with evident pleasure until his final couple of years when
his health failed him in some measure. Carl Sauer, one of America's
two or three most eminent geographers, taught freshmen with the
same gusto he gave to advanced graduate students in seminars and
field trips. Ira B. Cross, known nationally for his writings in money
and banking, lectured for many years in the introductory course in
economics. Where lecturing to students, however tender they may
be in years, is honored and where students show by their occasional
applause that they appreciate it, such lecturing—i.e., *teaching*—
will tend to be markedly better than where such teaching is looked
at as a chore, to be avoided at all costs.

Of course there were those, chiefly in the small liberal arts colleges, who pretended to sneer at large courses taught by the lecture.
How, it was asked rhetorically, could a student learn anything
when he was sitting in a class of some hundreds and perhaps fifty to
a hundred feet away from the lecturer? Well, Abelard transformed
the mind of Europe in lectures he gave in the twelfth century in the
great public squares of Europe. Luther broke the back of Rome
with his lectures at Wittenberg university. Tocqueville's *Democ-*

racy in America, indeed his work as a whole was basically shaped well before he came to visit America; shaped, as he has told us, from listening to the great Guizot's lectures at the Sorbonne. Far from there being a metaphysical conflict between teaching and lecturing before hundreds of students, the greatest universities of the past thousand years in Europe—at Bologna, Padua, Salamanca, Paris, Oxford, Cambridge, and other places—were quite literally founded on the lecture. It is sometimes said that the prominence of the lecture in the university's early stages of development was owing to the fact that students didn't have the advantage of text-books published in large numbers. This is nonsense. There was reading galore in the universities where Thomas Aquinas and his many hundreds of contemporaries taught. But the students never-theless listened to lectures. The great scholars of the day wanted to be heard, and their fame spread, with ever-wandering young schol-ars making virtual pilgrimages, as the medievalist Helen Waddell has so brilliantly and charmingly told us, from one great teacher to another.

The lecture, no matter how large, seemed to me a crucial element in the atmosphere of freedom of learning at Berkeley. I hadn't realized how sick to death I was of high school and its small classes in endless recitations or dialogues with the teacher able to keep his or her eye constantly on each pupil, until I signed up for my first classes at Berkeley in the fall of 1932. I had Ronald Olson in Anthropology along with a solid three hundred in the class and I had Franklin Palm in European history with at least that number. Both men were excellent lecturers and taking notes on their lectures was very good training for the students no matter what vocations they would follow after college. Herbert Eugene Bolton in Spanish American history would have, autumn after autumn, a thousand in his class, filling Wheeler Auditorium. David P. Barrows did like-wise in the introductory course in Political Science. The teacher I would in time pledge myself to as my mentor, F. J. Teggart, could have had when I first heard him a thousand, I am sure, had he been willing to depart the choicest room in Wheeler, Number 312, the Academic Senate room, with much better appointments, and which seated but two hundred. And it was close to his office, and he was thus saved steps.

Good lecturing had been around for a long time at Berkeley when I first went to class. There were still people around, albeit creakily in the thirties, who remembered hearing the great Joseph Le Conte in his course in Natural Philosophy and the equally great Bernard Moses in what were then called the moral sciences, later the social sciences. George Holmes Howison, founder of Berkeley's philosophy department not long after the new university had been created, was famous abroad for his bold evolutionary philosophical writings, but he was famous too for his lectures in South Hall. Early in this century, Henry Morse Stephens, perhaps to this day the most renowned of all Berkeley teachers, came to teach history. His specialty was the French Revolution, and alumni loved telling of the expression and dramatic intensity with which Stephens declaimed on the Jacobins, the Terror, and the rise of Napoleon. Stephens was famous also for the religious veneration with which he treated his ever-present cigar. He was puffing it when he walked into the lecture room and always appeared regretful when he put it down in the ash tray on the podium. Fifty minutes later he looked happy when he picked it up and relighted it. No gentleman, he told his class, could be away from his cigar for more than fifty minutes.

Stephens' popularity as teacher was campus-wide; even engineers and architects came to hear him. The great result of this was his undying popularity with the alumni, to whom he was never averse to speaking on festival occasions. Doubtless he had, simply by virtue of his special charisma, a great deal to do with the gifts that began to come to the University in the forms of buildings and endowed chairs. His was the crucial force in conceiving the Faculty Club and in getting funds from the well off to build it and, with it, the beautiful glade in which the Club sits. He was the founder of the Order of the Golden Bear, the best known of all Berkeley's honor societies, the Berkeley equivalent of Porcellian at Harvard and Skull and Bones at Yale.

Another of Berkeley's teacher-heroes was Charles Mills Gayley in English. For years he was prized by students and young faculty for weekly evenings at his home in the hills close to the campus. Sproul told me that it was Gayley above anyone else who really taught him English, made him cherish it and learn to use it effectively in his public speaking. Gayley loved students and their extra curricular as well as curricular activities. He composed the lyrics —and, for all I know, the melodies—of several of Berkeley's best known rally and cheering section songs.

Better, it used to be said at Berkeley, to sit fifty feet away in a lecture hall from a teaching mind of genius than ten feet from a mediocrity. The students seemed to feel this way and so, I came to learn, did the faculty. By today's standards it doubtless seems a prostitution of mental power to subject its holder to large classes of freshmen and sophomores. It didn't in the thirties. There was, there must have been, an underlying feeling that the freshman was in certain respects the central individual on the campus. He was young, not yet constricted by prejudices, buoyant, eager to learn and get started on his life's career. How important, then, for him to be met, hopefully inspired, by at least a few towering intellects on the campus. Most freshmen were hero-worshippers—still are, I am sure—and it wasn't at all uncommon to hear a freshman solemnly assuring a friend that Professor Smith, or Brown, or Jones was "an outstanding authority" on, say, the seventeenth century in English literature.

The genius of Berkeley lay in its calculated exposure of the eager, deeply impressionable freshman mind to the personages of the great and the notable on the faculty, the Hildebrands, the Boltons, the Sauers, and the Teggarts. And they, the professors, obviously liked the experience themselves. I repeat; it was considered an honor and a sure way to fame on the campus to be given the introductory course with its several hundreds of students who came expecting something to be good and who weren't often disappointed. If they had been often disappointed, there would have been, in due time, a change in the professor-lecturer.

I have likened the good lecture at Berkeley in the thirties to a work of art, which it was. Teaching itself, as more than a few have noted, has a reasonably close kinship with the drama, that is, with acting. There is nothing shameful in this anymore than there is in striving for a good pace in the lecture, for diction appropriate to the subject, and enough grace to avoid coming awkwardly between subject and student. Few of the better regarded lecturers on the campus were above the use occasionally of the dramatic pause, the pregnant second's silence, the use of hands, even arms and shoulders to make a point. It was well known on the Berkeley campus that any professor lecturing before hundreds was much less likely to come unprepared than was one who taught a small course with much use (and overuse) of discussion from all of the students, however dumb or uninformed — or boring to their fellow students.

Once — so I learned in later, faculty years — the Academic Senate's Committee on Courses, which alone could approve and disapprove courses and which was charged with continuing monitoring of courses, decided to have a random selection of undergraduates meet with the full Committee and to distribute as they would praise and censure. Much to the surprise of the Committee nearly all of the students preferred the large lecture courses to small classes where, said the students, instructors came too often with minimal preparation, hoping to cover their dereliction with an abundance of class discussion. In a course with two or three hundred students, the professor-lecturer was not likely to tempt fate by coming unprepared to class. Berkeley students, I found from the beginning, were quick to praise but equally quick to condemn when they felt so disposed. And the great majority of them could spot a phony at a hundred paces and weren't fooled by gimmicks or by adoption of roles of Good Fellow or Chum.

More and more today one reads of recognitions honoring faculty members through reductions of teaching loads or through being excused from teaching altogether for a fixed time, sometimes, as in a recent chemistry announcement, for up to five years. To which one is inclined to say, what a kick in the teeth for teaching! What good does it do a university administration for it to insist upon the sanctity of its teaching but at the same time countenance awards in the form of reducing or wiping out teaching. In the thirties Berkeley was thought very liberal by academics around the country because it permitted a faculty member every seven years to apply for a full year off — and at one-third of his normal salary — on sabbatical to concentrate on a particular piece of research. Among the stipulations of any approved sabbatical request was that of promising to return to his teaching department at the end of his sabbatical. I believe that stipulation no longer exists.

Most faculty considered an ideal teaching load to be one in which his teaching was evenly distributed among lower division and upper division undergraduate courses and a third course in the form of a graduate seminar. One of the advantages of the Berkeley system of courses and degrees was that a graduate student in pursuit of an advanced degree, even the Ph.D., could earn at least half his course credits in upper division undergraduate courses. And it was not at all uncommon to find seniors taking introductory courses in distant fields simply for the intellectual interest.

Rivalries among faculty could be sharp, even hostile, for introductory courses. In part this was calculated; to enhance, through the sheer number of T.A.s one would thereby have, the probability of their electing for their Ph.D. program the research specialty of the professor in charge. In an age predating the contemporary paid research assistant, any professor wanted as many graduate students as he could attract to his seminar; willy nilly, their contribution as students was to the furthering of his research. But that wasn't by any means the sole reason for senior faculty members wanting, using influence if necessary to get, the department introductory course. Overriding all else was the sheer luster that accrued to a Barrows, a Hildebrand, Cross, or Teggart.

I gather that the introductory course today is not as charismatic as it once was. A friend at Berkeley told me several years ago that his own continuing partiality to this course generated a kind of crisis in his home. He had been something of a hero to his two sons until they began work as undergraduates at Berkeley. As quickly as they recognized the low status of introductory courses among faculty members, and observed too the degree to which such courses were assigned to the very young or the very mediocre or the ordinary graduate teaching assistant, the two young men couldn't help but think of their father. Was he, after all, one of the cripples on the faculty instead of the heroic figure he had once seemed? I thought of my friend's plight and of the lowered estate of the introductory freshman course a year or two ago when I read that the graduate students at Berkeley had gone on strike and that as a result 75 percent of the classes in the lower division had to be cancelled.

Not all the teachers at Berkeley by any means were successful in their undergraduate experiences. Three of the intellectual titans at Berkeley in the thirties who were unsuccessful in this respect were Ernest Lawrence in physics, A. L. Kroeber in anthropology, and

Edward Tolman in psychology. Each, I learned, had years before tried heroically to teach, to give the lectures, in their respective introductory courses. But without success. There was the story of the undergraduate who had complained at home about the awful teacher he had in his freshman physics course, someone named Lawrence. Whatever happened to that awful teacher, his solicitous parents inquired a year or two later? "Aw, he got the Nobel Prize."

Today, given the very different values on university campuses, the general distaste for undergraduate teaching and the ease with which good teachers can become damned for their virtues, it boggles the mind to think of names as great as these three even interested, actually desirous of the freshman course. What strikes our attention is not that they tried and failed that level of teaching but that they tried at all, wanted to try. And the fact that they were unsuccessful in the introductory course, were unable to rival the Hildebrands, Boltons, and Barrows on the campus, doesn't mean for a moment that they were overall failures as teachers. Far, very far from it! In their upper division and graduate seminar courses all three were as famous for the students they trained and sent out to the world of learning as they were for their research monographs. When, in the mid-twenties, Kroeber published his classic book, *Anthropology,* he was teaching. For prior to that work the whole field was notoriously formless, without the structure that a science should have. Kroeber, master of every specialty in anthropology, made it possible for the first time to teach, that is, really teach a course called Anthropology 1A-B.

I must not leave the impression either that all those who did lecture in the large courses during the thirties were, ipso facto, Demostheneses. There were a few, alas, who did masterful jobs of covering, through their own insufficiencies, the true gold in the subject they were teaching. Such teachers, without knowing it, were killing what they had hoped to bring alive in the student breast. But they weren't many at Berkeley.

The happy consequence of the Berkeley system of free electives and of liberality in the matter of dropping courses one discovered one didn't like, was that never in four years of undergraduate work did I ever once have to suffer through a term with a faculty member I didn't like, respect, and feel rewarded by. As I mentioned early, I could wind up some semesters with a mixture of courses that would have given a Meiklejohn or Hutchins acute indigestion at the mere thought. But I was convinced I knew what I was doing and was doing right, at least for me.

On the face of it there might have seemed nothing but discordance in courses, all taken at the same time, in Greek literature, industrial organization, Shakespeare, appreciation of art, and American political thought. But James Allen in the first was often discursive and wide-ranging in his lectures; Robert Calkins in the second was ever the civilized mind and made the modern corporation as important and versatile a structure as any ancient kingdom or fief; Guy Montgomery drew the best and, as it seemed, the juiciest from the Bard; Eugen Neuhaus was a superb lecturer in art, especially modern art, with special regard for structure, line and color; and Raymond Gettell, not a major scholar, had what I thought a splendid perspective from which to detail American political thought. I was left with ample opportunities to apply the insights acquired in one of these courses to opportunities presented in the others. I recall using Calkins' perspectives on organization in the final exam I took in Allen's Greek literature in which he had stressed tribal and local organizations as part of the background for Hesiodic and Homeric sagas. Whoever read my blue book, Professor Allen or a reader, seemed impressed by my little exercise in comparative literature and wrote a special little note on the post card I had left in the blue book for early notification of grade.

Good lecturers there were in abundance. There were two courses I thought superb in their utilization of departmental professorial talent: Philosophy 5A-B and English 56A-B. In each there were two lectures a week before anywhere from 150 to 250 students, given by a series of faculty members each dealing in three or four lectures with the aspect of literature or philosophy closest to his own heart, and a section once a week, taught by one of the faculty who lectured. Thus I had the great privilege of not only hearing George Potter lecture in 56A but also knowing him in section in his role of, so to speak, agent provocateur on the lectures and the reading.

Philosophy 5A-B, as I have already mentioned, was organized along almost identical lines—two lectures a week before the full class of two or three hundred and one class, a section numbering perhaps twenty-five. I thought George Adams, Stephen Pepper, and Jacob Löwenberg outstanding and was stimulated to take advanced courses from each of them later.

Adams and Löwenberg, close friends of many years were utter contrasts in manner and substance of teaching. Adams, it was said, bent exclamation points into question marks, Löwenberg the opposite. Adams lectured from few notes, and did a great deal of pacing on the platform in front of the room, which held about seventy-five students. His full name was George Plimpton Adams, and, native of New England, student at Harvard, he could easily have been descended from both the Adams and Plimpton families. At Harvard he had studied under James, Royce, Santayana among others. It was Royce's particular form of idealism that most influenced Adams at Berkeley. New England was still in his voice.

Löwenberg never strayed from his rostrum and clearly lectured from copious notes. They didn't interfere with his eloquence, however, or to any exclusion of the students from his eyes and attention. He was always responsive to a question or observation, phrasing his words in virtually the same way that his lectures from notes were organized. He had a still fairly thick German accent, and occasionally this could make for confusion. My favorite recollection is of the time he denoted a couple of ideas as "apposite," which however he pronounced "opposite." There was just enough of both appositeness and oppositeness in the two concepts to baffle the students over which word he meant, opposite or apposite. The matter was soon resolved of course by use of the blackboard.

David Prescott Barrows was an impressive figure on the platform in Wheeler Aud in the introductory course in Political Science. He wasn't noted as a scholar, though I believe his *Berber and Black,* written many years before on the basis of field work in North Africa, is still referred to respectfully in studies of the area. Barrows had been president of the University of California from 1919 to 1923 and he was also a general in the California National Guard, serving overseas in World War I as commander of American forces in Siberia after the Bolshevik Revolution broke out in Russia. He was thus a little different from the average faculty member. He was totally serious about introducing political science to undergraduates and his military bearing, presidential manner, not to forget his steel grey mustache and full head of hair, enhanced thoughtful lectures in political science. The Marxist left among students enjoyed labeling him a militarist, imperialist, and political reactionary, but that seemed only to amuse him.

George Guttridge in history was one of the most respected lecturers on the faculty. English born, a veteran of the First World War — heavy cannonading at Sommes and Ypres gave him a lifelong facial tic — he remained the ever-loyal Englishman to the end. He lived in Kensington Park in Berkeley, on Stratford Lane just off Coventry Road. And he listened to little else on his short wave radio but BBC programs, especially news. None of that, however, affected the high regard in which he was held as a teacher and scholar by his colleagues or his popularity among students, graduate and undergraduate.

Eugene I. MacCormac, one of the older members of the History Department, taught American history engagingly to upper division students. He was midwestern in manner, voice, and prejudices. He detested England and all her works and, it was said, had disinherited his daughter when she married an Englishman. He was the author of what is, I believe, still regarded as the best book on President Polk and his momentous policies.

One of the most admired teachers in the English department was T. K. Whipple in American literature. His course in contemporary American fiction was extremely popular. His underlying methodology in the study of literature was quasi-Marxian, which meant a considerable emphasis upon the economic and social backgrounds or contexts of American writers. He did not, however spin webs of background to the detriment of exposition of the individual writers, the Hemingways, Fitzgeralds, Jeffers, Frosts, Menckens, and others who ranked high in novel, poem, or essay. Whipple died suddenly at the end of the thirties but not before he had an opportunity to read a feature article on himself as critic and historian by Edmund Wilson in *The New Republic*. A quiet, modest man, he was overwhelmed.

There were naturally some characters on the campus in the thirties. Every university or college has them. I recall several: Buceta in Spanish; he was Castilian to his fingernails and God help anyone who failed to pronounce his name as Butheta. He was haughty in manner — perhaps the only person I have ever known on whom the word "haughty" fit perfectly. It was said that early on the Masonic Lodge in the city of Berkeley extended him an invitation to become a member. His reply: "I cannot, for two reasons, be a Mason. I do not believe in God and I am a Roman Catholic." He departed Berkeley on the day of his official retirement, having spent more than twenty years there, to return to his beloved Spain and live a good deal more comfortably than his retirement income would have permitted in this country. He had displaced a lot of atmosphere in his twenty years at Berkeley.

One more character, and I will stop. This was the celebrated Alexander "Captain" Kidd of the Law School. To meet him casually was deceptive. No man could have seemed more restrained, simple, and plain in manner, unexcitable, than Professor Kidd. But at Boalt Hall among law students it was a very different Kidd. He taught criminal law; it was rumored that he had written most of the California Criminal Code. In class he expected student preparation, nothing less. When occasionally a student would be delinquent in this regard, Kidd might decide the time had come to make an example of the miscreant. He would lose his temper, he would mock, caricature, and pillory the unfortunate student, his voice rising and rising until he threatened to become soprano. I never sat in one of Professor Kidd's classes but I knew law students with a gift of mimicry and they loved to do the Captain before any audience.

There were legends about Kidd, of course. I will settle here for one. Please note, reader, that it is the *legend* I shall tell, not whatever degree of truth there may be behind the legend: One year Professor Kidd had to leave immediately after his final examination in criminal law to go to important meetings in the east. He began reading the exams on the train, a train I must explain back in the days when one could open windows at will. Kidd began reading the exams; they were apparently awful, and got worse as he read them. His temper came on; he couldn't emote and scream the way he did back on the campus, but what he could do and did was, in a final fit of rage, throw the whole batch of blue books out the window. Without grades sent back by Kidd, the legend goes, the entire class was prevented from graduating. And, the legend continues, it required an act of the State Legislature to pass and thus graduate the class in criminal law.

I will conclude, leaving the veracity of the legend thus far told unexamined. The following year a plaque was struck off by a group of law students and presented in ritual manner to Professor Kidd. On the plaque were the famous words of Marshall Petain at Verdun in World War I: *Ils ne passeront pas.* End of legend.

I repeat one more time: legend, dear reader, not fact.

9

On a Note of Applause

Having praised the faculty for its commitment to teaching in the thirties, simple honesty demands that I now give appropriate recognition to the students of that day. It is a truism that art would be mute, locked up in the soul of the artist, if weren't for an abundance of patrons and viewers to show in divers ways their appreciation of that art. Shakespearean drama wouldn't be half so good had it not been for the existence of a theater-going public that recognized and responded properly to *Othello* and *Midsummer Night's Dream*.

Nor would the teaching at Berkeley have been half so good had there not been a student audience capable and willing to make evident their appreciation of good courses, good lectures, and good teachers. The Founders had done their part at the very beginning by aiming the new university at a select percentage of graduates of high school: 12½ percent was hit upon by the Regents of an early day which was about what the better private colleges and universities drew from in their admissions policies. As I noted above, it required some courage on the part of the Founders in a then-populist America to face possible charges of elitism in the state university. In almost all of the state universities of that day, a simple diploma from high school was all that was required for entrance into the university. A student might have majored in harness making and got no better than a D-average and, with his diploma, still be eligible to go to the state university. That is, until as the consequence of sheer lack of proper preparation, he flunked out of the university.

The mortality rate could be very high indeed for freshmen at most of the state universities, reaching in some cases close to 90 percent of the entrants with the pathetic, even tragic fate of majors in harness making or carpentering going, diploma in hand, to face the iron requirements of the university in fields of the arts, letters and sciences which many of the entrants had perhaps never even heard of, much less done any preparatory work in.

By setting admission standards for Berkeley which specifically entailed superior grades in bona fide college preparatory courses in high school, Berkeley was able to avert the academic carnage among freshmen I have just mentioned. Berkeley's constitutionally mandated autonomy and self-government made it possible to draw as students very much the same kind of high school graduates that a Harvard or Stanford drew. Thus from early times at Berkeley the faculty could confidently look forward annually to entering students who in native ability and general academic disposition weren't materially different from those they perhaps had known in Eastern prep schools and colleges.

Thus the famed teachers at Berkeley, the Henry Morse Stephens and Charles Mills Gayleys of an earlier day and the Hildebrands, Boltons, Guttridges, Barrows, and Teggarts of my own day, could and did put their best energies into teaching in confident anticipation that at Berkeley there would be students intellectually and academically prepared for their teachers' labors and properly responsive.

Berkeley students were responsive not only in the high-grade work they turned out in exams and papers but also in a way that is, so far as I have been able to find out, unique in American higher education.

I'm referring to the custom — a fairly old tradition by the time I got to Berkeley — of applause, real applause, the hand-clapping kind. The applause — in, of course, varying degrees of enthusiasm but always in some measure of civility and courtesy — was bestowed unfailingly at the end of a term when the course was over and the last syllable of the last professorial lecture had been heard. But it wasn't uncommon for individual lectures during a term to be similarly greeted. I speak from personal experience when I say that it was sweet to join the dozens or hundreds, as the case might be, in

highly spirited applause for a course solid in substance and elo-
quently, even feelingly given during the semester. But if one
elected, as I did, an academic career at Berkeley and was fortunate
enough, as I was, to land a teaching post there, it was far sweeter to
know that day, if it ever came, when you yourself were the object of
the applause. You walked back to your office, feet not touching the
floor, wondering why it was felt necessary to pay a salary for such a
privileged calling.

As I say, applause was by no means absolutely limited to the term
endings of courses. Sometimes during a term when the professor
seemed to have outdone himself and the class was perhaps in an
especially generous spirit, there would be applause at the end of a
lecture. That wasn't common, and I am sure there were many
professors who, good as they were, never had that kind of in-term
appreciation. Teggart would receive it once or twice in a semester,
Bolton at least as often, Hinds in geology perhaps oftener, James
Cline in his Elizabethan course pretty regularly, and so on.

I am not suggesting here that all students were responsive along
these lines. Berkeley had its clods. But a majority, certainly a critical mass of students fell in the applause tradition readily and seemingly happily. They may not have cheered as they did Saturdays at
the Stadium during football season, but their hands did yeoman
service nevertheless in the lecture hall. Naturally, even at a place
like Berkeley where a long tradition of teaching flowered into a very
considerable number of first rate teachers at almost any time, there
were the exceptions: Dr. Dryasdust who stood in front of the class
face down in his notes and never looked up or in any other way
acknowledged the existence of a class; Dr. Thespian, just a little too
polished and self-consciously histrionic and a little lacking in important subject matter. For these there was applause at the end of
the term but not a great deal and given as a common civility rather
than as an expression of genuine pleasure. There were courses
notorious on the campus for their dullness and emptiness of either
spirit or erudition. P. Orman Ray gave one of these courses in
Political Science, in American Government; he droned and the
students dozed; they couldn't help it. (I was told, though, that Ray
was excellent in his graduate seminar, which was nice to hear.
Teaching is indeed a many-splendored thing.

Just when the custom of student applause began at Berkeley, I cannot be sure. Teachers of an earlier generation, such as Stephens, Gayley, and others I have mentioned, certainly knew the pleasure of it. Teggart told me that it was well established on the campus when he came to it in 1910. All I know is that when I got to Berkeley in 1932, there was never any want of conversations specifically about teachers. There was difference of opinion inevitably in some instances, but it wasn't difference based upon different sets of values or criteria; only on issues perhaps of style and clarity. Most of us knew who the older members of the Berkeley hall of fame — an immaterial but very real hall — were; and we felt no diffidence in predicting who among the younger faculty were headed for the hall of fame.

Students are hero worshippers by nature; it is one of their endearing traits; but it is also a functional thing, for there is nothing more calculated to raise one's perhaps already high level of achievement to a still higher one than the certain knowledge he or she is respected, even admired, in the role of teacher-scholar at a major university, actually blessed with at least a few students who give their all for you.

Venerated though teaching was at Berkeley, there were no teaching awards, no faculty members designated as Teacher of the Year. There was the deeply coveted honor of being chosen Faculty Research Lecturer each year, one invariably described in the prints as "the highest honor that can be conferred on a professor by his colleagues." Why not, then, Teacher of the Year? I couldn't forebear asking the question after I became a junior member of the faculty, and the replies I got from my seniors were roughly along the following lines.

First, teaching is the sine qua non of universities, just as piety is of the church and courage is of the army or navy. "We come to teach," Professor Pepper used to say often at faculty meetings; he was himself a noted teacher and also an impressive scholar. Second, efforts to distinguish among teachers, especially at a place like Berkeley where there were so many good ones, would be fraught with uncommon difficulties of judging; too often, I heard Joel Hildebrand say, awards would go less to teaching of highest merit — so difficult to determine and verify — than to teaching gimmicks such as dramaturgic devices or techniques that attracted some attention. Looking back, I think of the zoologist in the "pop" course in that field who, when he came to Darwinism, dressed like Darwin and made his voice as lugubrious and as much like that of a martyr as possible. He did the same kind of thing when he came to Mendel, Pasteur, and other notables of the past. Similarly inspired there was a young English instructor who was given the non-majors course in Shakespeare to teach, which he did by dressing in Elizabethan costumes and bounding all over the dais in soliloquies and postures. The first may have been a good zoologist, the second a student of Shakespeare, but it is unlikely that either was of much account as an actor. If there had then been a teacher of the year award, would one or the other gotten it? Whoever knows for sure? But I fear he would have.

Nor did Berkeley at any level of administration ever indulge in formal teacher-evaluations given out to the students for completion and return to chairmen or deans. There was, I recall, an associate professor of German, Franz Schneider, who, although without any known luster himself as either teacher or scholar, nevertheless became a kind of zealot for the improvement of teaching at Berkeley. On his own, he sent out evaluation forms to students in other professors' classes. This lasted only a very short while; he was hauled up, so to speak, before the faculty privilege and tenure committee. The committee's vote of censure went before the full Senate where it was approved heavily, but not without a tearful apologia from Schneider plus prophecy of his own martyrdom.

The fault of evaluations of professors by students, I heard classics professor Ivan Linforth say one afternoon at a Senate meeting, is that they tend to persuade students that what they *are* competent to judge—such as neatness of attire, courtesy, faithfulness in office hours—is more important than what they *aren't* competent to judge: a professor's mastery of his subject, for instance. At the time I heard Linforth's words I tended to agree. But I was then at the beginning of my teaching career. I've learned since that if a professor regularly, say, every two or three years, solicits comments in writing, with full anonymity, of course, on his teaching, he can often learn of especially if stung by, faults he was unaware of, faults highly germane to his own standards of teaching. And on the whole I've felt that the comments critical of my teaching were more accurate, and helpful, than those in praise. Students can be first-rate gadflies.

Perhaps at today's Berkeley, at what is regarded and described as a research university, there is a need that was lacking in the thirties for stimulants to good teaching—University-sponsored evaluations of teachers by their students, prizes and awards of substantial money and with extra publicity, and the like. It could be worth while, for in the long run universities will survive against the often deadly competition of other kinds of research organizations—federal, state, private institutes and centers—solely by possession of what these organizations don't have in any measure whatever—that is, the systematic teaching of the young. And although the balance may change in the near future, given the astounding and fast-growing number of nonacademic research institutes and centers, the truth seems to be that up to this point at least, the very best research is still done in the universities—indeed the *only* research in some fields.

Awards alone, though, such as Teacher of the Year, unsupplemented by heady emoluments and other rewards—or perhaps even *with* these extras—aren't likely to compete against the lure of research awards and rewards anymore than today's faculty at a major research university is likely to ask for more teaching. The atmosphere isn't quite right. William Arrowsmith wrote some years ago, "If you want Druids, you don't offer Druid of the Year awards. You plant trees."

Berkeley had a rich stand of trees in the thirties, and as much of that stand came from students and their applause as from any disposition of the faculty.

10

Giants in the Hills

Even though Berkeley was still the Old Berkeley in the thirties, the Berkeley by law, custom and tradition pledged to undergraduate teaching above all else, there were some great, internationally renowned, research scholars and scientists. Special rewards for research, well endowed research centers and institutes on the campus, and 'Research professorships' clearly were not necessary in the production of geniuses, as Berkeley's roster made evident all over the world. Gilbert Lewis in chemistry, Herbert McLean Evans in biology, Ernest Lawrence in physics, and A. L. Kroeber in anthropology suggest what I am referring to.

There was no lightening of teaching loads, nor any other special stimuli, to make possible these and other giants in the Berkeley hills, as I still like to think of them. Ernest Lawrence was the first Berkeley professor ever to win a Nobel; but he knew and others knew that there were others around him quite as well qualified for that prize as he was. There was no perceived, much less lamented "conflict between teaching and research"; and, to repeat, no unique privileges handed out to the titans. Even research stars of the magnitude of Lawrence, Oppenheimer, and Evans knew the priorities: teaching came first, research second—but research! Rare the student, undergraduate included, who didn't take some pleasure and pride in citing, in campus bull sessions or in letters home, some professor as a "world authority" on whatever subject he may have been teaching. I cannot and do not claim to have

129

known all of Berkeley's research light and leading, but I did have the privilege of knowing some of them in varying degrees of closeness. What follows are brief and highly subjective portraits of the greater ones, the titans at Berkeley in the thirties.

Andrew Lawson. He was the oldest of the greats on the campus when I came up to Berkeley. Emeritus by then, he was nevertheless a familiar figure on the campus, his name adorned by numerous legends. He came to Berkeley in 1890, already a young geologist of world prominence. He was brought with instructions to build a first-rate geology department, which he did in a very few years. One of the advantages of research giants on a campus is their capacity, by their mere presence, to attract others of comparable mettle. Lawson did. So did the others I am singling out.

He had been born in Anstruther Fyfe, Scotland in 1861. He migrated to Canada young, and at age nineteen was a member of the Canadian Geological Survey, getting world attention for work in Precambrian Strata. His interpretations remained controversial for years, but such controversy didn't damage in any degree respect for the brilliant young man who had made the discoveries.

His next burst into public fame came with the earthquake of 1906. He was made chairman of an international committee to study that immense quake, and out of his report on behalf of the committee came the founding of the modern scientific study of seismic seizures of the earth. In the 1930s, Lawson once again became newspaper as well as scientific journal copy when, against the negative recommendations of other geologists he gave geological sanction to the engineer-designers of the Golden Gate Bridge, assuring them that the subsoil on each side of the Gate could support the enormous weight that a suspension bridge would put on the pillar or stanchion at each end of the bridge. It was a bold analysis and prediction Lawson gave the bridge-builders, and a half century has proved him right. Although emeritus in the thirties he was a familiar sight on the campus, with his bush of white hair, walrus mustaches also white, and ice-blue eyes that seemed to burn when they turned on you. He was notoriously quick-tempered. Probably the most famous story about his temper was when, back in the Wheeler administration, he had told a campus telephone operator to go to hell. When President Wheeler told Lawson that he must apologize to the young lady, Lawson called her: "Are you the lady I told to go to hell?" Tearfully, she acknowledged that she was. "Well, you don't have to go."

It would be unfortunate to conclude this appreciation without one more episode in his life that impressed, awed, the faculty at Berkeley. In his mid-eighties Lawson married again (his first wife had died many years before), the granddaughter of one of his oldest geologist friends, a Canadian. A little over a year after the wedding, a baby, a son, was born. The next day at the Faculty Club there was little talk about anything else. "He does honor to us all," boomed the President's voice at the opposite end of the room from where I was sitting.

Gilbert Lewis. A chemist, he had been brought to Berkeley in 1912 by President Wheeler — his mission, to create the best college of chemistry in the world. This Lewis did. By the 1920s the Berkeley chemistry department was excelled by no other in the world. It was Lewis who attracted such younger chemists as Hildebrand, Giauque, Bray, Latimer, Gibson, Branch, et al. Lewis had a master's touch when it came to recruitment. To be sure he was already a magnet. As much physicist as physical chemist, he was already famous in the research world. He was one of the earliest Americans to understand and appreciate Einstein's relativity studies; indeed wrote a book on them.

Glenn T. Seaborg, Nobelist student of Lewis, has described vividly the kind of teaching Lewis did best:

> Probably the high point of each week was the Tuesday afternoon Research Conference held in Gilman Hall, at which graduate students presented a research paper on a current topic from the literature, which was followed by a faculty member, postdoctoral scientist or an advanced graduate student describing his own recent research. . . . Here saw G. N. (Lewis) at his best, sitting at the head of the table which dominated the center of the room, chain-smoking his huge black cigars. He asked questions and stimulated discussion over the whole wide range of chemistry and physics in a manner which I have never seen equaled. . . . Another high point was the weekly evening Nuclear Seminar. G. N. always attended these which added to the excitement.

Like most geniuses Lewis was a prodigy. Born in 1875, he graduated as an English major from Harvard in 1895. Then realizing that science was his true passion, turned to chemistry, self-taught as much as by others, and got his Ph.D. in a mere three years, 1899. There followed stints of study and teaching at Leipzig and Göttingen and MIT. His special field of work was in the then new and exciting area of chemical thermodynamics and atom structure. His work was brilliant, and by the 1920s it was almost taken for granted that he would win an early Nobel. But he never did. He remained what in Nobel circles is labeled "occupant of the forty-first chair." This means a scientist regarded by his peers as, at very least, the equal of any actual Nobel Laureate but who for one reason or other never receives the prize. It must have been bitter disappointment when one year the Nobel went to a chemist for his alleged discovery of "heavy water" who had done his first work on the subject as a student-collaborator of Lewis. As their fundamental teacher, Lewis yielded up four Nobels in the persons of students.

As a nonscientist I had no preparation and therefore opportunity to appreciate his extraordinary discoveries and breakthroughs in physical chemistry and physics. His mind, however, was diversely constituted, and his energies were seemingly limitless. Thus one day (this was after the war and I had come to know him at the Faculty Club) he asked me if I would read something he had written in the ethnological areas of cultural diffusion. I did know something about ethnology and readily, gratefully agreed. For years, it turned out, Lewis had been studying the most thorough of the monographs and books on the supposed diffusion of basic culture from the Middle East to the Western Hemisphere. Lewis, on the basis of the same hard evidence, reasoned that the diffusion had been West to East. He ended up publishing it in the *American Anthropologist*. In its way it was a masterpiece.

Sproul had the very highest veneration for Lewis. When the City of Berkeley decided in the early thirties to confer a Man of the Year award on the citizen who had done the most for his city in preceding years, Sproul nominated Lewis. When the civic committee, after expressing its own regard for Lewis as a great scientist, asked Sproul what specifically he had done for the city, Sproul replied, "He lives here." Lewis got the award. He had already received all the awards which his fellow chemists in the world could give him. This, from the City, must have pleased him.

Herbert McLean Evans. The other Berkeley occupant of "the

forty-first chair" in Nobel circles, Evans, was theoretically entitled to three Nobels on the basis of the highly original and notable work he did in three areas of the biological sciences. Evans was born in Modesto, California and took his M.D. at Johns Hopkins University in 1908 when he was twenty-six years old. He commenced research immediately and when he was thirty-three Berkeley offered him a full professorship, an astoundingly young age in those years for that rank. During the next years he was responsible for at least three major, differentiable, Olympian contributions. Harriet Zuckerman, sociologist at Columbia University, who has made the authoritative study of Nobel winners and losers, writes,

> He identified both the growth hormone and the oestrus cycle in the rat, which made endocrinology come of age as a discipline. He also discovered the antisterility vitamin (Vitamin E) and determined its structure. His work on Vitamin E, according to the official history of Nobel Awards, "has been held to deserve a Nobel Prize, even if it has not victorious in the competition with others". . . . Still, although each of these investigations was of Nobel Prize caliber, he was never summoned to Stockholm. Occupants of the forty-first chair, like Evans, continue to be esteemed by their fellow scientists, and their standing is unimpaired by Nobel oversight. The Evanses of the world of science provide evidence of the imperfect operation of the reward system at the topmost level.*

I think I know why Evans was so egregiously passed over by Nobel committees. The reason is personal, inseparable from his character and some of his starker views of others. He was perhaps the vainest and most arrogant man I have ever known in academic life. He was also an unabashed, vocal anti-Semite. Once, sitting at the same table with him at lunch at the Faculty Club, with others present, he suddenly said in a distinct voice, anent nothing I had been aware of in the conversation, "I have never liked or trusted Jews." For all the sheer genius of his research, it is not unlikely that his normal arrogance and his blatant anti-Semitism didn't figure prominently in his lifelong failure to be awarded at least one of the three Nobels he was fully entitled to.

Arrogance or not, Evans was one of the great teachers at Berkeley in the thirties. He was already legendary. His Institute of Experi-

---

* Harriet Zuckerman, *Scientific Elite* (The Free Press, 1977) 43.

mental Research in the Life Sciences Building must have been one of the very first such organizations in Berkeley history. Graduate students, even occasionally precocious undergraduates, virtually fought to reach the level of work and study in his laboratories. He was in biology at Berkeley what Lewis and Lawrence were in chemistry and physics. Except for personality. But that almost never bothers the brightest and most ambitious of students. It's work with and under a genius that they crave.

Ernest Lawrence. He was already famous on the campus when I arrived in the early thirties. He had joined the physics department as an associate professor in 1929. The following year he became a full professor. He had not succeeded as teacher of the introductory course in physics, as I noted above, but he became magnetic to advanced students simply by his brilliance and buoyancy in experimental physics. There were two graduate students in physics in the first rooming house I lived in, and they talked almost incessantly about Lawrence and his atomic work. Through them I found my way to where Lawrence was beginning to reach fruition of his early cyclotron work. It was in the old, long since abandoned and razed, East Hall just south, as I recall, of Faculty Glade. Lawrence and his students and assistants occupied a very large room, the basement, I believe, and it was almost thrilling, even to a scientific illiterate such as myself to go by it at night and through the windows at street level watch the complicated paraphernalia with lights going on and off in dozens of places, it seemed, and, no matter how late at night, the shifting figures of those conducting around the clock the operations involved in the first cyclotron.

In 1939 Lawrence received the Nobel Prize, the first University of California scientist to win it. Naturally the news electrified the campus. Years later I learned that he had been put up for the Faculty Research Lecture somewhat earlier but was turned down on the ground that he was not yet fully matured as a scientist. When news of the Nobel hit the campus, though, the Faculty Research Committee met again and decided that Lawrence was mature enough.

One of Lawrence's tennis-playing friends was Edward Strong, then an associate professor of philosophy. When Strong, during a year's leave, built the beautiful house that still stands atop a hill above Euclid a few blocks up from the campus, it was the result of Strong's builder's genius and the Nobel prize money Lawrence had received, then, I believe, fifty thousand dollars, a substantial piece of which Lawrence lent to Strong at very low interest.

That contact between the two men proved to be fateful. So impressed was Lawrence by philosopher Strong's abundant and manifold building skills that during the war when the new radiation lab high on the hill overlooking the campus from the east became engaged in top secret war work involving the historic atomic bomb, Lawrence invited Strong to take a job that may have been lowly in title but immensely important in practice, that of general factotum in all matters involving carpentering — creation, plans, building, repair, whatever. I think Ed Strong was prouder of that deeply secret work he did under Lawrence at the Rad Lab on the hill than anything else he ever did, including distinguished service in the sixties as chancellor of the Berkeley campus.

Lawrence became a celebrity first with the Nobel Prize in 1939 and then with the ever-widening fame for "cracking the atom." Of a sudden, atomic physics of the Lawrence variety hit the American popular culture. "Cracking" or "smashing" the atom became overnight a familiar metaphor in a variety of areas of discourse. People became accustomed to variations on the cartoon showing a man of heavy muscles bringing a sledgehammer down on a wedge that split the pea-like atom. Throughout the international domain of high energy physics, Lawrence's became one of the best known and respected names in modern and contemporary physics. His position in the Manhattan Project was unique. General Leslie Groves wrote after the war that it was Lawrence over and over who by sheer brilliance of mind and steadfastness of character kept the project going at times when it looked as though obstacles had become insuperable. But nothing ever destroyed or eroded the genuine modesty he had been born with in rural South Dakota. He had one serious flaw: the genetic inheritance of so high a threshold of pain that he couldn't feel even the early ravages of stomach cancer until the time had been reached where surgery was useless. He died at age 57.

J. Robert Oppenheimer, "Oppie" to friends, was already, in 1932, after only a couple of years on the faculty, a campus legend.

His air of perpetual abstractedness, his walk, his dress, and natural charisma made him something of a god with many graduate students in physics. He held the combined images of genius-scientist, academic bohemian, and also radical neo-Marxist ideologue. Something of a child prodigy while he grew up in New York, he graduated from Harvard at twenty-one and two years later received his doctorate in physics at the University of Göttingen in Germany having on the way spent a number of months in the famous Cavendish Laboratory under Lord Rutherford at Cambridge University in England. Beginning the following year, in 1928, Oppenheimer held appointments in theoretical physics at both Berkeley and Cal Tech, dividing the year evenly between the two institutions. By the time I reached Berkeley he had, I believe, become a full-time Berkeley professor.

And a colorful character. His walk — a long stride, body slightly bent over, pork pie hat on his head, and a cigarette invariably hanging from his lips — was famous and subject to efforts at imitation of most graduate students in physics. Unmarried, living comfortably in spacious quarters, he had — by insistent rumor at least — a succession of lovers, one of whom was the beautiful Jean Tatlock, daughter of Berkeley's crusty Chaucerian scholar in the English department. Among his hobbies was the study of Sanskrit, which he pursued under Berkeley's one Sanskrit scholar, Arthur Ryder who wrote excellent poetry in Sanskrit. Within a year of study on the side, Oppenheimer became adept enough to read the classics and try his own hand at writing in the language. Oppenheimer, who had inherited a considerable amount of money from his importer-father in New York, lived, without question, the good life — handsome house in the hills, and, so it was said, the best of wines, foods, and women.

Oppenheimer also became, by his own admission, a student of Marxism and, for a time before the war, at least a fellow-traveler of the Communist party. It was, he said later, the consequence of his deep hatred of Nazism. At the time, Soviet Russia appeared to be the most reliable antagonist of Hitler's Germany. Whether Oppenheimer ever became, as did his physicist-brother Frank Oppenheimer, a full-fledged member of the Party, is, I believe, still an open question to those interested in his biography. He denied that he had become a member, and his full, detailed account of himself and his activities and relationships persuaded General Groves at least, the military head of the highly secret atom bomb project, of Oppenheimer's loyalty and trustworthiness.

All that, however, lay in the future. During the thirties when war and loyalty investigations were still ahead, Oppenheimer was probably the most recognized single figure on the faculty, what with his clothing style, inimitable walk, famed brilliance of mind, and, not least, his bohemianism, his Sanskrit poetry, and romantic radicalism.

Richard Goldschmidt. The least known of the geniuses in the hard sciences was this man, a refugee from Hitler's Germany, reticent by temperament, and the object of ostracism by a large number of American biologists for what was deemed to be his heretical rejection of certain key aspects of Darwinism. (In America among biologists Darwinism could be both a church and a scientific hypothesis.)

He was already world famous in genetics for his experiments when he came to the United States in 1936 and was made a full professor in that field. Among his major accomplishments was his demonstration of the genetic basis of geographic variety among the species. No biologist ever questioned his brilliance as an experimentalist or the value of some of his major experiments. He was nevertheless ostracized because of his refusal to enter into the so called Modern Synthesis in evolutionary biology. Theoretically, or hopefully, it was thought by nearly all in the field to be the reconciliation, at long last, between Darwin's absolute insistence upon a natural selection rooted solely upon slow, gradual, and continuous variations and the discoveries by some of those geneticists following in Mendel's footsteps that large scale, mutational, punctuational changes have been and are crucially involved in biological evolution. But Goldschmidt was one of the tiny few in the field to refuse to accept the "synthesis." His view was that it really wasn't a synthesis but instead a papering over of the evidence for large-scale, discontinuous changes in evolution in an effort to keep Darwin's basic theory of continuous gradualism alive and sovereign.

Some of his discoveries or theories were understandably too radical to have attracted much if any support from biologists, who, like the rest of the human race are sometimes given to unconquerable compulsions to orthodoxy, be it theological or biological. Steven M. Stanley, contemporary evolutionary biologist at Johns Hopkins University, has written of Goldschmidt:

> His ideas on large-scale evolution were widely derided. In retrospect some of Goldschmidt's views still appear extreme, yet many were no farther from the punctuational model . . . than the prevailing views of the Modern Synthesis were in the opposite direction. . . . Even so, he prophetically focused attention upon chromosomal change, on the role of single mutations in effecting rapid changes in growth gradients or developmental sequences, and on what we now call quantum speciation. Goldschmidt's most controversial construct was the "hopeful monster," the single animal supposed to constitute a new genus or family at birth. . . . In retrospect, it seems to me that Goldschmidt deserves posthumous accolades for his steps in the right direction, though they may have been steps too far.*

I had the good fortune to meet him in his office several times at the end of the thirties, after he had been at Berkeley for about three years. He was charming. He was also grateful to be out of Germany and at so fine a university as Berkeley. He didn't complain or lament about the ostracism and its inevitable effects upon his ability to attract good students and also reasonably adequate research funds. But it was obvious that he was professionally lonely. The Goldschmidt case was the second I became personally interested in. The first was Teggart, my mentor, who had also been effectively ostracized for many years for his radical views on the proper study of history. The judgment of heresy is not made as often, thank heaven, in science as in religion, politics, and ideology, but it happens just often enough to push ever farther into the future the dream of genuine human objectivity in knowledge and faith. It is painful enough to see religions establish inquisitions and punish transgressions from The Truth. It is almost heartbreaking to see this odious work done in the sciences. But like it or not, it is a grotesque reality.

A. L. Kroeber. He founded anthropology at Berkeley in 1903, having just obtained his Ph.D. in the field from Columbia University the year before, the first ever granted by that university. He had

---

* *The New Evolutionary Time Table.* (New York: Basic Books, 1981) 135.

been invited by the Hearsts to come out to San Francisco and classify their excellent collection of New World artifacts. While there he met President Wheeler at Berkeley who promptly invited him to establish a department of anthropology at Berkeley. For this mission Wheeler was able to guarantee Kroeber use of an ugly sheet iron building in a corner of the campus, promising him, however, in a letter long since framed for exhibition by the department, that use of the inadequate building would be "very temporary" and that new and proper quarters would be available shortly. It was, I believe, exactly fifty years later that the promised new building was built at last. I recall vividly studying my anthropology in the thirties in the "temporary" building.

Of all the great men at Berkeley in the thirties, Kroeber was the closest to a universal scholar and scientist. He was the very last — indeed could be called the first — to write professionally in literally every specialization of the field of anthropology: physical anthropology, linguistics, archaeology, ethnography, et al. Anthropology was a very loose field indeed prior to the 1920s, almost bereft of the unifying concepts that commonly identify a genuine science. It was Kroeber alone who remedied this situation in his *Anthropology,* published in the early twenties. Here he distinguished between the general theories of man and culture that differentiated the field and also, with astonishing precision, the special theories attending the subdivisions of the subject. A purely chance contact with the book one day sent me to the anthropology introductory course of which it was the principal textbook. Kroeber, alas, was not the teacher. As I explained above, he, along with Tolman and Ernest Lawrence, were failures at teaching in the introductory sphere. But Ronald Olson was an exemplary lecturer — he should have been; Kroeber told me that he had scoured the world to find not necessarily a top flight anthropologist but a top flight teacher of the introductory course. Like Gilbert Lewis, Kroeber thought it the single most important course in the department.

He is without question one of the three or four most influential anthropologists of this century; and I include the European scholars in that judgment. He once said in my hearing at a Faculty Club table that it was very important for every scholar or scientist to know one thing, however small or specialized, better than anyone else. Thereafter he should, "for the good of his old age," spread out, take on diversity. Kroeber was a living example of his advice. He published in his lifetime well over five hundred separate, classified studies ranging from articles and reviews to reports, monographs, and notable books. There is scarcely a department of the field as it has been known for most of the century in which Kroeber's writings are not to be found. Many of his larger pieces, such as "The Super-organic," published as a very long article in the *American Anthropologist,* could easily have been released in independent book form.

He was born of Protestant parents in New York City, a fact I cite only to stress that unlike the great majority of Protestant or ex-Protestant social scientists in this country early in the century, he was not only free of racial stereotypes — the kind which so often included anti-Semitism — but saw as one of the major goals of anthropology the demonstration to the world that the most significant differences among human beings are not racial, not even genetic, but cultural. When Kroeber commenced his writing on this, early in the century, his message was revolutionary. No one else I can think of in this century did more, did as much indeed, to shape and diffuse a new science.

He and my chief, Teggart, had never gotten along well; in fact, disliked each other. But that never affected in any way my relationship with Kroeber. He was interested in what I was doing, generous with his advice when I asked for it, all in all, it seemed to me a gentle human being as well as genius in his field.

Herbert Eugene Bolton. I shall be brief here inasmuch as I will be obliged to say more about Bolton in the context of my chapter on Teggart. The war between the two men was epic. Bolton came to Berkeley in 1911 after two years at Stanford and before that Texas where his primary teaching was in medieval history. At Texas he had become fascinated by the documentary and other riches of the history of the U.S. in its relationship, not to Europe, which was conventional, but with Mexico and other countries in Latin America. Spanish-American history had become very definitely Bolton's chief love when he went first to Stanford, then upstate a few miles to Berkeley, which had just received the magnificent Bancroft collection of Westerniana, formed of everything from old legal documents to personal diaries and letters.

For the next half century, Bolton's achievement was that of almost single-handedly creating a new and fully recognized field of history. His 1920 book (with T. M. Marshall), *The Colonization of North America,* opened and gave definition to his work and the new field he was opening up by dealing with the growth of America in the terms of non-English colonies and English colonies other than those making up the familiar Thirteen on the Atlantic seaboard.

It would be hard to locate any one area of his work at Berkeley in which his light burned the brightest. His skill and attraction as undergraduate teacher were well demonstrated by the very large classes he lectured to in Wheeler Aud year after year. There wasn't a major trail, road, historical site in Latin America that he hadn't visited for scholarly purposes. He knew how to extract the drama of the history he was teaching. But Bolton was equally impressive as a graduate teacher. His seminar was famous; it attracted some of the best history students at Berkeley. More than a hundred Ph.D.s and two hundred M.A.s were taken under Bolton during his career.

His work habits were celebrated. He was on the campus all day and well into the night. Bancroft Library, then a part of the fourth floor of Doe Library was the setting for him and his junior colleagues and graduate students. Bolton was there as late as anyone, working, conversing, looking for all the world like just what he was in fact: master of a milieu of study. He never left Bancroft before midnight to go home. In earlier years before a rule had been established requiring that the library be vacated by that hour, it was possible for him, quite literally, to spend the night working (napping occasionally, he said) in his office and immediate surroundings. For years, prior to the midnight-clearance order, he could be seen by early arrivers on the campus leaving Wheeler to go down Telegraph Avenue for a shave at a barber shop and breakfast at the nearest cafe. Somehow his family life was unaffected significantly; he and his wife were a devoted couple, she active in many campus affairs, and there were several children, one of whom, Jane, was very much a campus leader in the Thirties.

Bolton, with his prodigious scholarly accomplishments and his unyielding, untiring devotion to teaching, starting with the thousand students he lectured to in Wheeler Aud in the introductory Spanish-American history course and culminating in the literally hundreds of graduate students he had over a lifetime, was as impressive a walking demonstration as one might ever see of the truth that intrinsically there is no conflict whatever between the demands of research and the demands of teaching.

Joel H. Hildebrand. Of all the greats in Berkeley's faculty history, this man is probably the most versatile. He was a notable chemist, one of the very first young men chosen by G. N. Lewis after his arrival as chairman in 1912. I have heard knowledgeable chemists say that in terms of creative discovery and synthesis, Hildebrand was not the equal of Wendell Latimer and one or two others of that generation. Perhaps so. But Hildebrand became a member of the National Academy of Sciences in less than a decade after his arrival at Berkeley in 1913; during his lifetime he won most of the prestigious chemical prizes and awards and became president of the American Chemical Society. He was, in sum, no mean scientist in his research.

He was also, as I have mentioned several times, an outstanding teacher. He was given the introductory freshman course that the chemistry department took such pride in, and he held on to that course from just before 1920 until his retirement in the 1950s. He was revered by thousands of alumni who had taken his introductory course. No one at Berkeley in the thirties had greater fame or luster as teacher than Joel Hildebrand and he was proud of it, prouder, I think, than even of his research recognition internationally.

He was also proud of the Academic Senate he had helped create in the Faculty Revolution of 1920 in which he, then still young and relatively new at Berkeley, took a prominent part. He believed strongly in academic freedom and democracy and saw the Academic Senate at Berkeley as virtually his church. He served repeatedly as chairman of the most important and time-consuming committees of the Senate. Additionally he accepted the post of Dean of Men for a time in the twenties and Dean of the Faculty of Letters and Science in the late thirties. Several times he was offered presidencies of other universities, but he chose to stay at Berkeley, in whatever capacity. I was reliably informed, I believe, that he was highest on the Regents' unwritten list of those at Berkeley qualified to succeed Sproul were he to resign the presidency.

Hildebrand's talents went well beyond the academic and administrative. He and his wife Emily and their four children were inveterate Sierra campers. (He was an early, ardent member of the Sierra Club). With the participation of his family, he wrote a charming as well as utilitarian book on camping in the High Sierra. He was one of the earliest serious California skiers, forty years old when he first put on skis. When the United States first entered the Winter Olympics, Hildebrand was made manager of the first team. He was also a gifted photographer, and several times there were exhibits of his work on the campus and elsewhere.

His final gift was longevity. I have never known a person who in middle and old age seemed more likely to live forever. Joel didn't make that, but he was a 101 when he died. Up to the final weeks of his life he was driving himself from his Kensington home to the campus, in the late years directly up to a parking space in the Hildebrand Hall area, thence to his laboratory where, well into his nineties, he was at work and turning out professional papers. When he reached 100, the campus was virtually put on holiday status, and there were festivities to have tried the strength of one half Joel's age. I could not be there, but I learned that he was in his car driving to the campus the next morning.

One final event. He adored his wife, Emily, almost as old as he. By dint of her early marriage to Joel, she had not, as I recall, been able to finish college. Joel was a member of Phi Beta Kappa, so were all of the four children. On that basis Joel proposed at an annual meeting of the Berkeley Alpha chapter that Emily Hildebrand be made an honorary member on the ground that "she married one Phi Beta Kappa and gave birth to four." With great applause she was so honored.

11

Teggart

For the last of my "giants in the hills" I turn to Frederick J. Teggart. I knew him best by far of that illustrious group; knew him from 1934 when I chanced to take his notable introductory course, through three years of work under him for the Ph.D., and finally as his tyro-successor when he retired from active teaching in 1940. He remains the finest scholarly mind I have known in my life. It is hard to think of very much in my own teaching and writing that doesn't bear the trace of his influence. Students, in their informal, word of mouth ratings, placed him high among the best of the Berkeley faculty. They liked him for his eloquent and serious lectures, and also for the radical cast of his philosophic-historical mind.

The originality of his mind was known on both sides of the Atlantic. A. J. Toynbee credited Teggart with being the principal force in his own conception of *A Study of History,* a classic, if still controversial work in comparative history. Teggart's work, he wrote in 1965, "more than anyone else's opened the door for me." When Spengler's *Decline of the West* came out in English in this country in the late twenties, it was to Teggart that the editors of the then eminent *Saturday Review of Literature* turned for what became the authoritative review of that grandiose and flawed piece of Teutonic obscurantism. Most other reviewers took Spengler at his word: that he was the most original mind to come along in a hundred years. Not Teggart. His review is still, after sixty years, the most penetrating and, it must be said, devastating of all written in this country. When Harvard University decided sometime in the late twenties to create for the first time a sociology department, it was to Teggart the University went not only for counsel but leadership if he could be persuaded to take the chairmanship. Teggart couldn't. He loved Berkeley too much.

I came on Teggart by accident in 1934; more specifically by the laissez-faire system of course selection that I have already lauded. I had 11:00 open on my schedule for that semester and on searching the Schedule and Directory for what was available at that hour saw Progress and Civilization taught by one F. J. Teggart. The catalogue description was seductive: "Major theories of history; cycles and the idea of progress; the nature of change and revolution." I got myself over to 312 Wheeler in record time and the rest is history, meaning my own personal history.

Teggart was impressive. Never did he have to wait for the hubub of conversation to cease, Daily Cals to be folded and put down, binders snapped to prepare for note taking, and the like, all of which could in some classes take up to a couple of minutes to subside, letting the lecturer begin. Teggart began without slightest delay. Not that he was overbearing. He simply personified in his bearing and voice The Professor at Berkeley. Teggart was adamant in his refusal to allow attendance to be taken at the lectures, as was the case in at least a couple of large lecture courses at the time. "They are in a university now, no longer a school; they're mature or at least should be treated as such; if they want to cut, it's their business, provided they pay any consequences." The result was that the students who were at the lecture—and this was always the vastly larger part of the class—were serious about being there. Teggart lectured with force, sometimes passion, and sounded as though he considered what he was lecturing about to be the most important thing in the world. It was not unusual for Teggart to receive student applause for a lecture several times during a semester and a rousing accolade at the end of the semester.

Granted that his most celebrated course, Progress and Civilization, was at bottom an introduction to Teggart's broad and diverse learning as revealed in his books and articles, rather than to a national intellectual discipline such as economics or political science or anthropology, granted, in all truth, that the course was introductory to Teggartism and was not infrequently so described on the campus, the students still got something that was a great deal more than one man's preoccupation with his idiosyncrasies, which is so often the case in introductory courses no matter what they are purportedly introductory to.

Each year Progress and Civilization (Fall Semester, MW 11 and additional section) took up the history of the idea of progress in the West, an idea I had never heard of. It was a good deal more than eudaemonic in Teggart's hands, being, in his view, the master idea, going back to the Greeks, under which modern conceptions of philosophy of history, social evolution, and what Karl Popper calls "historicism" fall. (There was nothing in Popper's *Poverty of Historicism* when it came off the press in 1957 that I was not fully prepared for, even on top of, as the result of Teggart's course a quarter of a century earlier.) This led him to the fixation in the West on purely narrative history instead of comparative histories, making it necessarily an art form instead of scholarship with scientific potentialities. He dealt too with the classical and Renaissance theories of cycles in history, pointing out how derivative Spengler's vaunted *Decline of the West* actually was and how meretricious so much of the touted learning. All this for beginning undergraduates!

The second semester of the course covered major problems of historical change and with some of the processes of change that the philosophy of progress and its offspring social evolution so blandly overlook. Here we learned of the role of migrations in Eurasian history, of the clash of peoples and their cultures, of the periodic rise of great ages of culture such as that in Athens in the 5th century B.C., in Paris in the thirteenth century, and in London during the Age of Elizabeth. He poured heavy criticism, sometimes acidulous, on race theories of achievement, pointing out how to the Romans of the first century A.D. the inhabitants of Great Britain were nothing more than savages destined to remain savages, or at least highly retarded people, forever. But he condemned equally other determinist theories of history, geographic, climatic, and economic foremost. He dealt with Marxism but only as a form of determinism in history which he found as fallacious as other determinisms.

What the French Annales school of history today calls, critically, *l'histoire evénementielle,* that is, history as "first this, and then and then and then . . . " was emphasized critically by Teggart as far back as 1910 when he published "The Circumstance or the Substance of History" in *The American Historical Review*. This seminal essay was followed by his *Prolegomena to History* in 1916 and *Processes of History* in 1918. In both books but in dramatically different ways, Teggart drove home the point that as long as the unilinear-narrative format is used for the study of history there is no way in which the discipline can become a science. In the social sciences of the time, Teggart noted, the format of unilinear social evolution played the same role. In each instance a unitary pattern was imposed by the historian and social scientist upon a subject matter inherently plural. "History is plural" was Teggart's tireless injunction, whether in his introductory course or his books and articles. It is Procrustean to force the diverse, plural phenomena of the human races onto or into a theoretical framework identical with the literary epic or simple story.

Teggart essentially educated himself into the life of scholarship once he had earned the A.B. degree in English at Stanford. He was born in Belfast, Ireland, one of eleven children. His father, a distiller, brought the whole family to the United States in 1889; Teggart had by then completed courses in Methodist College in Belfast and then Trinity College in Dublin.* About the time the Teggarts were settled, Stanford University opened its doors to its first class, and Teggart (along with Herbert Hoover who, Teggart once told me, wasn't a "friendly person") began work toward the B.A. degree. Stanford had been dedicated to helping the worthy poor to a college education, and along with scholarships and loans, offered jobs on the campus to help pay their way. Hoover's was in the laundry, Teggart's in the library. There was no tuition at Stanford in those years (not indeed until just after World War I), and Teggart said he managed nicely with his job and a dormitory room.

English was Teggart's major at Stanford. When he graduated in 1894 he had already published small pieces on one or other aspect of English, but, marrying in that year, he needed a job; graduate

---

* For certain biographical details I am indebted to the late Grace Dangberg and her *A Guide to the Life and Works of Frederick J. Teggart*. Reno: Nevada, The Dangberg Foundation, 1983.

work was out of the question. The librarian left suddenly for a better job in the east, and Teggart was lifted from student assistant to acting librarian. The library would be his platform for the leap into scholarship. The B.A. would remain his only degree prior to an honorary LL.D. from Berkeley upon his retirement in the spring of 1940. There is no doubt in my mind that he wanted, when he graduated, to go on for graduate work leading to the Ph.D., for despite the strenuous opposition to this new, German-exported degree from American scholars of the towering fame of William James at Harvard, the degree was spreading fast at the end of the nineteenth century in the United States as a condition — soon as *the* condition — of academic appointment in the institutions of higher learning. Teggart's reason for not pursuing the degree had to be his marriage within weeks after graduation and the absolute necessity of earning a living.

This he did with gusto. Such was his early fame as librarian that a year later, while still holding the acting librarianship of Stanford, he was made librarian of the Hopkins Railway Library, very much of a treasure for Western scholars. He also began his career as scholar-writer. He had majored in literature, combining English with the Greek and Roman classics. In 1896 he published an article, "The Plot of Lyly's Sapho and Phao" in the journal *Poet-Lore* and two years later "Caesar and the Alexandrian Library" in a German scholarly series. In the same year he published in the *Library Journal,* "Contribution Towards a Bibliography of Ancient Libraries." Clearly he was something of a natural scholar, without actual need of Ph.D. training.

In 1898 he was appointed head librarian of the prestigious private library in San Francisco, The Mechanics Mercantile Library, conceived by its donors especially for the working men of San Francisco but not in any degree thereby lowered in scholarly objectives. Teggart regarded the years immediately following this appointment as by far the most stimulating and intellectually rewarding of his life. From the beginning he was caught up in some of the circles, literary, dramatic, philosophical, that formed the sociological fundament of the turn of the century renaissance the city enjoyed in literature and the arts. His writing broadened and deepened. In addition to a continuing volume of learned pieces on

library and bibliographic history, he turned his mind to philosophical ventures, particularly ones having a historiographical edge to
them. He told me he had come across F. H. Bradley's *Methods and
Presuppositions of Critical History,* and it had quite literally shaped
the rest of his intellectual life. Historiography and its relationships
to literature, philosophy, and science became, it is fair to say, the
governing interest of his life. But Teggart would go well beyond
Bradley, especially in his famous *Theory of History,* published by
Yale University Press in 1925.

While librarian at the Mechanics Library, Teggart kept up a
continuous flow of lecturing, participation in scholarly sympo-
siums, and writing. The last included an audacious history of civilization, one in which, he told me, he dealt with Western Europe in a
full Eurasian context, featuring the great movements of peoples
throughout the Euraisan land mass. This was when historical geography, cartography, and the study of migrations as key elements in
the rise of civilizations became dominating interests in Teggart's
life. Alas for the drafted history of civilization, however, it became,
along with the 200,000 precious volumes in the Mechanics institute he headed, a total casualty of the 1906 earthquake and fire. As
was the city's equally famous public library.

Teggart's connection with the University began in 1905. He was
appointed lecturer in the Extension Division, giving classes in literature and history in San Francisco. At some point in his life Teggart
seems to have become one of the paid "nameless scribes" the
famous H. H. Bancroft engaged to assist him in writing his gigantic
(thirty-nine volume) history of the West, U.S., and Latin America).
If so, he made a hit. For when Bancroft presented his magnificent
library, numbering more than 60,000 invaluable items, to the University it was stipulated that Teggart go with it. Thus in 1911
Teggart became associate professor of Pacific Coast History and
Curator of the Bancroft Library, a notable step in the professional
life of this remarkable man. Teggart and his family had moved to
Berkeley in 1905, buying a house near the campus; it was as though
he anticipated not only the devastating earthquake and fire (which
destroyed the house the Teggarts had lived in before the move to
Berkeley) but also the appointment to the faculty of the University.

Here began the saga for which Teggart was best known for many years, one that encompassed the great Henry Morse Stephens, chairman of history, the equally great Herbert Eugene Bolton, founder of a whole school of Southwestern American history, and other lesser-known but active members of the Berkeley faculty. When Teggart arrived on the Berkeley scene he almost immediately became one of Henry Morse Stephens' devoted followers. The acidulous Arthur Ryder in Sanskrit, no admirer of Stephens, referred to him and his circle as "a sham giant surrounded by real pygmies."

Stephens encouraged Teggart to do the work necessary to winning a Ph.D. from Berkeley—then, unlike today, acceptable within the bylaws. As Stephens saw it, there would be no need for special examinations, which would be embarrassing to colleagues and candidate alike, and quite unnecessary since by the nature of his post there would be no necessity of getting insight into his mind. All that would be necessary was a dissertation in the field of history. Teggart wrote it; it was published by the University of California Press in 1916 under the title, *Prolegomena to History: The Relationship of History to Literature, Philosophy, and Science.* It attracted considerable attention in Europe where the interest in philosophy of history and in the possibility of historiography ever becoming a science were very strong. A. J. Toynbee and John Linton Myres were among those who read it and approved of its boldness.

But not, alas, Henry Morse Stephens at home. For whatever reasons—real reasons plus public reasons—he changed his mind; also, at least in Teggart's highly interested perspective, lied about what he in fact promised in the beginning. Mrs. Teggart told me one day that nothing she had seen in the way of his Irish moods during their forty years of marriage equaled his fury and bitterness at what he believed Stephens had done to him.

Teggart's Irish genes converted the bitterness into an implacable antagonism that quickly spread in the history department and then in some degree to the campus as a whole. As late as 1940 there were still tensions in History that went back to the rift between Teggart and Stephens and then between Teggart and his backers and Stephens and his backers. What contributed most probably to the conversion of a feud into campus war was the presence in the

History Department of Herbert Eugene Bolton, from the start a rival of Teggart's in Spanish-American studies and in due time an outright enemy. Bolton was considerably the more distinguished historian in this area; he had won fame at the University of Texas for his step-by-step retracing of some of the greater trails and roads of Spanish-American history and also for a notable literary style, one that Samuel Eliot Morison of Harvard would publicly compliment. In 1909 Bolton had gone to Stanford, but in 1911 when the Bancroft Library, under Teggart's curatorship went to Berkeley, Bolton did likewise.

From the start, the two men disliked each other. It would have been dislike even if the riches of the Bancroft Library hadn't provided ample reason for rivalry. Professor Van Nostrand who taught ancient history had been a beginning instructor in the Department when Teggart and Bolton collided in their ambitions. Van Nostrand told me in the very late thirties when I was pressing him one day at the Faculty Club for recollections of the earlier period, that by chance he was in his office late one Saturday afternoon in 1915, as he recalled, and began to hear Teggart's and Bolton's voices in sharp altercation over the Bancroft. Teggart told Bolton that he, as curator, could keep Bolton out of Bancroft if and when he decided. (One's mind reels at the thought of Bolton either being actually kept out or threatened with being kept out of the Bancroft, given his spectacular, path-breaking utilization of its contents over the several decades.) Bolton's reply was that if Teggart ever did, he would knock his false teeth down his throat. Happily, there were no fisticuffs; each man was big and strong and quick to high temper, and it might have been a true knock-down. It wasn't; something intervened, and the meeting broke up.

But not the feud. Teggart, by 1916, was engaged in two feuds; one with the chairman, Stephens, the other with Bolton. Obviously something had to give, and what gave first was Teggart's curatorship of the Bancroft Library; his resignation was requested by the Regents and President; and, second, his position as member of the faculty in the history department. He remained in history as associate professor through 1917, teaching, however, in comparative history with much stress on migrations, not in California or Spanish American history, the fields that had brought him to Berkeley.

Teggart relieved the heavy air of tension in the department by taking leaves of absence during most of 1918 and 1919. Work and presumably salary were provided him by Arthur Lovejoy, professor of philosophy at Johns Hopkins, then strenuously engaged in getting the newly founded American Association of University Professors off to a strong start. The AAUP, under the leadership of Lovejoy, John Dewey, and other eminent academics in America was, at the start at least, a good deal more than a mere union for professorial rights and advantages. It was a consecrated, wholly serious effort to lift the level of academic work in the U.S., to improve research libraries, conditions of teaching and research, incentives, and the like. Teggart's specific responsibility was what was called "the apparatus of scholarship" in America, that is, the fundamental resources, the structures of research, and the vital groundwork. Germany then was the world leader in scientific and humanistic scholarship, and although Teggart had never been to Germany he was intimately acquainted with its great bibliographies.

In addition to Lovejoy, another Johns Hopkins eminence, Isaiah Bowman, premier geographer, courted Teggart and with him worked out a scholarly program for the study of world migrations, especially in Eurasia. Teggart during his two years spent mostly on the Boston-New York-Washington axis became a familiar figure among scholars and scientists and also intellectuals of the kind who founded *The New Republic* just before the war. The editors honored him with a lunch. He said that he had chided the editors of the new weekly for their subtitle: A Journal of Opinion. Why not, asked Teggart, a journal of *knowledge?*

That is characteristic Teggart. He was a man obsessed by the quest for knowledge. *Knowledge,* not mere compendiums of facts, not boneless generalizations of cosmic spread, not the manufacturing of concepts like the Germanic, especially Hegelian, entelechies, not thinly disguised sermons under the rubric of sociology or psychology instead of Protestantism from which so many of them were actually derived, not, in fine, pseudoknowledge but knowledge; comparable to the knowledge that was so plainly being yielded by the physical sciences. He was contemptuous of the German distinction between the *Geisteswissenschaften* and the *Naturwissens-*

chaften. The method underlying the studies of chemistry, geology, and physics is at bottom quite as applicable to the study of human behavior as to the behavior of molecules, fossils, and atoms.

Teggart was never shy about expressing his convictions on almost any subject. He feared no one as his conduct in the history department — bringing him into deadly conflict with the magisterial Henry Morse Stephens and the redoubtable Herbert Eugene Bolton — abundantly demonstrated. It is shocking to realize that it was not until 1925, when he was fifty-five years old, that he was elevated to the full professorship. Chairs for the distinguished, or assertedly distinguished, existed in philosophy, economics, history, and elsewhere, but never was one created for him. He had a fame in European scholarly circles that very few at Berkeley ever had. He paid the price, in short, that is so often paid by the genuinely innovative and principled.

Yet it would be false to leave deliberately any impression that he was a prophet without honor at Berkeley. Even after the war in the history department led to his separation there and the beginnings of a feud that lasted for years on the campus between those who gave their moral support to Stephens and Bolton and those who favored Teggart, he was treated with high respect on the campus. At the height of the battle, the Cosmos Club, a select, invitational group of eminences in science and scholarship, and of which he had been a member for years, honored him by electing him president. Few if any outside the physical sciences received funds from the Board of Research as generously as Teggart did. This had nothing to do with sympathy or compassion; it had everything to do with the high respect in which he was held for the originality and power of his research, not only on the Berkeley campus but, as I have said, at Johns Hopkins in the east and at Oxford across the Atlantic.

When Teggart decided to return to Berkeley in 1919 he was given the appointment of associate professor of social institutions without, however, any department affiliation. Going back to the history department was completely impossible, and it is just possible that there was at first a sticky problem in finding a welcoming department. His temper and his epochal battles with Stephens and Bolton were of course very well known. For a year his only academic tie was with the President's Office. There was a single page in the catalogue of courses with his name at the top—but without the name of any department—and a listing of several courses that he would be teaching in the academic year 1919–1920. Barrows became president, and he persuaded his own department, political science, to take Teggart as at least a temporary member. Teggart taught "political Geography, The Origin of the State, and Migrations." Everything appeared to be going well and at the end of two years Teggart wrote President Barrows to say that as far as he was concerned, permanent membership in that department was quite acceptable to him. It may have been, however, that he wasn't acceptable to a majority of the department. After all, Teggart by that time had built up a formidable reputation for being his own man and for displacing a considerable amount of atmosphere. Add to that the fact that he had been in 1920 one of the key figures in the faculty revolt which I mentioned briefly above and will say more about below.

Thus it was that the Regents—who didn't want to lose Teggart —created for him a department of his own in 1923, naming it Social Institutions. From many comments I heard in later years, including some from Teggart himself, I deduced that there was some consideration given at the time to naming it Sociology—no such department then existed at Berkeley—and that Teggart himself was not strenuously opposed to that label. There was opposition to it though, particularly from Jessica Peixotto who taught social economics in the Economics Department and who regarded most American sociology of that day as a mixture of social uplift and metaphysical nonsense. Teggart told me one day in his office, only months before his death—and he had a twinkle in his eye— "Miss Peixotto and I decided it was best not to use Sociology as the name of the new department." The final decision was "Social Institutions" as the name of Teggart's department.

People could well have been forgiven for thinking that, title notwithstanding, sociology—de facto, if not de jure or de nomine —had at last come to Berkeley. The commonest definition of sociology in the U.S. was "the study of social institutions." Second, almost from the outset there were courses such as "Progress," "Social Evolution," and even "Introduction to Sociology." Third, during Teggart's seventeen years as founder-chairman of the department, all but two of the graduate students working under him for the Ph.D. did their dissertations on subjects clearly sociological. Fourth, again with the exception of two, all graduate students taking their Ph.D.s under Teggart got their jobs in sociology departments—at Yale, Smith, Minnesota, Utah, Idaho, et al. Fifth, when Teggart's department began bringing in easterners to teach summer session, as most departments did, they were unfailingly sociologists, and very well known ones such as Kelsey, Hankins, Bernard, and House.

Thus, on the homely theory that if something quacks like a duck, waddles like a duck, and flies like a duck, it must be a duck, Berkeley's department of social institutions was substantively and operationally sociology; a different form of sociology, to be sure, than that existing at Stanford or Michigan or Yale or any other university, but not, as I think of it, much more different than, say, Yale was from the common run, or Wisconsin, or North Carolina, each of which had known a strong, Teggart-like figure who put his own personal stamp upon a national academic discipline. By the time I left for the army in early 1943, with the department under Margaret Hodgen's chairmanship, our standard response when someone suggested instituting a new department on the campus to be known as "Sociology," was that although we were not ourselves Sociology, our presence nevertheless made it unnecessary to found a new department to be called Sociology. But once Teggart was gone (he died in 1946), that answer no longer sufficed.

It is enough to say that after his death the name of the department was changed by the addition of "sociology" to the title, thus making for the highly redundant label of Social Institutions and Sociology. In a few years the "Social Institutions" was dropped, and by the mid-1950s Berkeley was known as one of the top four or five departments of sociology in the U.S. Thus flow the waters of academe.

Quite possibly the years following 1923 and the creation of a new department for him and his research and teaching interests were the happiest in Teggart's so often beset and beleaguered career; possibly as happy as the years at the turn of the century when he lived in San Francisco and, as chief of the prestigious Mechanics Institute Library, took his place in the society of San Francisco's most celebrated epoch. When I came on the scene in 1936 as his teaching assistant and aspirant to the Ph.D. I found him generally austere, even aloof, but not without capacity for occasional conversations in which I gloried and from which I drew a good deal of learning. By 1936 he had retired largely from the extracurricular affairs of Berkeley, retreating to his office on the fourth floor of Wheeler and to his home, a not particularly large apartment that he shared with his wife and son Richard, a librarian on the campus. The Teggarts had had a fine, large house on Scenic Avenue in the Berkeley hills until it, along with around 650 other houses in the hills burned to the ground in the terrible fire of 1923. The Teggarts lost everything, including the draft manuscript of the book he had been working on as a sequel to *Processes of History.* He had lost heavily of research and bibliographical materials of his own in the fire that followed the 1906 earthquake. I suspect that after the Berkeley fire seventeen years later, there was no longer a desire for anything but simple living quarters, together of course with his office on the campus.

As I say, Teggart was aloof, had become so by the time I knew him. There was something about him that discouraged anyone from ever making the mistake of seeking intimacy of relationship with him. Familiarity, he used to say, "doesn't *breed* contempt; it *is* contempt." Never once in our years did he call me anything but "Nisbet," usually mispronouncing it to "Nesbit." Once when I left something for him with a note I signed it "Nisbet." The next day he explained to me that such a signature was proper only for a British aristocrat. I was momentarily at loss. I knew that "Robert," most certainly "Bob," would be rejected. So I signed thereafter, as he always did, my three initials.

Yet he was not cold. All Irish, in temper and even sense of humor, he could and usually did act like a son of Erin. When he believed or was convinced of something, any change of mind, it was widely said of Teggart, made the earth tremble. But he had wit and the continuing capacity to laugh. Sometimes I could hear his laugh half way down the hall from his office. When I went up to his office to say goodbye on the eve of my joining of the army in early 1943, I could swear that his eyes looked a little moist and he threw his arms around me for a second or two. He also presented me with a handsome, military-looking wallet he had bought for me. All he said was "Come back."

Above anyone I have ever known or seen during more than a half

century of association with university people in this country and in
Europe, Teggart best personifies the scholar-teacher. He almost
worshipped the university as an historical phenomenon in the
West; it was his church, his state, his profession, his real love. It is
probably true — as one often heard on the campus about him —
that Teggart controlled more temper in any ordinary day than most
of us do in a lifetime. His fierce Irish nature had almost cost him his
academic career in his tenure in history at Berkeley. Doubtless the
Wanderjähren in the east allowed him necessary time and context
to contemplate past and future. The contemporaries at Berkeley
who knew him best, such as George Adams in Philosophy, Eugene
McCormac in History, and William Popper in Near Eastern Languages told me that there had been a definite change in the temperament of Teggart after he came back to Berkeley in 1919 to become, so to speak, a marginal man — without department or even
conventional academic identity. This, however, didn't constrain
him from joining with respected colleagues and friends in the Revolution of 1920 at Berkeley when the modern Academic Senate
with all its extraordinary powers was founded. He was allowed to
keep his office, 432 Wheeler, after his retirement at seventy and
there, as he had for so many years, he kept his daily schedule of 7:30
to 5:00 or thereabouts, writing a great deal on what engaged his
interest. One of the finest articles he ever wrote was a study of
Hesiod and the idea of progress. *The Journal of the History of Ideas*
took it immediately but what with backup of learned articles at that
estimable journal, it was several months after Teggart's death in
October 1946 that the article appeared in print.

Amusingly Teggart, who was deeply conservative in his political
views, voting for Hoover in 1932, Landon in 1936, and Wilkie in
1940, was frequently visited in his office by student Marxists, socialists, and communists. They had heard he was "radical," which
in the purely intellectual-scientific sense he was, profoundly radical. After all most of his life's work had gone into assault on the
dogmas of unilinear narrative history and unilinear social evolution. But, although Teggart was polite he was not long in disabusing
them.

12

Years with the Octopus

A few months before graduation in the spring of 1936 I had a summons from Teggart. Would I be willing to take over the teaching assistantship in his introductory course and at the same time work toward the Ph.D.? I had vaguely thought of entering Boalt, the law school, the following fall, but it was only that—vaguely. I accepted Teggart's offer immediately and to this day, to my dying moment indeed, will consider it a great windfall in my life. I would receive a salary or stipend of six hundred dollars a year, quite enough to support anyone, I thought proudly, and at the same time work, as an apprentice, to the distant but now realizable day when I would ascend to the ranks of the annointed ones.

The thirties was the first decade in Berkeley's history when the graduate student became wholly accepted by the academic hierarchy. Prior to the thirties the undergraduate walked tall and supreme. The graduate student was regarded by many departments —though not the physical sciences—as an odd duck, neither fish nor fowl actually. Even in the twenties, from Harvard to Berkeley, there were still those in faculty service with only a B.A. after their names. At the turn of the century no less an eminence than William James had strongly opposed Harvard's establishing the Ph.D. In an article in 1903 James referred to "the Ph.D. Octopus."

James had several reasons for opposing the new degree. It would be regarded surely as a pretentious Teutonism, an aping of a people with too many demonstrated flaws of character. Second, most

Americans would treat the degree for what it was, an idle bit of decoration. Those who were natural scholars and teachers wouldn't need or be benefited by it. They would go, as their forefathers had, straight to the classroom and teach from their innate strengths. Finally, James said, only the inferior students in any graduating college class would be even mildly interested; the best undergraduates would go straight to the world of business and professions and make their marks early. The graduate student, staying on and on and on, would be inevitably an object of either pity or derision.

William James, it must be recorded in honesty here, would change his mind somewhat after writing the "Octopus" piece, but neither he nor a great many of college contemporaries lost altogether their suspicion of the new degree. The late George Stewart, for many years a member of the English Department has written that when he first set foot on the Berkeley campus, in 1919, aiming at a Master's degree, out of seventeen members of the English teaching staff, only four had Ph.D. degrees. Stewart chose to go to Columbia University for doctoral work after getting his M.A. at Berkeley. He had fallen in love, though, with Berkeley and came back not long after he had gotten the Ph.D. and stayed on to become one of Berkeley's most respected teachers and scholars. He also became a novelist of considerable fame.

By the late 1920s the place of the Ph.D. and of the graduate student was a secure one in the humanities and social sciences as well as in the hard sciences. But it wasn't much more than that: secure and accepted but scarcely lauded. The undergraduate still ruled Berkeley within the limits laid down by the administration. In this Berkeley wasn't different from other major universities. To be a Harvard man or Princeton man was to be, or to have been, a full-fledged undergraduate in Harvard College or Princeton College. Four or five, even ten years of graduate work didn't make a demigod of you. The same was true at Berkeley. A true Cal man was one who had spent four years at Berkeley and emerged proudly to begin his life's career. All the mores and sacred traditions, the offices in student government, the best scholarships, and the annual awards and medals were for undergraduates, never graduate students.

Not often in the years prior to the thirties—or even then, come to think of it—was the brightest student on the campus a graduate student. That is one reason why the Berkeley faculty took their greatest pains and luxuriated in what they felt were their greatest rewards in their undergraduate courses, including, as I have stressed, freshman and sophomore courses. Among undergraduates one was, as teacher and mentor, far more likely to strike gold than among graduate students. Undergraduates who came to Berkeley were drawn from precisely the same national stratum of demonstrated high school or prep school academic talent as were the undergraduates who went to Harvard, Yale, MIT, and Stanford. Whereas for a great many years in the American university it was a rare graduate student, no matter how zealous his ambition and assiduous his seminar work, who came very close to the best of the undergraduates. It was quite as William James had predicted: the best in Harvard College would go, on graduation, straight to business or to law school, less often medical school, in other words, straight to career. Graduate students on the other hand were those who seemingly lacked the gumption, the drive to do anything but go on and on taking courses, ever preparing and preparing until, often after ten years of such bondage and drudgery, they were finally certified as doctors of philosophy and, every one of them, budding, burgeoning scholars, and scientists. The feared Doctor's Oral had been passed, sometimes after half a decade of preparing for it, the almighty Dissertation had been completed—or at least well started and covered by promises of early completion—and now ready, they all hoped, for a few of the rewards they had been for so long deferring, such as job and income, marriage, family, status, and so on. But when they did at long last begin in their first jobs, it was commonly at the rank of instructor, at the bottom of the heap, surrounded by those who had once been lowly instructors but were now assistant professors, associate professors, full professors, representatives of the grades and ranks the tyro had yet to conquer. It was not uncommon be reach age fifty before one was at long last made a full professor. It is no wonder that George Bernard Shaw said, "Those who can, do; those who can't, teach." Or become a bonded worker in the Ph.D. mill.

The Depression thirties changed much of this second- and third-class citizenship of graduate students. Not all the bright undergraduates left at graduation for careers. There was heavy unemployment; jobs were few. The attraction of a few years spent in graduate work became greater. True, there were Ph.D.s in physics, chemistry, mathematics and other fields going jobless, desperately searching for jobs as clerks, anything to stay fed and lodged. One heard of X or Y who after anywhere from six to ten years getting the Ph.D., wound up teaching in a junior college, a high school even, in some cases, or worse. But, all this recognized, graduate school was still a good place to be if you could possibly swing it financially during the Depression.

Graduate students were advantaged by the Depression in another way, one that went to the very heart of the nature and purpose of the American university. In brief, they were upgraded while many courses were downgraded. The Depression had severe impact on university budgets, what with reductions of tax revenue for the public universities and the drying up of alumni giving for the private. Enrollments continued to increase, but there was insufficient money to meet these increases with increases in the number of bona fide faculty members. Under pre-Depression conditions, faculty, including full professors, taught sections in larger courses. Chemistry 1A-B, in which the two lectures a week were given by Joel Hildebrand, presented laboratory sections taught and supervised by faculty members as eminent as Hildebrand. In the early thirties when I took the history of English literature, two lectures a week by a series of senior professors were accompanied by a section also taught by a faculty member, ranging from assistant professor to full.

But by the end of the thirties that kind of use of faculty talent— in sections, I mean—was virtually gone from the campus; gone forever as events have shown. Increasingly—and here lay the boon for graduate students—graduate T.A.s were used for the sections in all courses. For whereas each of them cost only 600 dollars a year for teaching up to five and even six sections a week, a faculty member cost anywhere from $2000 a year as instructor to $5 or $6000 as full professor. The strange (to the academic mind) and horrid concept of cost-effectiveness was at long last invading university accounting offices and thus in a short time trustees' rooms.

Why not, it was asked, first doubtless in whispers within executive sessions, subject the university to the same cost-criteria one used for his steel plant, bank, or mercantile establishment?

Thus was born the prosperity of graduate students. By a constantly increasing number of departments they were recognized at long last as important people, ready to spring to the help, at a mere fifty dollars a month, of section-classes not very long before taught by full-fledged members of the faculty. With the aid of the Depression and sharply reduced University budgets that cut down on the size of faculty, especially in humanities and social science departments, the graduate students came into their own, to a degree hardly imaginable during the twenties when the undergraduate was sovereign, forever as it must have seemed, and the graduate student was a kind of ne'er do well.

Graduate students were thus a new class on the campus in the thirties. The new class was identifiable from several perspectives: economic, political, cultural, and ideological. At the base, giving a certain solidity and also fertility, was the married couple. This last was indeed novel, at Berkeley and every other university in the country. Through the 1920s marriage was as seldom found among graduate students as undergraduates. Through the thirties marriage among undergraduates remained taboo, a gross violation of the mores. I recall one fellow student in my undergraduate years who was married. Once I accepted his invitation to have dinner with his wife and himself at their small apartment. To me there was something eerie about it. It was too strange to be assimilable. Once marriage by an undergraduate had been ground for expulsion. I believe that strictness of ban had disappeared by the thirties, but it was still considered unthinkable.

But not, by this same decade, among graduate students. The faculty didn't approve of marriage among graduate students even then; they saw it just as the Roman Catholic Church has seen marriage among its priests, as a distraction from the main objective, which for graduate students was serving scholarship, or the scholarship of the masters at any rate, and the demands of their own careers. In the typical marriage, the graduate student (invariably male, then) was supported by a working wife unless he was fortunate enough to have a teaching assistantship or income from family. On the basis of the small sample stored up in personal memory, I can report that most of the marriages were successful; that is, they lasted and, contrary to the prejudices of older faculty members, were complementary to, not distractive from academic work.

All classes have their subclasses, and the new class of graduate students was no exception. At the top of the heap was the research assistant, a rara avis in the thirties. Below him came the teaching assistant, more numerous but still scarce. Below these beings came the lowly readers, the lumpenproletariat, paid by number of blue-books read or the hour. The total compensation didn't come to much unless the reader covered several courses. The English department, I recall vividly, had one such reader, Mr. Diamond, who had been a graduate student for twelve years, still had his doctor's orals ahead (theoretically at least — he had probably lost all ambition toward that end after a dozen years), and read for at least four English courses a term. As William James foresaw, the Ph.D. could well be an octopus.

The political culture of graduate students in the thirties was very much to the left, often Marxist among the humanities and social science graduate students. I remember two more or less charismatic graduate students, also teaching assistants, both in economics. The first was Harry Conover, ebullient Marxist who proudly claimed to subvert, as a T.A., in section the lectures given by the liberal, middle-of-the-road, Ira B. Cross. The other was Robert Merriman. He too was of heroic mould among graduate students; and he would go to Spain to fight for the socialists, die, and eventually become the prototype of Hemingway's Robert Jordan in *For Whom the Bell Tolls.* Although I knew Conover slightly, I never chanced to meet or see Merriman. John Kenneth Galbraith who was a graduate student in agricultural economics at Berkeley in the thirties, has written in his autobiography that the only really interesting mind he found at Berkeley was Robert Merriman. Perhaps so, but, as I have said above, Berkeley's Marxists, unlike those at City College in New York were a monolithic lot; not a Trotskyist or Lovestonite in a carload; all convinced that Stalin was just a slightly more discipline-oriented Franklin Delano Roosevelt.

Graduate students were, as I have said, typically married in the thirties. But I cannot recall a single graduate household in which so much as a single child could be seen. Contraception was considerably more makeshift then, before the pill, than it is today, but somehow, despite all the solemn warnings before marriage of "accidents," graduate couples remained childless. Birth rates were of course low all over American society in that decade.

Graduate students were endogamous, living with, marrying, studying, enjoying and cohabiting among themselves. Ties with others, including recent undergraduate friends, were null and void. Get-togethers were common on weekends. Playing host would be by turn among couples in a group. But the food and wine would be brought in considerable part by the guests. It was usually a huge pot of spaghetti, a round loaf or two of San Francisco's sourdough bread, a large salad, mostly chopped up lettuce and, of course, plenty of red wine from gallon jugs filled from barrels at the nearest liquor store. There was always a radio—almost anyone could afford to buy or rent one—and one by one the Bay Area bands would be heard, hotel by hotel, until midnight, conversation never flagging, however, from the impact of Anson Weeks, Phil Harris, or Tom Coakley.

Once or twice a semester, the group would splurge in San Francisco—by ferry and street car, of course—usually out in North Beach, with one or another cheap bistro the setting. A six- or seven-course dinner, including filet mignon and wine could be had in the depth of the Depression for a dollar at both Ripley's and La Favorite. If there was a bar, and there usually was, drinks never more than a quarter, beer a dime a bottle of the local brands. Thus for ferry and streetcars, drinks, a sumptuous dinner, and maybe a snifter of brandy on the house afterward, not more than five or six dollars a head. But of course those dollars were plucked from T.A. incomes of fifty a month; if married to a working wife perhaps twice that but not more.

I should add that contributing to the career expenses of the graduate teaching assistant on his fifty dollars a month was the unwritten—but puissant—law that T.A.s must dress like the faculty; that is, in suits or at very least jackets, trousers, and necktie. Just as any student at Berkeley today would be first shocked on going back to the Berkeley of the thirties in a time machine, by the all-whiteness of faces on the campus, such a student might well be shocked again by the unvarying attire of the faculty in suits and jackets with necktie, all looking very bourgeois indeed. The day hadn't come, for T.A.s or their masters, when jeans, dungarees, sweatshirts, exotic, flowing-collared shirts, and the like were standing operating procedure among faculty as well as graduate students. Anyone returning from today's Berkeley to that of a half century ago would surely have found the faculty a stuffy-looking lot.

That is, with the exception of course of the maverick bohemians whom I mentioned above. But they were few, and even their dress — berets, neck scarves, and soft shoes — was somewhat conventional by today's post-Sixties faculty attire.

As a graduate school in the thirties, Berkeley was uneven to say the least. There were privileged and underprivileged departments. Berkeley's greatest strength as a graduate center was in the sciences. Chemistry and physics could hardly have been improved on by the early thirties. They were internationally renowned for the research done by such minds as Gilbert Lewis, Wendell Latimer, and Ernest Lawrence and J. Robert Oppenheimer, and they attracted some of the cream of the graduate student population. In the biological sciences there were areas similarly blessed: genetics and the complex work done by the genius Herbert McLean Evans in endocrinology. The agricultural sciences were strong almost across the board and notable for the fact that unlike so many colleges of agriculture in the country, they were privileged to maintain an even balance between pure or theoretical science and the practical or applied work that most farmers and legislators preferred.

The humanities and social sciences ranked a good deal lower as areas of graduate teaching. There were some exemplary individuals: Teggart, Kroeber, Sauer, Tatlock, Ryder, Bolton, et al. But almost without exception departments in these areas were, and were regarded nationally as, weak compared to the sciences. For the most part in the humanities-social sciences area, Berkeley as a graduate school was regarded as behind such universities as Harvard, Yale, Princeton, Chicago, and also Michigan and Wisconsin. Stanford, never strong as a graduate school until well after the war, was particularly weak in the Depression.

The trouble with Berkeley in the social sciences and humanities was lack of faculty noted for their research. A strong reputation for scholarship and research is vital to the success of any department that presumes to offer itself as a medium for graduate teaching. To be and be known as a graduate student of a Merriam at Chicago, a Kittredge at Harvard, a Commager or Nevins at Columbia was a long step forward in a graduate student's career. Berkeley had a few in the areas I am writing about here; I have already named them. But they stood out as lone individuals; not as strong members of strong departments.

Political science at Berkeley in the thirties was very good as an undergraduate medium. But there was literally no one in the department of stature then; not until Hans Kelsen came for a short stay during and just after the war did political science at Berkeley have a scholar with national luster. Political science at Berkeley could not have ranked nationally in the top twenty through the thirties, considered as a graduate training center. There wasn't a V.O. Key, a Lasswell, a McIlwain, or Corwin in the lot: not even close. A number of the Berkeley political scientists wrote and published, but it was mostly textbooks, and this was precisely what the department was known as across the country: a herd of textbook writers, as someone put it.

Economics was scarcely better, if as good, through most of the thirties. There was no one to be compared seriously with John R. Connors at Wisconsin or Milton Friedman at Chicago, Schumpeter at Harvard, Samuelson at MIT or Viner first at Chicago, then Princeton. Leo Rogin was generally thought of as the theorist in the department, but he held only the rank of lecturer until after the war, published almost nothing, and was unknown nationally. Both Brady and Gulick published, but their work was institutional in character and that was a persuasion fast going out of economic respectability. Just before the war Howard Ellis was brought in and a little later William Fellner, both of whom would become presidents later of the American Economic Association. Fellner, however, left Berkeley for Yale early on.

Anthropology was, small though in number of faculty, easily the best known of Berkeley social science departments for graduate study. No department in the country outstripped Berkeley's department. Kroeber and Lowie ranked very high.

Sociology, or social institutions, had Teggart, everywhere recognized as a maverick genius, but by his own dictate the department was small and specialized. The one other full-fledged faculty member in the department was Margaret Hodgen, a splendid scholar and teacher but not, or not yet, of national note. Teggart had reached the point by the thirties where for his own well being and comfort he wanted a department as small as possible in faculty, and graduate students as few as possible.

The humanities departments at Berkeley varied considerably in quality in the thirties. History, except only for the Spanish American wing under Bolton and Priestley, which was outstanding and internationally known, was fairly weak through most of the decade. One man, not a genuine scholar, though popular as a teacher, represented the whole of ancient history. Prior to the arrival of James Westfall Thompson in the mid-thirties, a refugee from Hutchins' Chicago, there was only a longtime assistant professor teaching medieval history. The arrivals of Frederick Paxson, Thompson Raymond Sontag and John Hicks in the middle or late Thirties added considerably to the strength of the department. I should mention both Kerner and Guttridge, European and English history respectively, who were there, and especially Guttridge, respected. But in the thirties, with the conspicuous exception of Bolton and the Spanish-American wing, the Berkeley history department was not among the best departments in the country.

English was very uneven, to say the least. The star was Tatlock in Early English and Chaucerian Studies. He had been brought from Harvard in the early thirties. Everett Hughes, in Milton Studies, was a major research figure and graduate teacher, but, presumably alienated by the presence of too many nonscholars, he left in the mid-thirties for Wisconsin. There were some outstanding—as later accomplishments would demonstrate—younger members of the department. Bertrand Bronson perhaps was foremost—he would achieve stardom in three areas of literature—, George Potter, T. K. Whipple, the then very youthful James Hart, among others. Lehman, a superb undergraduate teacher and gifted administrator, had done no real work as a scholar since his Ph.D. dissertation on Carlyle. The other language-literature departments, excepting Spanish which was excellent, were adequate, no more.

The reason for the two nations among departments was a combination of money and scholarly leadership. The physical sciences were stronger in both. Money is required for research support. The University didn't have it in the thirties. Since there had to be a choice made, it was in favor of the sciences, of departments such as physics and chemistry, biology, and the ever-vital agricultural sciences. After the war when tax revenues were high from wartime prosperity and appropriations to the University by a friendly Governor Warren were considerably enhanced, stars began to appear in the nonscience departments as well as the sciences. But if there is one generalization that holds firmly and universally true in the academic world, it takes time and luck for departments long mediocre to rise, even when money becomes more abundant.

Philosophy was a kind of paradox on the campus among departments in the thirties. It had early carved out a very strategic place for itself in respect of curricular requirements in the College of Letters and Science; it had a top flight group of faculty members, considered as teachers, that is. Stephen Pepper, Adams, William Dennes, Jacob Löwenberg, to cite only four, were strong individual presences in the Academic Senate at Berkeley. No department was more highly respected on the Berkeley campus. But it was singularly weak in scholarship. Except for Pepper in esthetics, who began writing seriously and copiously in the late thirties, the majority of members had only their published Ph.D. dissertations of long ago to offer as books.

Philosophy's principal research offering at Berkeley was its Philosophical Union, so called. It had been founded many years earlier by Berkeley's early and greatest philosopher, George H. Howison, known as well in Europe as in the U.S. for his writings in the philosophical aspects of evolution and also in psychology which was then a part of philosophy at Berkeley and most other places in the early part of this century. The Philosophical Union consisted of lectures, usually every year in the spring, by some of the members of the department on some overarching theme; Being, Process, and Civilization come to mind. These were public lectures and invariably filled 312 Wheeler at nights. The lectures were then published and distributed widely across the land. There were some good titles conceived by the Berkeley philosophers for their contributions. My favorite after fifty years is one of Löwenberg's: "The Factitiousness of Qualified Factuality." The Union was an old Berkeley tradition by the time I reached the campus and it still had an impressive following.

In the humanities and social sciences, unlike the physical and biological sciences, it was a rare graduate student who came from afar. Most came out of the ranks of Berkeley's own undergraduates. Even so it was possible to get good Ph.D. training in the thirties in the areas of the humanities and social sciences as well as the natural sciences despite the absence in the first named of departments of the strength of Chicago, Harvard, and a few other universities. But you had to work on it yourself, supply all necessary motivation yourself. Doing that, there was always something you could learn from almost anyone on the faculty. Gettell, for instance; he was not a sparkling mind, he never got beyond writing textbooks for the money, but he ran a disciplined seminar in political theory. Each student was obliged to select a topic at the beginning of the year from a list he passed out to the fifteen or so who were in the seminar. What was expected was a one-hour paper to be read by the student, followed by an hour's criticism and discussion of the paper and its topic. Willy nilly, I was getting my first education in how to write an article. I realized that fact poignantly two or three years later when I was at work on my first article for publication. In demanding papers for reading aloud at seminar and for criticism by others, Gettell was preparing us for apprentice and journeyman status as faculty members when life and promotion depended upon articles one wrote and managed to get published.

No doctor's oral ever went better than mine did on 27 November 1938 between the hours of three and six in 405 Library before a committee composed of Teggart, Hodgen, Kroeber, Gettell, Emily Huntington, and Adams. A graduate student thinks of little else but the oral in advance and remembers nothing more vividly during all the years that follow, especially if it has gone well. I was prepared; I had saturated myself for many months in all that I could imagine to be relevant. But there was the luck factor. There always is. Suppose the first two questioners had, as is easily imaginable, led with subjects I had somehow missed, for all my diligence. Would I have somehow righted my precarious balance for the next questioner? And then the one after that? Who knows?

During the past fifty years I have served on dozens of Ph.D. orals committees. It is painful indeed when one of them turns sour early on in the interchange with the committee. Despite possible lore among graduate students to the contrary, most faculty members dread having to fail a student in the qualifyings. Trouble can come from several possible sources. First, the candidate simply hasn't learned enough; he was put up or allowed up prematurely. Second, he may know enough but find himself seized by a near-paralyzing case of nerves; almost unable to think of his name if asked. When this happens, faculty members will sometimes outdo themselves in the effort to get the student settled down. Not often, I have observed, does any such effort work. Or, and this is rare, there may be an obstreperous member of the faculty committee who in the interest of prosecuting a feud with a fellow-faculty member on the committee, usually a departmental colleague, will use the student as the means of getting at, through tendentious questions, the faculty member concerned. Robert Kerner of the history department was perhaps the most notorious offender on the faculty at Berkeley in this regard. He was a fairly well respected scholar and a popular undergraduate teacher. He was inordinately vain and quick to be resentful or jealous of colleagues, among them, beginning in 1940 when he came from Princeton to Berkeley, Raymond J. Sontag. Sontag was, and Kerner knew it, the abler historian, and, even worse for Kerner, Sontag was brought to the Ehrmann Chair in History, the chair Kerner had virtually appointed himself to once its first occupant James Westfall Thompson, the medievalist, had retired. In his desire to sting Sontag, Kerner could be ugly at times in his treatment, bullying, of a Sontag student up for his qualifyings.

One of the best members of the Berkeley history department from the point of view of his scholarship, and also his gift as a writer of the English language was Herbert Priestley, in Spanish-American studies. He had come to Berkeley in the teens to work under Bolton. This was at the time of the height of the fight between Teggart and Bolton. Teggart had not only flunked the young Priestley in the Ph.D. oral exam but apparently done it rather humiliatingly, out of his desire to get at Bolton. Priestley of course never forgot it, and I believe he meant it when, during a conversation at lunch at the Faculty Club, just after I met him, he said with not an iota of humor in his words that he "came very close in earlier years to killing your chief," meaning of course Teggart.

Bolton whom I came to know also at the Faculty Club (Teggart had ceased altogether going to the Club) was of a different temperament. Despite the onetime fury of his relationship with Teggart in the History Department, Bolton had mellowed to the point where he could talk about Teggart to me without a trace of malice or continuing hatred. Once he told me a delightful Teggart story, one at the expense of Teggart but not vengefully. Back about 1915 when Teggart was still in the department, he served on the qualifying examination committee for one of Bolton's students, a Mormon from Salt Lake City. The student's proposed dissertation was one on Mormon history. Bolton said that when Teggart's turn to question came, he began as follows: "Mr. Jones, is it true that you are a Mormon?" "Yes sir." "Well, do you think that as a Mormon you could write an objective history of the Mormons." The student thought a moment, Bolton said, and then asked: "Professor Teggart, are you a Mormon?" "NO," was Teggart's immediate and emphatic answer. "Well, then," said the student, "could you?" Teggart, I was glad to hear Bolton wind up his story, had passed the student without qualification, and had even seemed to enjoy the humor of the exchange. On the whole, though, in my fifty years of attending doctor's orals, there wasn't much of this kind of badinage. Too risky.

When an oral goes as well as mine did — and many others seen as faculty inquisitor over the years, I am happy to say — it is a pleasure to everyone. Within minutes, usually, it is fairly clear whether the subject is well prepared and also whether the faculty committee is a congenial one. It is always a problem for the student and his graduate adviser to know with any certainty whether the student is ready, after two, three, or five years of grinding study. But when everything comes out right, a doctor's oral is a privileged conversation.

I have heard the story of an exceedingly hard working graduate student, also bright, alert, and knowledgeable, who even after three or four years couldn't believe that he was yet ready for his orals. Almost everyone else knew he was ready. The trick was getting him before a committee. The chairman of his department called the student one day, asking him to stop in about three o'clock; he had something to go over with the student. The student arrived; within a few minutes he and the chairman were engaged in a learned conversation; other faculty members drifted in and participated, questions and answers floating all over the office. After three full hours the by now fatigued student was notified that he had just passed his prelims, his orals, and many congratulations!

There were faculty members who with the best of intentions could be unbearably tedious and miniscule in their questions. The language departments were generally reputed to be the worst in this respect. Apparently George Stewart, member of the English department and also a novelist, thought so. For, in the late 1930s he published a small novel titled *Doctor's Oral* in which he dealt sardonically with this academic pettifogging. Over and over Professor Smith in the novel presses student Jones on incredibly picayune aspects of Dickens' vocabulary, syntax, phrasing, everything about Dickens, in short, except for all that is truly important.

As I say, the best of the orals exams are those which early on go so well that what follows is more like an elevated conversation than an examination imposed by one's superiors. It is no wonder we, the erstwhile subjects of such exams, find ourselves—when we have passed with flying colors—looking back for many years on the experience. How often, after all, in a scholar's life does he find himself the center of attention for a three hour conversation about matters everyone is interested in? That was my happy experience; for years memory of it was galvanizing to me. And, as noted at the beginning of this section, I still have no memory difficulty with the event of long ago.

Few things in the academic world have been subjected to more derision and also hot criticism than the Ph.D. dissertation. It was this aspect of the newfangled degree that aroused most of William James's contempt for the degree and led him to refer to it as "the octopus." He fairly hooted at the requirement of "originality" for the dissertation, predicting, not inaccurately over the last century, that the search for originality by a babe in the woods would necessarily culminate in triviality. Europeans, especially the English but also the Germans who did more than any other people to popularize the doctorate in the nineteenth century, were amused by what had become by 1900 a near-obsession with both the degree and the dissertation in America. Leading lights from William James then to Jacques Barzun today have waxed merry about the pretensions of the degree and the absurdity of a college youth still wet behind the ears essaying an "original work of scholarship" (even when he didn't want to essay it) when he ought to be plunging into studies of great works in his field and applying himself to the dedicated teaching of undergraduates.

Charles A. Beard had the Ph.D. dissertation very much in mind when he gave his sardonic advice to a student who, just graduated, came to him for counsel about a career in history. "Tin," said Beard, and repeated it to the mystification of the young man. Beard went on (I am paraphrasing from memory) to say that to succeed in academic history in the U.S. it is vital to have subject, no matter how tiny and uninteresting to the majority, on which he could become "the outstanding living authority" with endless future academic honors, promotions, chairs, and salary increases ahead. Take the mining of tin in the southeast corner of Patagonia during the years, say, 1783–1805. That will doubtless strike a few gray-beards in the department as a recklessly large subject. One of them may ask icily, are you trying to be a Mommsen or Macaulay? Take no account. Do your dissertation (after several seminar reports) on tin, as suggested. That should land you your first job. Then begin to widen. Do a five-year study of tin mining in the whole southern part of Patagonia. That will broaden your reputation and very probably endow you with tenure. After that continue valiantly with tin; not only in the rest of Patagonia but perhaps in a couple of neighboring countries also. You will have the pleasure of seeing yourself heralded as "the greatest living authority on tin mining" and no one will dare discuss world tin at the faculty club lunch table without due deference to you.

I am bound to say that I knew graduate students in bondage to tin or some comparable entity in their Ph.D. researches. I recall one, a graduate student of Frederick Paxson, who was in this third year of dissertation research on a thirty-mile stretch of railroad track in northeastern California. I don't know whether he ever finished it. The required number of dusty records, due bills, acts of town councils, and letters, to be duly run down among the oldest living inhabitants of the area, must have been mountainous. Dear God, one may imagine the great Frederick Jackson Turner saying as he rolled over in his grave: "Is *this* what I wrought when I opened up the Western frontier to effete eastern historians?" Who knows? But one would hate to count the numbers of theses and dissertations written, especially in the Midwest during this century, written, it was said solemnly, in the Turner school of American history, which dealt with tiny towns, villages, individual school houses, early American retail shoe stores, foundries, railway depots, etc etc. In any library of a university at least a century old, dozens and dozens of shelves contain the bound double-spaced typescript pages of both master's and doctor's dissertations.

I don't mean to pillory the Turner school of American history alone. I can't think of a single field of history to be found in an American university in this century that hasn't piled up tons of tons of such bric-a-brac across the country. Columbia University took its Ph.D. dissertations so seriously in the early part of the century that among the requirements for the degree was that of publication of the dissertation, that is, by a regular, bona fide publishing house. One may imagine the tumult occasioned by publishers' representatives bulling their way onto Morningside Heights in order to get first refusal of one of these dissertations. But Columbia was stubborn. When the enormity and fatuity of the publication requirement finally struck home, what did that great university do? Create a division of its own university press which would publish nothing but the University's own Ph.D. dissertations. Occasionally one made good reading.

The bulk of individual dissertations could boggle the mind. One of a mere hundred and fifty pages—no matter how genuinely important its subject and how able the writing—was generally regarded as unacceptable at Berkeley in the humanities and social science departments. Two hundred pages was about the lower limit and even that would be regarded by some faculty members—such minds as M. M. Knight, P. Orman Ray and William Morris leading the way—as dangerously thin especially if the number of footnotes was also low, meaning at least several hundred. The longest dissertation I ever saw ran 2,200 pages; I was the outside member of the dissertation committee and my heart sank when I went by for it to take home and read. Quite apart from the reading necessary, there was the logistical matter of carrying it home by bus. But it turned out to be first rate in intellectual quality and, when it had been reduced in length by half or two thirds, it was published by a major American press. The shortest Ph.D. dissertation I have ever heard of was one in zoology; it consisted of a seventy-word cablegram sent from distant shore back to the department at Berkeley. Whatever it was, it had to be close to phenomenal. Typically, dissertations were much shorter in the sciences than in the humanities, often consisting of little more than an account, successful or not, of a significant experiment done. The most amusing title of a dissertation I ever saw was in Flexner's great study of American and other world universities: "The Bacterial Content of Cotton Underwear Worn in the Iowa Summer of 1938." Needless to say, Flexner was acidulous in his description of this magnum opus.

There was the absurd requirement of "originality." But who is original? Newton? Einstein? Perish the thought. There are major pieces of scholarship in the history of science to demonstrate the degree to which each was dependent upon earlier discoveries and formulations. Anyone who claims to be original in almost anything he may do at this point in the history of the human mind is tempting fate and virtually asking to be referred to earlier works which disprove his originality. Bernard Malamud, the American novelist, writes of his short experience in an English department in which the average member's idea of research was spending a weekend in the library in order to try and catch a graduate student in some plagiarism. Shakespeare and Milton, two of the very titans, stole shamelessly from contemporaries as well as predecessors. It used to be said cynically at Berkeley that to base a book or an article on one book by another person is plagiarism; to base it on at least three books is research.

I was struck by a major difference in graduate study between the scientists and the humanists. My friends and other contemporaries at Berkeley in chemistry, physics, or biology began "doing" their field immediately upon becoming Ph.D. aspirants. That is, they began without delay experiments or observations which with any luck would in time mature into dissertations. To be a graduate student in chemistry was to *be* a chemist from the very outset, to commence under proper guidance, of course, the kind of work that characterizes professional chemists. One did not spend two or three or more years circling in outer periphery of the field by reading books and articles *about* chemistry.

Very different were the humanities—in which I include the social sciences of the 1930s. To so much as raise the question of research, that is, research in the sense I have just described in the sciences, was absolutely forbidden until after one had passed one's qualifying exams, one's orals. One must first demonstrate one's capacity for taking courses and reading books *about* English literature—or French, Spanish, or history, or philosophy, or whatever—and take written examinations all along the way. After three or four years of this peripheral, dependent status, how many graduate student minds, one wonders, were still buoyant enough to successfully complete a project leading to one's Ph.D. dissertation?

The differences in average lengths of time taken by humanities and by science students were instructive then, and I don't doubt today as well. It was not at all uncommon to find Ph.D. aspirants taking up nine and ten years to complete all requirements— courses, seminars, qualifying exams, dissertation et al.—before they were allowed to go out honorably into the workaday world of the professoriate. English was appalling in that respect. An old joke was paraphrased at Berkeley into "A father with two sons sent one off to sea, the other to graduate work in English. Neither was ever heard from again."

This indeterminateness, lack of structure, has been the greatest flaw from the beginning in the Ph.D. Unlike law and medicine in each of which there are firm curricular requirements and also a publicized norm of time to be spent—three years in law, four in medicine, usually—there are neither course requirements nor ter- mini of time for the Ph.D. A student simply begins, knocks around, taking courses here, there, and everywhere, waiting, praying that at some time he will be found "ready" for his doctor's orals and then advancement to full candidacy and the privilege at long last of beginning what, in his naivete, had attracted him in the first place: to do serious study of something.

The worst of it all is the terrible waste of one's mental powers. Nearly all studies of creativity, no matter in what fields, from

mathematics to zoology, indicate the vital role of sheer buoyancy of
mind—in distinction from the older, static concept of
"intelligence"—and of opportunity during one's twenties to turn
innate buoyancy without delay into constructive channels, channels in which one is "doing" one's subject whether this be the
writing of history, literary criticism, drama, novel, and poetry, or
starting at the bottom in business or profession. The important, the
vital thing to a gifted, ambitious mind is *getting at,* as soon as
humanly possible, whatever it is that burns in him as the means of
making his mark on the world.

That is why the best and brightest students, especially in the
humanities and social sciences, tend to bolt, to depart the campus
once the B.A. degree is awarded. The thought of spending anywhere from five to ten years in pursuit of a Ph.D. and only then be
stamped "Qualified" for the beginning at last of one's life's career,
is odious to say the least. That is, I repeat, for the minds of first
quality, not for the drones who are only too happy to stay on and
on, thus putting off indefinitely the harsh responsibility of facing
life directly, without blinking.

Suffice it to say by way of conclusion of this chapter that I,
neither genius nor drone but buoyed up by an acquired love of
university life, by a desire to become as much like my heroes on the
Berkeley campus as lay within my capabilities, and, far from least,
the promise by Teggart of an instructorship in the department if I
finished my Ph.D. dissertation in timely fashion, managed to finish
it on schedule. No doubt it would have been a better piece of work
with another year's nurturing, but whoever knows for sure in such
matters? Another year's fussing over it might well have robbed the
dissertation of such little distinction as it had. In any event, mine
received the approval of the faculty committee and thereby the
final approval of the Graduate Dean. I was ready now for the life of
a professor.

13

The Faculty, Yes

My ascension took place in July 1939 at rank of instructor, salary two thousand a year, three courses to teach. Among the three was the introductory course that, six years earlier had thrilled me as taught by Teggart and that had turned my mind to becoming one of his followers. Teggart was in his final year and ordinarily would have held on to that course, which he was deeply attached to, but his health was ragged from persisting respiratory troubles and he was also bringing to completion at last the book *Rome and China* to which he had given so many years of work. I, brashly, was only too happy to relieve him of the course.

Before the end of July, though, I had sobered up somewhat from the intoxicating joy of becoming, so suddenly as it seemed, one of the Brahmins on the campus; a member of the faculty. I began to think about the realities of being a faculty member, a teacher, a lecturer, someone whose responsibility henceforth was that of having, or seeming to have, enough knowledge or information to dole out in each course fifty minutes an appearance for approximately forty appearances — making a hundred and twenty for three courses — during the term immediately ahead. What kind or mass of notes would I need? Teggart and other faculty heroes of mine had lectured from a single page of notes. The mere thought of that terrified me. But how many pages: four, five, six? And suppose you ran out of notes when lecturing before two hundred students in the beginning course? What did you do? For lines to speak, that is. Horrors!

Mercifully, August and the commencement of teaching came soon and within a week nightmares were succeeded by the hardest work I had ever done, that is, keeping three courses going, one of them a large lecture course, the other two smaller but still calling for basically the lecture even though some dialogue was possible from time to time. I reflected bitterly on the widespread misconception in the minds of the lay public about the number of hours faculty gave to teaching: "Imagine! Only eight or nine hours a week! And they call that hard work! I have to work anywhere from forty hours up in my job."

So, dear citizen, did we. Those of us, at least in our early years. At a place like Berkeley where good lecturing and conscientious teaching were taken for granted by the students—including me up to this point—you put a good many hours of demanding work behind and in between the lectures to avoid the ignominy of being found thin in substance, awkward as if in stage fright, and somehow unlikable as a teacher. Students were, at least at Berkeley, good critics. As I have noted, applause, its presence, its absence, its volume when turned on, mattered a great deal. So much about teaching at Berkeley that had for years delighted me now, because I was overnight, the cynosure, intimidated me.

It was, or seemed, terribly important to be known as soon as possible as a good teacher. You had about two years in which to manifest such natural abilities as you may have had, natural abilities and also, of course, conscientiousness of preparation. By the third year, when a decent backlog of lecture notes and class preparations had been built up and you were no longer under the daily gun, you were expected to show serious interest in research, not publication necessarily, just serious interest. But research was on the average a distinct second, to teaching. Research was a sine qua non at Berkeley and other major universities—unlike the colleges, public or private—but it never filled in the holes left by an inferior teaching performance. It is different in today's heralded Research Universities which, from Harvard to Berkeley declare research (invariably pronounced REEsearch) the primary if not actually exclusive obligation owed to humanity. A few years ago I received a letter from an unusually candid young assistant professor at a midwestern research university that expressed nicely, I thought, the ambiguous position the tyro is in today when he begins his academic career. He wrote: "I don't overdo the teaching thing. It's better, I've found to have a merely so-so record as classroom teacher. Then your chairman and the director of the research institute you're in don't have to worry about whether they'll have a Teacher of the Year on their hands instead of a good, reliable grant-getter in research." Translated: A good teaching record, complete with popularity among students, may suggest that it covers a mediocre research promise; whereas an indifferent record as teacher leaves open the exciting possibility that one might be outstanding in research.

In the thirties it was never teaching vs. research, but teaching *and* research. On the whole, to the degree that Berkeley erred in the thirties, it was on the side of giving more relative weight to teaching than to research or research promise in the candidate being considered by a confidential faculty committee. Or so I found myself thinking after I began to serve on review committees. But that was a venial fault at worst. I saw other cases in which a solid and profuse research record — a couple of books, a couple of dozen research papers, frequent attendance at research conferences — virtually blinded committee members to unsettling reports that the subject was not only an inadequate but an indifferent teacher, frequently the object of student complaints.

Again I iterate the falsity of the teaching *versus* research simplification that fills the public mind today. The best teaching is rooted in ongoing research, in the teacher's desire to keep up with the best of knowledge and information in his field; that is research whether it flowers or not in a multitude of articles. And, as I have discovered over the past few years, the best research is done for the most part by men and women who teach and enjoy teaching. Few things are more salutary in the teaching process than when an instructor tries out for effect and possible criticism his ongoing research before a class of, say, upper division and/or graduate students. Such a fusion of research and teaching is a very heady experience for the students and an energizing one for the teacher-researcher.

As I write, there are hundreds of nonacademic research institutes and centers in America, not to forget the research divisions of our major industries, especially those in the high-tech areas. In these research is the only significant pursuit; there are no interruptions of research by the necessities of going to class or student office hours from time to time. Prior to World War II such nonacademic research bodies were few in number in this country and almost totally in the fields of science and technology. Since the war, however, research centers and institutes have mushroomed in all fields of study and research, in the humanities as well as the social sciences. It is possible now — as it wasn't before World War II — for the gifted scholar and scientist to weigh realistically the comparative advantages of doing one's research in a university. The resolution of the matter is usually a function of one's interest in and regard for teaching. For a long time the ablest scholars and scientists for the most part preferred the university with its students to the research division of IBM or GE or the research institute or center. But that condition appears to be changing rapidly, the more so as the suspicion has begun to dawn on scholars and scientists that the most original and innovative research is being done these days in institutes, even in certain industries.

The Berkeley faculty had the reputation — it may still have — of being cold socially, of lacking the kind of welcomings of newcomers that are almost standard in most American colleges and universities. There was, in the early fall of each year, a President's Reception for new students, one in which faculty members introduced themselves to students and chatted amiably with them as they moved up to where President and Mrs. Sproul stood for introduction. It was a fine event, one that I had enjoyed as a freshman and enjoyed all over again after I had become a faculty member and received an invitation from the Sprouls to assist them at the Reception.

Nothing comparable, either formal or informal existed for new members of the faculty at Berkeley. Individual departments varied in the amount of social recognition that was given to newly arrived members. Of course, in the thirties, for budgetary reasons there weren't very many new faculty. For some departments there were none, throughout the decade. But all this was true of every university in the country. Yet these universities, private or public, didn't suffer from the reputation of coldness that Berkeley did.

At Berkeley, unlike so many other universities, there were no welcoming groups of resident faculty, groups prepared to make certain that no newcomer, be he the new Sather Professor in History or an instructor very wet behind the ears, suffered from lack of a dinner invitation early in the first term. There were no faculty wives organized to pay early visits on the wives of new faculty, to help them get acquainted in both the campus and the surrounding town. I had the sense that the science departments looked after such social niceties more conscientiously than did departments in the humanities.

I recall that John Hicks, in American history, decided to leave, to take himself and family back to Wisconsin, which they had left when Berkeley offered him a prestigious chair. This was in his third year. The social factor was paramount in the Hicks' lives. Sproul didn't want to lose Hicks and persuaded him to stay, quite possibly covertly stirring up the channels of social intercourse on the Berkeley campus. The deanship of the Graduate Division became vacant at the time, and Sproul appointed Hicks to the deanship. That may have helped. I remember Carl Bridenbaugh, a considerably more distinguished scholar than Hicks, also felt frozen socially and, seeing no letup, went back to the Ivy League after two years at Berkeley, a major loss to the campus.

Old timers said it had been different in earlier years in the century. Stuart Daggett, professor of economics, had been on the faculty since 1905 when he came as an instructor; he said World War I had made a substantial difference, for whatever reasons which somehow involved human beings in their interrelationships; Daggett wasn't sure. He said that in the early days spontaneous faculty get-togethers were common. Most faculty lived in the hills behind the campus and there was a great deal of relaxed, off the cuff gregariousness. Daggett seemed wistful when he cited one custom of the early days: a faculty couple would drop in after dinner at another couple's home up Euclid Avenue; then the four couples would do the same at yet another faculty home, and so on until presumably a company too large for anyone's house had accumulated. Daggett, as I say, thought the First World War had made a difference, but he bethought himself of the Berkeley fire of 1923 that destroyed nearly a thousand homes in the Berkeley hills.

Things, he thought, were never the same after that holocaust in which so many valuables, among them manuscripts and other vital research documents were destroyed in a matter of hours. Afterward people tended to live more and more to themselves. Consensus and community declined.

What conceivably saved me from any feelings of angst and of solitariness in the universe was the Faculty Club. Not once in the last fifty years of living in or visiting other universities in America have I found one in which a faculty club meant as much to its members, in which it loomed so importantly in university affairs as the Berkeley Faculty Club. It was literally in this beautiful building, located at the east end of equally beautiful Faculty Glade that the Faculty Revolution of 1920 — was hatched. I knew nothing of that uprising when I first saw the club, within days of becoming a freshman in 1932. But I knew it and its gardens to be of striking architecture. Bernard Maybeck, I learned, still the most famous of all Berkeley architects, designed and supervised the building of the club. I had admired it from the outside and also the inside in my first year as student; the inside was when I tried to get a hashing job as a first year student; without success, for those were the most sought after jobs serving tables anywhere in Berkeley.

Teggart, who had been a lunchtime habitué for many years but for reasons of failing strength had quit going, urged me to join immediately upon becoming an instructor. He loved it and predicted I would like it also. I did. For all the years I was at Berkeley thereafter I doubt that I ever missed a weekday lunch at the Faculty Club unless I was out of town on visit or leave.

The club was considerably smaller than it is today following substantial additions made in the 1950s. Then it consisted of the great main dining hall with its vaulted ceiling and incomparable windows on the north and east sides of the room; a small guest dining room on the north side together with a couple of committee meeting rooms, the Stringham and O'Neill, named after lustrous personages now gone; a large members' lounge immediately south of the great hall, one with abundant easy chairs, magazines and newspapers, card tables, and, in an annex, the billiard room. There were then two good-sized rooms above the west end of the dining hall; these were rented by bachelor members of the faculty, Thomas

Buck of Mathematics and Robert Lowie of Anthropology when I first became a member.

Lunches and dinners were then sit-down-and-order affairs; never a buffet as is regular, I believe, today. You wrote out your order from the menu at the table and it was nicely served by one or other of the student waitresses and waiters, all of whom, understandably looked happy in their jobs. Faculty members were rarely if ever less than courteous, even convivial with them, and they looked as they were serving demigods instead of mortal teachers.

The wonderful Berkeley spirit of laissez-faire in curriculum extended to faculty relations and specifically to the Faculty Club. There was nothing that smacked of a high table, reserved for the eminent. There were perhaps fifteen tables, each seating anywhere from six to ten, and you sat wherever you wanted to, or an open seat was to be seen. Dues to the club were graduated by rank; mine as an instructor were two dollars a month; lunches ranged from a quarter to fifty and sixty cents.

In the main, the tables in the great hall were loosely, very loosely, associated with departments or fields. The table at the west end of the hall, seating about ten, was known as the history table even though nonhistorians often predominated in number. The same was true of the languages table, the economics, the biologist and chemist tables. As a natural-born table hopper I sat one time or other at all of them, never once feeling unwelcome. At lunch time perhaps a hundred filled the hall, with a dozen more using the small guest dining room and another dozen or more combining lunch and committee meetings in the Stringham and O'Neill private rooms. The club hummed with conversation and other activity for about an hour and half each week day, considerably fewer on Saturdays and none on Sundays. Not often did members stay on the campus for dinner, and when I did occasionally the atmosphere seemed almost sepulchral.

It pleased a number of members to come at lunch not to eat but to get early occupancy of one of the two bridge tables, always "at ready" with cards and pads in the lounge. Some, I learned, were outstanding at bridge, starting with Gilbert Lewis, a genius at everything it seemed, and including Wendell Latimer, also Chemistry, and Gerald Marsh of Speech.

I was one of the great majority of members who went for lunch and for good conversation. Mostly I sat at the "history table" where I found myself welcomed not in spite of but, or so it seemed to me, because I was Teggart's student. It was Bolton who sat every day at the head of the table and he couldn't have been more pleasant. If he ever chanced to mention my chief, it was in a friendly manner as in the tale I told above about Teggart and the Mormon student. At this table also were regularly Guttridge, Sontag (with whom I hit up warm and lasting friendships), Paxson, Priestley, and J. P. McBaine, the only member of the Law Faculty who came regularly to the Club. Conversation was pleasant, interesting, and sometimes edifying on world affairs. That I was an instructor and they senior professors made not the slightest difference in my participation in the talking.

I enjoyed, though, some table hopping: Sometimes at the "Languages table" where I met, with close friendship to follow, Ronald Walpole in French among others including Harold Small, senior editor at the University Press and raconteur nonpareil. This was where Kroeber often sat and also, on the rare occasions when he came for lunch, Max Radin, learned teacher and scholar in Roman Law. Conversation could be sparkling at that table. Guttridge sometimes sat at this table instead of with his fellow historians. One day H. R. W. Smith, professor of classics and, like Guttridge native of England, told a story about a man named Pars whom he had known in England many years earlier. Smith said the last he had heard of Pars was that he had gone to France to live. At which point Guttridge said with perfectly straight face, "There were three of them in France." "Oh," responded Smith, "really, how do you know?" "Simple," said Guttridge, "It's in Caesar: *Omnia Gallia est divisa in partes tres.*" (Laughter).

Another table I enjoyed sitting at occasionally, though most of the conversation was far beyond me, being about chemistry and physics a good deal of the time. Here sat almost every day the youthful Seaborg, Pitzer, Calvin, and the brilliant, charming Ruben who would die very prematurely but enlivened as well as edified many lives. They were a friendly lot; I never felt like a stranger in their paradise even though much of what they said was unassimilable by me. Camaraderie was delightful. Like all scientists headed for fame, they were brimful of their work. There were frequent references to G.N. (Gilbert Lewis, their master teacher) and some to Ernest Lawrence with whom, I gathered, the young assistant professor Seaborg was working occasionally. They all had a sense of humor, and funny stories about colleagues and students were frequent. I listened much more than I spoke, which was fitting enough given the commonest subject of their animated conversation. I became a friend of both Seaborg and Pitzer, the former as much down at football practice field in the autumn as in the Faculty Club. He was, like me, a football nut, and I often joined him in the late afternoon to watch Stub Allison put his excellent teams through their paces.

The high point of each year at the Club was the Christmas dinner, always on a Tuesday night about two weeks before Christmas when finals were winding down and term reports and seminar papers being read. The main dining hall was beautifully decorated with boughs from campus trees, and there was a great air of seasonal festivity. It was the one time of the year then when the mile limit law concerning alcoholic beverages was overlooked. There were no pre-dinner cocktails but lots of excellent wine with dinner, chosen by the professor of Oenology who also served as wine panjandrum for the Bohemian Club in San Francisco. The food was always good; the kitchen staff were as up to the annual event as were the Club members. Four or five members dressed in monkish habit and possessed of decent voices occasionally strolled around the dining hall to sing carols. It is a pleasure to recall Ed Strong as one of the carolers; he was tallest and sang the most spiritedly. Inevitably a few members quaffed more than their due and slightly tipsy, uproariously funny incidents could occur (only a tiny few incidents unfunny). Naturally the student waiters and waitresses loved every minute of the whole banquet. The Christmas dinner was an ancient custom at the Club. I was told that in older times it was a more serious (but never solemn) affair, with one of the grand old men of the faculty such as Lawson, Lewis, and especially Walter Morris Hart of English offering a few words appropriate to the dinner. There was no room for that at the Club dinner during my years, starting in 1939. Too many happy sounds from the well-wined and dined members.

Not by any means all of the Berkeley faculty took to the Faculty Club. There were those who didn't like it; even those who positively disliked and disapproved of it. Carl Sauer, eminent geographer, was one of these. He told me that the Club had and had had a pernicious effect on the campus. In the first place, he said, it had been at the core of the faculty uprising in 1920; Sauer disapproved of that uprising for its having turned a great deal of the administration of Berkeley from administrators such as the president, provost, and deans of colleges and schools to the faculty, its Academic Senate and the committees created by the Senate. Sauer also thought — and I believe he was thinking of me as much as of anyone, for I early became active in Senate committee work — that the Club had the effect of taking too many young faculty members' ideas and interests away from their professional fields of teaching and scholarship and stimulating ideas and interests instead in administration. Administration, he said, had an emasculating effect on first-rate scholarly minds. The combination of the Academic Senate and the Faculty Club misled bright young teachers and scholars into thinking a deanship was the highest goal, second only to the presidency, in academic life.

Many years passed before I found myself coming reluctantly to the conclusion that much of what Sauer said was true.

Few aspects of Berkeley were more celebrated or, as the case might be, deplored than its system of dual administration. What was called the administration — a president, vice president, provost, chancellor, dean of college or school, and department chair — was present at Berkeley just as could be found in every other mainline university in America. But, so often to the consternation of administrators in other universities. Berkeley's official administration seemed to range from the impotent to the crippled. The Presidency at Berkeley was, as I have twice noted briefly, relatively weak by comparison with the presidents of Harvard, Michigan, Stanford or any other university that comes to mind. In so many respect the president of the University of California found himself limited, even checkmated by unpaid, unofficial faculty committees. The president's weakness resonated to all other parts of the official administration: chancellors and provosts of the several campuses, deans and department chairmen. They couldn't rule or govern their respective principalities; they could only reign, like a king or queen of Great Britain.

To understand this peculiar system it is necessary to go back to the first of the six Berkeley revolutions I identified early in the book: the Faculty Revolt of 1920. It was a quiet revolution, unreported in the press, even in the Daily Cal. But for all that, it was undoubtedly the most potent of all Berkeley revolutions, at least as measured in its comprehensiveness and, above all, its endurance to the present moment. The revolt began in a power vacuum that opened up in 1919 and extended then into 1920. Benjamin Ide Wheeler, greatest of U.C. presidents had governed the University since 1899, governed it somewhat autocratically (most university presidents at that time in America were effectively ruling monarchs) but brilliantly and wisely. He lifted Berkeley from an essentially regional-college institution to a university in the full sense of the word. His leadership extended to creation of new professional schools, to strengthening of weak departments and, above all, preternaturally wise and sure appointments of new faculty. Most of those I noted above as giants at Berkeley in the thirties had been found and appointed as young men by Wheeler himself. Wheeler was loved by faculty, students, alumni, governors and legislators, and, not least, by citizens proud of the university he was creating.

Obviously, it couldn't last. It rarely does in history. From 1899 until about 1917 Wheeler was both strong and popular as president. Then the fall, eventually collapse, began. He was seized by recurrent illnesses and incapacities of office and also, pathetically, with baseless charges of being pro-German after America went into World War I in early 1917. The nearest to a basis of the absurd whisperings was the fact that as a young man he had studied in Germany, formed a high regard for the greatness of German culture at its best, had many friends in Germany whom he saw regularly before the war broke out and, given this background, refused to do what so many American philosophers and scholars did in 1917–1918, under the fevers of war patriotism, condemn publicly all German culture, the culture of Beethoven, Brahms, Kant, and Goethe included. For this Wheeler found himself among those suspected, even alleged "pro-Germans" whose property and at times very lives were in jeopardy during America's superpatrioteering madness. Additionally, perhaps relatedly, Wheeler's health was rendered feeble by a series of ailments. He was no longer, during his final two years in office, the great president who had, almost single handedly brought Berkeley within view of future greatness.

During Wheeler's final months and before David Prescott Barrows was appointed president by the Regents in 1920, there was near chaos at Berkeley so far as the official affairs of the University were concerned. As a means of not appearing to hurry Wheeler out of office, for which he was no longer fitted by 1919, and not rushing into appointment of a new president, a committee of three—immediately known on the campus as the Triumvirate—was created as an interim government of the University; all told, it lasted scarcely a year, but during that period it became the focal point of a great deal of animosity on the campus. The initial triumvirate consisted of one regent and two deans; the regent was Ralph Merritt who was an Old Blue to his marrow, one of President Wheeler's favorite students as an undergraduate, and very successful businessman; Charles Mills Gayley was one of the group and Dean William Cary Jones of the Law School the other.

This was the body the Faculty Revolution of 1919–20 was primarily aimed at. Three-headed executives are rarely successful in history, and this one at Berkeley was no exception. As is common with such bodies, the Berkeley triumvirate acquired a reputation ranging from ineptitude and anarchy at one extreme to arrogant authoritarianism at the other.

A small but powerful group of faculty, numbering some of the university's finest scientists, scholars and teachers, arose, led by Andrew Lawson, Gilbert Lewis, Joel Hildebrand, Teggart, and others of equal luster. Within the revolution was a prestigious fellowship known as Kosmos Club, still extant, I believe. It consisted of perhaps thirty of the more notable members of the faculty, humanists and scientists in about equal proportion. No administrators, not even the president, were eligible for membership. The club was self-perpetuating. Every two or three years as older members retired and dropped out of campus affairs, new, younger faculty members were elected by the club. It was considered a high honor to be elected. The club met once a month for dinner at the

Faculty Club, a half-hour for sherry beforehand, and afterward one of the members, chosen along with the others who would perform that academic year by the small Program Committee, would give a talk or read a paper of about thirty minutes length on some part or episode in his own field of study; following the paper, there would be discussion among the members present, and after that general retreat to the Faculty Club billiard room, its bridge tables, or abundant newspapers and magazines to read. Inevitably there were small conversational groups some of which might go on until midnight or later. The club was founded around 1900, and by dint of elections from time to time of new, younger members, stayed prosperously in existence. Teggart had been elected president of Kosmos for the year 1920–1921. Other members included the most prominent of the Berkeley faculty; such as Lewis and Hildebrand in chemistry, Adams in philosophy, McCormac in history, Walter Hart in English, Lawson in geology, et al. It was not unlike a Jacobin Club, as I recall twitting the very conservative Teggart one day when he had answered some of my questions. It was the same combination of interest in ideas and action.

Thus began the revolution. I will spare readers the details. It suffices to say that a majority of the Berkeley faculty, led by members of Kosmos Club who met regularly in the Faculty Club, called for direct meetings with the regents. Insultingly, they gave scant attention to the Trivumvirate through which the faculty leaders were, under University regulation, supposed to go in any official contact with the regents. The luster and sheer individual power of many of the insurgents led the regents to take them very seriously. Several of the regents, well aware of the mess things were in during the interregnum and power vacuum, seem to have been sympathetic from the beginning.

It was, I must stress, a silent revolution, one conducted by faculty leaders with full respect for the authority of the regents and largely in confidence. No one sought headlines. A committee of the faculty, led by Lawson and Lewis, chiefly, met regularly with a committee of the regents through much of 1920. (Even if the newspapers had known about the academic revolution going on, they probably would have tended to yawn, for 1919 and 1920 were the years of the colossal, precedent setting Wonder Teams at Berkeley.)

Out of the peaceful meetings came a republic of letters on the Berkeley campus that was without parallel in the United States. Whereas in all other universities, including the Harvards and Yales of the land, all trustee power, when delegated either to the president and his administration or to the faculty, had to pass through the president. No faculty member was privileged prior to 1920 to seek official contact with the regents or any single regent except with permission of the president. This was standard in academe at the time.

But not at Berkeley after 1920. In effect two separate administrations came out of the revolution. The first was that symbolized by the president, provosts, deans, directors, et al. This was of course *the* administration, the body known everywhere in the American university. The second administration, the outcome of the revolution, was the Academic Senate which included for its membership every faculty member from rank of instructor up to full professor. To the newly created Academic Senate went all of the following authorities and functions:

1. The power of scrutinizing all nominations for the appointment or promotion of faculty members. Only the regents actually appointed or promoted, but from now on the recommendations of the Senate's Committee on Budget and Interdepartmental Relations would accompany the president's own recommendations to the regents for final consideration. Sproul differed from a Budget Committee's recommendation occasionally on an appointment or faculty promotion, but it never went beyond 1 or 2 percent a year of the total number being considered.

2. The Senate had exclusive and full power with respect to courses, their inception, discontinuance, and supervision.

3. The Senate had full authority with respect to admissions of new students. No member of the administration, not even the official director of admissions, served as a voting member of the Board of Admissions. The president was given a limit of 3 percent of students he could admit "for the good of the university," meaning needed athletes and also the sons and daughters of people very important to the University, including alumni.

4. Only the Academic Senate could approve degrees in course: that is, the B.A., B.S., M.A. and Ph.D. Honorary degrees were left to

the president who, however availed himself of the advice of a faculty committee that he appointed.

5. All monies, starting with those emanating from the State Legislature, given the University for research had to be turned over to a new Board of Research, a Senate body, for allocation to individual faculty members.

6. All matters in any way affecting educational policy such as new professional schools and colleges, new curricula, research procedures, relations with other colleges and schools, had to be submitted for recommendation to the Senate, specifically to the Senate's Committee on Educational Policy.

7. All Academic Senate Committees would be appointed by the Senate's own powerful Committee on Committees, a body elected by the full vote of the Senate.

The effect of the Revolution of 1920 was not solely upon the president, although all the new powers vested by the regents in the organized faculty represented in the first instance sharp cuts in his traditional powers, the kinds of powers known virtually everywhere else in academic America. The larger, if derivative, effect of the faculty revolution was upon the administration that descended from the president and that was appointed by him: chairmen of departments, deans, directors, provosts, et al. The same authority endowed by the regents in the faculty that cut into the president's authority, cut as well into the authority and autonomy of every chairman and dean, leaving each, notoriously around the academic world, singularly bereft of the powers which mattered the most.

The Revolution of 1920 came close to emasculating U.C. presidents. What was left of their authority? Not much compared with other university presidents. Power over buildings, grounds, nonacademic personnel, alumni matters, student affairs of noncurricular sort, and of course the right to be the sole representative of the University in external business. University of California presidents have been, ever since 1920 and the faculty revolution, essentially weak figures, at least by comparison with presidents of other important universities in the country. Correspondingly subpresidential administrators such as provosts and deans have, by comparison with their counterparts elsewhere, relatively little power and function. I have always been struck by the avidity with which distinguished members of the faculty at Berkeley accepted deanships. That acceptance automatically cut them off from further membership on Senate committees and the revolution had denuded deanships of responsibility for much of anything besides applying and interpreting Senate rules with respect to courses and student scholarship.

I think of Joel Hildebrand: outstanding chemist in research and teaching, one of the leading figures of the 1920 revolution, thereafter an extraordinarily influential figure in the new Academic Senate, frequent member, by Senate appointment of the powerful Budget Committee, and active, leading influence at meetings of the Academic Senate. In 1940 he was made dean of the College of Letters and Science. As such he was no longer eligible for membership in the Senate committees, which were strictly faculty in composition, and he was thus transposed from Senate positions of genuine importance in the life of the University to an essentially sterile deanship. Until well after the war, deans had absolute no input in matters of appointment and promotion of faculty, in admissions, research allocations of money, even degrees in course.

The remarkable thing about the Unpaid Bureaucracy, that is, the Academic Senate system was — down until after World War II — its costlessness. This important sector of the University government did not have a single paid secretarial or stenographic assistant. The secretaryship of the Academic Senate was for many years — down until after the war — in the hands of Thomas Steel, Registrar. He attended every meeting, took notes, wrote the official minutes and served also in like capacity on two or three other Senate committees; courses for one. There wasn't even an Academic Senate office until about 1950.

The danger of as fully democratic a faculty system as Berkeley's was that some members of the faculty would succumb to the allure of faculty administration and politics; that is, gradually begin to shirk their most fundamental duties, which were those of their professorial roles of teacher and scholar in favor of undeniable prestige and sheer political interest of Senate committee work. It was thought that in promotions a faculty member's record of Senate work could count almost equally with, say, research as grounds for promotion. On the whole, though, I think the pure democracy of the early Senate system escaped the perils of such temptations. There were a few exceptions, to be sure, but in the far greater number of cases those who were placed on the more important Senate committees were well known as excellent teachers and serious research minds. The illustrious origins of the Academic Senate in 1920, with internationally noted scientists and scholars assuming leadership in the revolution and then in the operations of the new system did a great deal to keep the system clean for a long time thereafter. The leaders for at least a quarter of a century were individually scholars and teachers first, then only citizens of the academic democracy.

I must make one emphatic point here. Nothing I have thus far written should suggest that all the Berkeley faculty were avid participants as well as automatic members of the Academic Senate and its committees. Dean McMurray of the Law School once wrote on behalf of his faculty to the president and to the current vice-chairman of the Senate requesting that henceforth no further reports, not even calls to meetings, be sent to Boalt Hall. "We have no interest whatever in the political processes of the Academic Senate. We consider ourselves separate and distinct from the Senate." Few of the faculty of engineering and architecture ever attended a meeting of the Senate or showed any other kind of interest. Sauer in geography took pride, I learned, in never having attended a meeting; I believe that was true of Bolton and Kroeber, both distinguished members of the faculty, noted teachers and scholars but cold to the idea of the dual administration.

To the present moment the dual administration thrives. With the advent of new campuses since the war and the establishment in each of them of the Senate modeled on Berkeley, and with the normal intercommunications of the eight campuses, the Academic Senate has become huge, what with its cross-channels of communication from campus to campus, its establishment of a large Senate legislative assembly composed of members from each of the campuses, and a secretariat that is today larger than the staff of the president's and provost's offices in the thirties, the Senate has become a splendid illustration of the theories of bureaucracy associated with the names of Tocqueville, Weber, and Michels.

14

Berkeley Goes to War: The End of an Era

The Second World War broke out almost to the day with the beginning of my teaching career as faculty member at Berkeley. Of the two events, it was the second that I deemed the more important. In the first place I was convinced that it was just another one of Europe's recurrent wars, fought at bottom for the usual nationalistic and imperialistic reasons, all of which we had seen exposed from the First World War in a continuing, stark and vivid literature running all through the twenties and thirties. I detested Hitler and Nazism; who didn't? But what could he do, given the formidable Maginot Line and what we were sure was France's highly superior army? It would be, I was confident, a short war and one that would not implicate me or make the slightest difference on Berkeley, indeed the whole American university.

There is no need to detail my smug errors of insight and foresight. Suffice it to say that when it ended I was a staff sergeant on Saipan, having spent the two previous years in the Pacific and somewhat changed from the feckless young academic I had been when Hitler struck Poland. So was the University changed, and that is what I want to deal with here.

The First World War had had little impact on the American university. President Wilson was not loath to prosecute the war. Government, society, and economy all attest to the zeal with which Wilson pursued the war. Even the schools, churches, and civic organizations were invaded by the American government with war propaganda. But when it came to the colleges and universities it is as though the ex-President of Princeton University, despite his wartime role, was determined to spare them as far as possible. Their students and faculty members were drafted like all other citizens of the nation, but the structure, the basic significance of the university in America was left alone.

Very different in this respect was the Second World War. Not in the beginning. Germany's invasion of Poland, the declaration of war on Germany by England and France, and the events of almost the entire year following had seemingly little impact on the American mind. At Berkeley, as I learned from daily lunches at the Faculty Club, the faculty was overwhelmingly of noninterventionist mind. Even the dispatch of war materiel to England and France aroused little if any enthusiasm; tolerance up to a point but nothing more. There was intense dislike of Hitler and Mussolini and almost universal hope that both would be destroyed by the Allies. But the old negative sentiment in America toward British and French imperialism was very much a reality through most of 1940. The Battle of Britain, following the surrender of France, perceptibly influenced thought and conversation at the Faculty Club. The number of outspoken interventionists began slowly to increase. Even during most of 1941 there was almost a total lack of spirit for actual armed intervention in the war. But FDR's policy of Lend Lease had many followers on the Berkeley faculty. His Four Freedoms speech before Congress at the beginning of 1941 had a considerable effect on the Berkeley faculty—though not student—mind. So did the Atlantic Charter of August 1941. The German invasion of Russia in June 1941 had the almost instant effect of legitimating the war for the more radically minded in America as elsewhere. Without doubt a considerable development of the American war mind took place in 1941 prior to Pearl Harbor. One heard more and more faculty members speaking out for American armed intervention as well as full Lend Lease.

Even so, I will always believe that all else equal, the preponderant sentiment of the Berkeley faculty, and of course also the student body, would have remained negative toward a policy of armed intervention in the European war. But, as we know, all else didn't remain equal. The Japanese, in an uncharacteristic stupidity of strategy at Pearl Harbor made it absolutely certain that America would go to war in the Pacific. Would the outbreak of war between the U.S. and Japan have made it certain, all else equal again, that the U.S. would have turned also to Japan's two Axis partners, Germany and Italy? No one will ever know for sure. I recall vividly that both across America and in the Berkeley Faculty Club there was a decided difference of opinion. Not only was there the lingering animosity on the part of many to British imperialism but also, perhaps much more important, there was the fact that the "godless" Soviet Union, author of the Ukrainian genocide, of the Great Terror, and of the Pact between themselves and the Nazis, would necessarily become an ally of the U.S.

Again, however, all did not remain equal. To our astonishment, Hitler, with Mussolini quickly following, declared war on the U.S. within a very few days following Pearl Harbor. There was nothing that American isolationists could do about that unexpected event, and the result was of course all-out, fully armed American intervention. The Second World War had dawned at last in America.

So did it dawn on the Berkeley campus. Gone now for good the internecine hostilities of isolationists and interventionists, of conservatives or liberals and the Communist Left, of pacifists and militarists. President Sproul immediately put the University of California at the service of the American government for the duration. I remember a meeting of the Academic Senate two or three days after Pearl Harbor in which much the same position was taken by the Senate. An emergency committee was quickly approved and staffed that could in military emergency speak for the entire Senate.

In many respects the atmosphere at Berkeley became militarized in one or other degree. Every student, male and female alike, was required to carry at least one "war-related" course a semester. The initial list of such courses was limited pretty much to ROTC, certain physical education courses, and the like. But, with the thought of declining enrollments in their courses faculty members in ever-enlarging number sought to have their own courses, no matter what they were — English Poetry, German History, American Nationalism, whatever — so hallowed. A course called America at War appeared, required attendance, one unit, no exams or grades. I found myself one of the lecturers in the course. I knew nothing about war and little about matters of foreign policy apart from newspaper stories, but I did know quite a bit about the Peloponnesian War between ancient Athens and Sparta as written up by that master historian Thucydides. No less an authority than the journalist Elmer Davis had recommended to Americans the reading of Thucydides as the best means of finding out what the current war in Europe was all about. I thought when I completed my lectures on the Peloponnesian conflict that I had acquitted myself creditably. The thousand students were polite at least.

The most colorful effect upon the campus of the war after we were thoroughly in it, was the sight and sounds of the ASTP units in their army uniforms marching, hup-hupping all the way, to their classes. By the beginning of 1943 one could summon up images of West Point just by looking out on the Berkeley campus. Mathematics up to the level of calculus was required by the Army for all these cadet-like college students, and that took some doing. The Mathematics department even with graduate students to use simply couldn't come up with the necessary number of teachers. So the call went out for faculty in any department who might possibly exhume what they had learned long ago about math. A sad innumerate, I couldn't help.

Conspicuously lacking, thank heaven, in World War II was the morbid hatred of everything German, including Beethoven and Goethe and Kant, that had seized the American mind in the First World War. That hatred and the fear of pro-Germans swept the American mind. As I noted above, even the great President Benjamin Ide Wheeler had in some measure fallen victim to the hysteria. On a personal note, as late as 1926 I was using, in grammar school, texts from which all German literature, including poetry and music, had been carefully razored out during the First World War. There was none of that in the Second World War.

What there was, though, was unreasoning, almost terrified fear of the Japanese-Americans, including the large number of them who were bona fide American citizens. Most Japanese-Americans lived on the Pacific Coast, largely engaged in farming. There were virtually none of these, as I explained earlier, on the campus; not as students, certainly not as faculty. In perhaps the single most unconstitutional action of the American government in all its history, these Japanese Americans were rounded up summarily by Federal and State authorities and dispatched to internment camps in eastern California, Arizona, Nevada, etc. Such action went far beyond anything happening to German-American citizens in the First World War. It signalized not a political-national but racial war.

By far the greatest effect of the Second World War on Berkeley — and the American university generally — was the conversion of the university's essential mission in society from teaching to research, more particularly big research. The effects of the war on teaching — the special "war-related" courses, the presence of soldiers on the campus, the oddly shaped teaching terms — disappeared immediately after V-J day and the end of World War II. By the time I got back to Berkeley in early 1946, all these deformations of teaching were but dim memories.

It was a different story with respect to the war's impact on research and its place in the university. It is no exaggeration, I believe, to say that what we today refer to as the "research university," meaning institutions like Harvard, Berkeley, Stanford, Michigan, and scores of others located throughout America, had its origin in the Second World War. It was the war, total war as it quickly became, that lifted research to a level of prestige it had never known before in its history, not even in the bitterly fought First World War. In the interests of quick and total destruction of Nazi Germany and Imperial Japan, we made research — only for duration, it was thought — the arch function of academe.

After the war public fascination with research, starting with the atomic bomb and its dramatic implications for the peaceful use of atomic energy was nearly boundless. J. Robert Oppenheimer, first known to us at Berkeley as renowned young theoretical physicist, bohemian, student of Sanskrit and Marxism, and as far from war and the military as one could possibly be, of a sudden loomed up in the final months of 1945 as a war hero in the same proportion that General Marshall and Eisenhower were. He had commanded, hadn't he, the making of the two bombs that fell on Hiroshima and Nagasaki and had materially shortened the length of the war in the Pacific? Oppenheimer had a charismatic impact upon Congress, the public, as well as the scientific world for some time after the end of World War II. Everything that had made him almost a cult figure to physics students before the war — his attire, especially hat, his way of walking, his reputation for being both a genius and a bohemian — now, after the way, widened his audience to the whole nation.

When to the publicity given the atom bomb was added the publicity of radar, penicillin, and a host of other scientific "miracles," all in large measure the products of highly secret research conducted by university professors, the way was wide open for a public interest in university research that had been almost nonexistent in America prior to the war. Before the war it is fair to say, I think, that in the average American mind research and development were associated chiefly with such nonacademic figures as Thomas Edison, Luther Burbank, and even Henry Ford. *They* would see to it that we would keep getting better automobiles, potatoes, electricity, and the like and allow the college professor — always cartooned as someone with his head in the clouds or playing the fool to college students, especially the fraternity boys — to teach.

It is really not surprising that in some measure the institutions of higher education in this country followed the public mind in this respect. The man who walked tallest among faculty in American colleges and universities was more likely to be the classics or philosophy professor than the physicist or chemist. American science would have been in parlous shape indeed had there not been the German universities to go to for advanced work. Joel Hildebrand told me that when he graduated in chemistry early in the century at the University of Pennsylvania, he was told by the senior chemistry professor that all important laws and principles had been discovered and that there remained nothing for Joel or other young chemists to do but apply these principles in the betterment, say, of soap and bread.

But when the Oppenheimers and Lawrences and Rabis received the plaudits due them for their contributions to the defeat of the Axis powers, the repercussions were clear and almost immediate. The contribution of research to the winning of the war was a stark reality, not to be seriously doubted by anyone. Why not, then extend these remarkable contributions from wartime to peacetime, applying to major national problems — ranging from poverty to air pollution and cancer—the same kind of genius that went into atomic energy and radar? "If we can make an atom bomb," went the national refrain, "why not a cure for the business cycle, unemployment, and all the dread diseases of mind and body?"

Thus was born, in war, the legitimation of research, especially in the sciences, in the American popular mind. No longer did we think solely of the teacher when the word "professor" was uttered. No longer was the main and essential function of the university unanimously held to be teaching. Aiding the spread of popularity of university research in the national mind was the creation of literally dozens of new foundations, led by the enormously wealthy Ford Foundation, nearly all of which made the financial support of research—rarely teaching—projects their prime business.

The nature of research in the universities changed. Once it had been almost entirely *individual* research. Now, with memory warm of the Manhattan Project and of many, many other research projects formed for war purposes, scientists and scholars began to think of *project* research as the proper function of universities in peace time. As the result of postwar fascination with research grants— from the armed services, Federal departments, and agencies and the new, sprawling foundations—and research projects, the idea of fixed, permanent institutes and centers on campuses began to grow as the proper framework or infrastructure of university research. Research institutes were beginning to flower at Berkeley when I came back in 1946 from the Pacific.

There was no teaching revolution following the war to rival the research revolution. The number of students at Berkeley soared to close to thirty thousand; there were lots of willing students and serious teachers. But there was never the same spirit of enthusiasm and enterprise to be found in teaching measures and reforms that one found in the dozens, even hundreds of research ventures, one and all with the model of the Manhattan Project in mind. Minus the secrecy!

Before the Second World War, the *department*—from Art to Zoology—was the key unit in all universities. It was and is essentially a teaching instrument. The chairmanship of a department was an honored position. Faculty members not uncommonly would actually compete, struggle for the prestige of a chairmanship as they would for the equal honor of being entrusted with the introductory freshman course.

How different things were following the war. Anyone with eyes to see couldn't miss the declining prestige of the department and the rising prestige of the purely research organizations—the novel institutes, bureaus, and centers, all progeny of the war and of the university research specially conducted for the war. Had one asked a professor, normally ambitious, which he would prefer, a department chairmanship or a research institute directorship, there wouldn't have been a moment's hesitation by 1950. Directorship, of course. Department chairmen were coming more and more to seem like custodians shuffling teaching schedules just as janitors shuffled paper trash. Research was the thing and the institute was its shining symbol. The new era of the research university was not established by trustees and administrators, but by faculty. The prestige of research and of grants and projects in research in the physical sciences together with at first millions, then tens and hundreds of millions of dollars coming from the armed services, federal and private foundations, was not lost on members of departments in the humanities and social sciences.

If there could be an Institute of Nuclear Dynamics and a Center for Biophysics, why not, it was inevitably asked in the humanities and social sciences, institutes and centers for the study of Shakespeare, of existentialism, the business cycle, poverty and unemployment? It wasn't long before the Berkeley campus along with dozens of other campuses in the country was virtually dotted with such newfangled corporate entities. If it was nice to teach Renaissance history, how very much nicer to be known as a senior fellow, or God willing, the Director of the Center for Renaissance Studies. Rarely in social history, I believe, have new groups and strata conferred so quickly status and power upon individuals as these research entities did in American academe.

There were instant boons for individual professors who were inducted, willy nilly, into the new institutes and centers: guaranteed summer income for doing the research under the rubric of some institute or center that otherwise would have had to be done —as it had universally in academe before the war—without continued salary. Even more mouth-watering to academics in institutes was the considerable reduction in one's teaching responsibilities. Three courses a term, at least two undergraduate, were the norm at Berkeley and most if not all other universities prior to World War II. But now, if one was so fortunate as to be tapped for an institute, his responsibility as teacher, his "teaching load" as it was widely called, was diminished by 33⅓ percent. In sum, within the new research aristocracy that blossomed from the war, increased income *and* substantial reduction of teaching.

Such differential of status, far from awakening any outcry from noninstitute faculty members, only whetted desire to have more institutes, ones in which the have-nots could become themselves haves. To become the founder and head of your own institute—funded by such soft and credulous entities as the federal bureaucracy and the Ford Foundation—gave the ordinary professor feelings of euphoria and power. One had a carpet perhaps on one's office floor, certainly a secretary or two who could repulse or intimidate any hapless student who might have wandered in the front office. By very nature and purpose the new institutes were anti-teaching.

There were two kinds of capital or currency on the campus once the institute system of research came into being. There was first the historic and once sole capital furnished by the annual state appropriation and by loyal alumni and of course university investments. But after World War II a brand new currency, if not capital, flowed copiously. This was the very substantial funding that came more or less directly from the federal government and the new, gushing foundations to the institutes and centers. Any institute director or member could, with some real truth, see himself as a proud member of two nations in his loyalties rather than one. Inasmuch as the government and foundations gave their money, not to the university as a whole except as a station, but to an institute, it was always the privilege of the institute director to take his wealth with him, so to speak, if and when he chose to depart one university for another. This could make for a certain degree of arrogance.

Very few if any of the new foundations chose to follow the distinguished example of the John Simon Guggenheim Foundation and award its research money to *individual* scholars and scientists. "We don't like to retail, we prefer to wholesale our money," I recall hearing a vice president say—I thought haughtily—who represented one of the new eleemosynary behemoths.

Prior to World War II universities and their faculties were exceedingly cautious about accepting money from the Federal government—most especially the armed services—or the big corporations. A few foundations such as Rockefeller, Carnegie, Russell Sage and Rosenwald were considered clean—that is, free from the pressure of some special interest they were riding, but there weren't many. I remember learning from a chemist friend in the thirties about the effort of Shell Oil Company to add to its luster by funding at high salary for those years what would be known as "The Shell Professorship of Chemistry." If I recall, a million dollars would accompany the professorship. Gilbert Lewis and a united Department of Chemistry turned it down, spurned it, despite the severe need for additional research funds in the Depression thirties. From their point of view such money was tainted as it would have been had it come from the Vatican, the Republican Party, or the Department of Commerce.

No such rectitude existed during and then after World War II. It was only patriotic for scientists to accept big money from the armed services and other agencies of government. The war for democracy had, it was widely and comfortably thought, sanitized money from the federal government. The quick onset of the Cold War after the defeat of the axis powers provided useful continuation of what could continue to be thought of as patriotic (and secret) research. When President Eisenhower delivered his now famous Farewell Remarks at the end of his second term, he warned against what he called the "military-industrial complex." Everybody remembers that. What fewer remember, and especially in the universities, are Ike's immediately succeeding words of warning about what he called the "military-university complex" where, he said, "the research contract has replaced individual curiosity."

Thus the contemporary research university was born of World War II and its immediate aftermath highlighted by the Cold War. Administrators relished the money, cheered on of course by professors dazzled by the new sources of money and the new titles and statuses that went with the new era.

There was, to be sure, a large vein of naiveté found in universities; naiveté rooted in administrations. Since every new research grant to a professor or research center or institute could be skimmed — that is anywhere from forty to sixty percent of the dollar value taken by the administration in compensation for the building space and services utilized by grantsmen and institutes — couldn't, just possibly, universities so enrich themselves that they could steadily reduce the amount of tuition paid by students, or enlarge salaries of those such as classics professors, poor souls, once the mainstay of all universities, now virtual beggars by dint of their not being a Policy Science?

It was a noble dream or hope on the part of university trustees and presidents. But in the end a gigantic and costly illusion. We have seen the financial problems of universities double and redouble since the Era of Research was born. And as hundreds of thousands of middle-class parents know, tuition costs rise correspondingly. Even worse, if that is possible, is the status on campus of the individual professor who, without disparaging, or flinching from, research, who in fact enjoys research, especially the kind of research that he can manage alone, thank you, without the bureaucratic impediments constituted by elaborate research institutes and centers with their iron hierarchies of research managers and fund-raisers operating on the fringes of academic government. And, believe it or not, there are still professors at Berkeley and Harvard who actually enjoy, who want, undergraduate teaching — including introductory courses. But they have to be very careful. Too great a familiarity with undergraduate courses might arouse suspicions in the minds of peers that they aren't serious about their research. The great physicist Enrico Fermi had to await a Nobel Prize and the heroic status he enjoyed in the Manhattan Project before he could safely indulge, at the University of Chicago after the war, his desire to teach introductory physics — to undergraduates! Essentially the same experience was enjoyed by Linus Pauling at Caltech.

Even before the war ended, one could hear occasional references to a Berkeley or MIT as, not a mere university but increasingly a Research University. The Era of the University as foremost Teacher came to an end alongside the rise of the Era of the University as Discoverer. Of course personal discovery had always been a part of the lives of the better professors on a university faculty. But such discovery could be and was for the most part harmonized with the claims of teaching—and the recognition of teaching as the university's first and major responsibility.

It is evident that equilibrium has not yet been established between the function of teaching and the function of research in the contemporary university. The Research University is not without problems, some of them increasingly worrisome. Scandals and embarrassments increase steadily with respect to the heavy emphasis on research and to the large amounts of money required to sustain much of it. The rising intensity of competition among university research stars leads occasionally to outright scandals in the struggle to be first and supreme—more like professional sports and the head-hunting in corporate enterprise in the marketplace than the academe of old. The fight among universities for stars—in such fields as English as well as mathematics and physics—has led inevitably to substantial increases in salaries. A half century ago, as I wrote above, minds of the genius quality of Kroeber, Lewis, Evans, and Teggart earned well below ten thousand dollars a year. More than simply monetary inflation is involved in the increasingly common salaries running between $100 and $150 thousand a year at this writing; such salaries, be it noted are for teaching periods within the normal academic year that don't go beyond about eight months of actual residence. The research star can do pretty much what he wants to do if he like Ricky Henderson, Michael Jordan, Wayne Gretzky, Bill Cosby, or Johnny Carson can call himself the "greatest."

The heavy dependence of universities on large funds for research from the federal government—most often from the military branches of government—has put the universities precisely in the position so feared by scholars and scientists down through the thirties; that of being subject to Congressional inquiries into the once sacrosanct domain of higher education. The disposition then to allow universities and colleges a maximum of self-government within American society was heightened by the fact that these institutions were paying their own way, not developing a parasitic dependence upon the Federal budget.

I have no doubt that there are teachers today at Berkeley, MIT,

Stanford, and Michigan fully the equal of those back in the Era of Teaching. But there aren't as many of them. And by the very nature of the Research University there simply isn't much encouragement to develop one's teaching proclivity. What good does it do to offer a half a dozen teaching awards a year, as Berkeley does currently when awards of tens of thousands of dollars a year — in increased salaries and in the literally hundreds of research prizes now existent in this country — are available to the research star? We have learned that there are exceedingly bright young scientists who very early on select a field of specialization and make other strategic adjustments in their work as means of increasing their eventual chance of a Nobel. When your average multimillionaire faces death, what better monument to himself could there be than a substantial trust fund set up to make possible each year the award of The Jones Prize in physics or even sociology. Prizes, like endowed chairs, are like sandwich boards: they flatter both the giver and the receiver of the award or chair.

More and more university presidents and boards of trustees are thinking, sometimes desperately, as at Stanford, of ways by which the current, increasingly problem-infested research university can be replaced by a rejuvenated teaching university. It is said that the President of Stanford has set aside five million dollars for the exclusive purpose of ascertaining the best means of returning Stanford to the position in which teaching is once again the highest function. I don't like to be the thrower of cold water on the hopes and plans of decent, well-motivated executives, but it will be a freezing day in July before the faculty of any research university will even consider giving up their current emoluments and privileges, all of them anchored squarely in research and the aristocracy of research. In every major university I know of, the teaching responsibility is now down to a mere two courses a year. May God help the poor university president who decrees that faculty will once again teach, as they did in the best universities before World War II, three courses.

Not that I think the research university is here to stay indefinitely. There are two sets of forces that conjoin to make somewhat perilous the future of the present Berkeleys, Stanfords, and Harvards. The first set of forces is external. I am referring to the hundreds, the thousands of private and public organizations built solely around research, without even a gesture toward teaching. There are the multitudinous and huge federal research fiefs spreading from the National Institutes of Health all the way to the currently beleagured but undoubtedly permanent NASA. For those who love research and haven't the faintest interest in being a Mr. Chips, there are a great many institutes and centers, both private and public, small and large, with large budgets, places where no student, particularly undergraduate student, dares enter. For many years such organizations—and they were few and tiny before World War II—didn't enjoy a particularly good reputation, least of all the so-called research divisions of the big auto and electric industries. But most of that is changed now. What was once left to the universities in the way of research, to combine with teaching, has now enlarged and developed into a whole knowledge industry, one comparable to the steel or textile industry.

The second set of forces capable of destroying the research university in the interest of a return to teaching is that belonging to students, chiefly undergraduate students. The power of students was made manifest as students in the 1960s and again in the early 1980s, not to forget the largely student-centered ethnic minorities revolt going on at Berkeley. But student revolts have been legion in the West's universities since the Middle Ages. Almost invariably the students win their insurrections; they did at Bologna and Oxford in the thirteenth century and the evidence from around the world suggests that they still do. Berkeley students would, I believe, have won their revolution in the 1960s at Berkeley had they stayed firmly with strictly academic objectives and not gone astray over Vietnam and civil rights in San Francisco. Students are slow to rouse; their most endearing trait is their loyalty, their desire to be loyal, to their teachers in college. But the research university hasn't since the war been quite as loyal to its students. Its cynical use of graduate students—sometimes deficient in the English language—where full-fledged faculty once taught betrays, consciously or unconsciously a contempt for teaching, most especially that below the graduate course level.

Once again I emphasize that nothing in what I am writing here should be interpreted as bearing animus toward research on the part of faculty. A university in which there was quite literally no research, only classroom teaching, would be a monstrosity. There simply can't be teaching at the true university level by anyone, physicist, philosopher, economist, whoever, who eschews research. It is vital to the content of proper university teaching and it is ever-refreshing to the individual faculty mind. Once the early enchantment of the tyro-professor with the faces of students before him begins to wane, once the romance of the rostrum commences to disappear, it is individual research, research combined with teaching classes, that offers the best hope for avoiding the kind of malaise that so often strikes teachers in midlife, rendering them unhappy bores in the classroom. Research, individual research, that is, not research embottled in walled institutes and centers, is a marvelous tonic to not only university professors but people in all walks of life, for what is research but discovery and happy is he who seeks and seeks in the hope of finding something previously unknown. Students love that kind of faculty research.

Index

Dual Administration, 188–89
Duerr, Edwin, 84
Dyer-Bennetts, 42

Edison, Thomas, 202
Eisenhower, Dwight, 206
Eliot, Charles W., 18–19
Eliot, T.S., 83
Ellis, Howard, 77, 167
Euclid Apartments, 79
Evans, Herbert M., 78, 129, 132–34, 166, 208

Faculty Club, 184–88
Fellner, William, 167
Faculty Revolution, 49, 102, 189–93
Flexner, Abraham, 176
Football, spell of, 86–88
Ford Foundation, 203
Foster, William Z., 56
Foundations, 206
Friedman, Milton, 167

Galbraith, John K., 164
Gayley, Charles, 112, 124, 190
General Strike of 1934, 51–52
Gettell, Raymond, 117, 170
Gladding, Hope, 70
Golden Bear, Order of, 112
Goldschmidt, Richard, 137–38
Gordon, Walter, 61
Greek Letter houses, decline of, 92–97
Groves, Leslie, 135, 137
Guggenheim Foundation, 205
Guttridge, George, 119, 124, 186

Harper, William R., 87–88
Harrison, Maurice, 57
Hart, James, 67, 168
Hart, Walter M., 187, 191
Harte, Bret, 36
Hearst, Phoebe A., 25–26
Hearst, William R., 25
Hicks, John, 183
Hildebrand, Joel H., 19, 49, 101, 109–10, 142–43, 162, 190, 191, 194
Hinds, Norman, 125

Hodgen, Margaret, 70
Hoffer, Eric, 46, 51
Hollywood, 12–13
Honor System, decline of, 89–92
Hook, Sidney, 59
Hoover, Herbert, 32
Howison, George H., 112, 169
Hughes, Everett, 168
Hume, Sam and Portia, 42
Huntington, Emily, 70
Hutchins, Robert, 20–21, 88, 106–7

Jackson, Ida, 61
James, William, 159, 161
Jones, William C., 190
Jordan, David Starr, 30

Kael, Pauline, 76, 85
Kaun, Alexander, 41, 42
Kerner, Robert, 168, 171
Key, V.O., 167
Kidd, Alexander, 62, 120–21
Kosmos Club, 154, 190–91
Kroeber, Alfred, 78, 115–16, 129, 138–40, 166, 167, 186, 195, 208
Kurz, Benjamin, 67

Landauer, Carl, 53, 56
Laski, Harold, 83
Lasswell, Harold, 167
Latimer, Wendell, 166, 185
Lawrence, Ernest, 77, 115–16, 129, 134–35, 166, 187, 202
Lawson, Andrew, 69, 130–31, 187, 190, 191
Le Conte, Joseph, 30, 112
Lehman, Benjamin, 41, 42, 67, 168
Lewis, Gilbert N., 102, 110, 129, 131–32, 166, 185, 187, 190, 206
Lipman, Charles, 67
London, Jack, 36, 37, 85
London, Joan, 52
Los Angeles, 1, 45–46
Lovejoy, Arthur, 153
Löwenberg, Jacob, 118, 169–70
Lowie, Robert, 67, 167
Loyalty Oath conflict, 104
Luther, Martin, 110